FOR THE GOOD OF THE COMPANY

FOR THE GOOD OF THE COMPANY

Work and Interplay in a Major American Corporation

By Isadore Barmash

GROSSET & DUNLAP
Publishers • New York

A Filmways Company

Copyright © 1976 by Isadore Barmash
All rights reserved
Published simultaneously in Canada
Library of Congress catalog card number: 74-5629
ISBN 0-448-12245-6

Printed in the United States of America

To Reba and Harry Jasnoff,
who left beautiful memories

Contents

FOR THE GOOD OF THE COMPANY

Introduction

This is the story of an actual company and its people.

Founded more than ninety years ago in a tiny Pennsylvania town, the company is today the result of a merger of a merger of a merger. In almost a century, it has undergone so many levels of change—not to mention different ownerships—that it is as different from any other American company as one huge boulder on a mountainside is subtly different from another. A few years ago, it reached the growing circle of businesses with sales of $1 billion a year, a pinnacle sought after by many. But, like many, it ran into trouble.

The reasons are the classic ones for the quarter-century that began with the 1950s. One was a difficulty in keeping up with the times. Another was that the company became involved in conglomeration, the buying of other types of businesses which had little relationship with the original company or with each other. A third was that still newer owners appeared on the scene but lost basic interest in the company.

But, to keep the matter in balance, they took pains to turn the stewardship over to the right man—and then lost interest again.

The people in the company are typical of the American white-collar worker. Immersed in a conservative industry which had seen no upheavals or major changes in techniques for decades, they were unaware that their biggest problem was their lack of productivity. They weren't even worried when the company was acquired by a holding company run by a mercurial, temperamental financier. They were convinced that their longtime superiors would protect them. And they weren't completely wrong. The bosses did protect the staff as much as they could until they themselves were fired.

In addition, since at their core businesses are never more than the people who run them or work for them, this is the story of two men. Two egocentric, dominant personalities who created separate waves of fame, notoriety, innovation, and drama. They grew apart from each other, however, with unforeseen results, and eventually all 50,000 employes felt the tremors.

So those are the three elements of this book—a company, its people, and the two men who were its prime movers. But in essence, this is also the portrait of a social experiment carried on in the pressure crucible of New York's financial and merchandising world.

As a member of the business and financial news staff of *The New York Times*, I was fortunate in being involved in the coverage of this drama during the decade in which it unfolded. But I was even more fortunate during the writing of this book. The off-again, on-again business merger which is the major complication in this real-life story turned on-again and was actually consummated in the final weeks of the writing. It adds a real conclusion to what would have been in a sense an unfinished account and it is gratefully used that way.

A variety of narrative methods is used here, including a frequent semifictional approach, since a sense of authenticity can only come from both objective and subjective means. And, besides describing their actions, I have also taken the liberty of putting myself in the hearts and minds of a number of those in this book. I have done this on the basis that while it is presumptuous, close knowledge of the circumstances and pressures that surrounded them allow me to re-create reasonably the workings of the inner as well as the outer man.

Finally, I wish to make a major acknowledgment to Robert J. Markel, editor-in-chief of Grosset & Dunlap, whose idea formed the subject of this book and whose patience and encouragement were boundless during the three years of research and writing.

I.B.

One THE WAVES OF CHANGE

1. Here I Am

The short, stocky man with the bald head walked briskly from the doorway to the long, oval table. He stared briefly around at the crowded room of curious and hostile faces. Smiling, his lower lip pouting a bit, he said:

"Well, here I am. My name is Samuel Neaman, Sam Neaman. I'm fat. I'm ugly. I'm Jewish. And I'm your new boss."

He waited a few moments for their surprise to dissolve. Almost everyone in the room was either middle-aged or older. A few were young. All were Gentile. Some were smiling, and some of those smiles held admiration. Yet, a few frowns lingered. They would not, he guessed, ever be erased.

"I'm your new boss," he went on. "But I'm here mainly to help you. I believe that people can help each other." After a pause, he added, "This is, of course, my friends, if you will allow me. I have helped people before."

A tall man in a dark suit in the back scowled. As the man muttered to a neighbor, the speaker pointed a not unfriendly finger at him and said, "Sir, I don't know your name, but I think you want to say something. Please?"

The man in back straightened up. He seemed even taller and

3

more angry. "My name is Henry Werner," he said in a deep voice. "You're right, there is something I want to say, even though it may cost me my job. I don't think you can help us. We don't need any help. All we need is a little more time. We don't need this merger. No way."

Neaman's smile grew. His hand slapped the table hard, and he turned to a stolid man sitting nearby. "Walt," he said, "I like him. He's a man with guts. Let's make sure he gets the kind of assignment such a man deserves." He addressed Henry Werner again. "I like a man that speaks up," Neaman said. "Unfortunately, the merger is a fact, a *fait accompli*. But if you will bear with me, I think you will find that everybody needs somebody."

He nodded in a friendly manner to the fifty men in the room and moved away from the table. It had all lasted less than five minutes. He left with his arm around the shoulder of Walter Straus, the man he had turned to. As he did, Neaman's face displayed satisfaction at the ripple of applause that followed him out of the packed room.

Fifteen or twenty minutes before, he had emerged from his chauffeured black Cadillac and taken the elevator to the third floor of the Manhattan building. "Would you be so good as to tell Walter Straus that Sam Neaman is here?" he had told the receptionist. Her eyes had widened at the mention of his name. A few moments later as he entered the office with the sign on the door, "Walter Straus, Chairman of the Board," he found Straus standing in the middle of the room, a tight smile on his square face.

"Hello, Sam."

"Here I am."

"How do you want to do this, Sam?"

"I should meet all the people."

"I'll call a meeting of the entire management team in five minutes. I told them all to stand by."

And that was how the merger between McCrory Corporation (Neaman's company) and the J. J. Newberry Stores Company (Straus's firm) was sealed on a human basis. Some weeks later, Neaman confided to an interviewer why he had elected to make such a frank introduction to a "roomful of stiffs."

"I was very nervous that day," he recalled. "I didn't sleep so well the night before. The merger had taken place. Already, the news was old. But, still I had to meet the people, and they had a name for being anti-Semitic. When I began to shave that morning, I looked at myself in the mirror and what did I see there? Sam Neaman. He's fat. He's ugly. He's Jewish. And he's the new boss. There was only one way to get around the problem. I would put all my cards on the table, the faces up, and that would break the ice."

It had worked, Neaman decided, back again in the Cadillac. The national headquarters of both McCrory and Newberry were less than five blocks apart in mid-Manhattan, but it could have been a world. At that point, late October 1972, Neaman's firm had just reported nine-months' sales of $766 million and record net income of about $4 million. Straus's company in the same period had a loss of $1.4 million on sales of less than $284 million. A truly miserable performance on top of earlier losses. Sixty-one years in existence, the Newberry stores, 740 in all, were virtually in bankruptcy. The McCrory takeover was a lifeline being thrown almost humanely to a drowning company.

As Neaman's limousine threaded its way through the midtown traffic, Walter Straus sat back in his high, leather chair and mopped his sweating face. Good-bye $100,300 in earned remuneration, he thought, and good-bye $50,000 in estimated annual retirement benefits. He realized that too much expansion into different types of stores and into foreign endeavors, all based on bad advice from his colleagues, had done him in. Outside his door, he heard a stirring, a murmuring of voices. He knew it was some of his top executives, loose after being emotionally drained but with enough residue of frustration to want somehow to exhaust it. What could they do? What could he do? They—and he—had had their day. Now, the day was Neaman's.

Meanwhile, the sleek Cadillac arrived at the door of the McCrory Building. Hugh, the young chauffeur, bounded out and opened the car door. "Come back at two," Neaman told him as he entered the building. The twelve-story structure, remodeled by an all too willing landlord, housed the administrative and central buying offices for all of McCrory's 1,100 stores. One of America's largest retailers, McCrory had once been moribund itself but was now vital, perky, thriving, and innovative. As he progressed into the building, Neaman told himself that even the lobby—with two smiling women receptionists, two stern security guards, and a number of anxious salesmen waiting to get in—exuded a smile and a smell of success. Perhaps success was a state of mind, he thought, but that was only after success had become a reality. Everything else was a myth.

He smiled at the eager greetings of all in the lobby. In the elevator reserved for top executives, he gestured in a friendly if restrained way as the door opened at various floors to expose other eager or surprised faces. By the time the elevator had reached the ninth floor, where he stepped out, he had made several decisions. Henry Werner, the protestor, was a malcontent whose continued service would be like a boil on the neck of the company. He must go and soon, guts or not. Walter Straus, though cooperative and philosophical about his failure, would have to be relegated to a minor post at a cut in salary, but quietly. Any prominent exposure of such a prominent failure would hurt progress. Neaman had no doubt that Straus, like a branch withering away from the rest of the tree, would soon fall away altogether.

Heavy, well-dressed, his stomach beginning to rumble despite the bleak prospect of an unchanging lunch of two scoops of cottage cheese and two pieces of Ry-Krisp, Neaman moved confidently through the clean, smooth hallway to his office at the end of it. Here again, as he passed the various offices, faces bent to desks looked up with respect, fear, awe. He nodded at all and savored the satisfaction that this created. Good, good. As Margit Bergklint, his secretary, glanced at him with her usual, impassive expression but this time with a concerned question in her eyes, he nodded firmly at her, smiling his answer. Yes, it had gone well. He had carried off his entry into Newberry with neatness and aplomb as he had everything else. McCrory had come a long way, as had Neaman. As part of McCrory, Newberry would also come a long way. With such a bright past, such a bright present, such a bright transition, how could the future look anything but bright for him, for all 50,000 of them?

But that didn't matter so much to him. Consciously, Neaman knew he was very much an operator in and a product of the present. It's what you did now, every moment of the now, that determined how well you did later. Why is it so difficult for everyone to grasp that simple fact of life? He sighed at the sheer inability of people to think clearly. He moved to his desk and impatiently tapped his intercom button to get the meeting started.

2. No Wrenchings, No Agonies

Margit Bergklint does everything well, without fuss or undue gestures. A taciturn, stocky Swede, within five minutes she has summoned everyone and has all the food distributed before each of them, with the help of an aide from the company kitchen. Quietly, she closes the door, and they begin.

But they eat first, taking their cue from Sam Neaman, who pitches into his cottage cheese as though it were a feast and he vitally needs its fuel. He pushes the empty plate aside, stares thoughtfully at an optional dessert plate with a large canned peach-half swimming in thick sauce and pushes that away too. The others with full, more calorie-loaded dishes, have tried to keep up with him but have failed. He smiles indulgently and says, "Eat, eat, gentlemen. You will need all your energy. I will talk."

Before each plate, folded like a tiny tent, is an angled card. Sam nods at the cards. "Gentlemen," he begins, "because of the importance of this meeting, I want to make sure that you have my aids to successful management in front of you, even though you may have seen them so many times that they are already embedded on your brains. Let me read while you eat."

Clearing his throat, Neaman recites:

```
Key to Successful
Management.
    * Facts
    * Plans
    * Execution
    * Supervision
```

He pauses and says, "Now, gentlemen, please reverse the card." They do and he reads:

> Directives for
> Supervisors.
> * Detect
> * Correct
> * Prevent

Neaman glances around the table. "I hope that you will all bear these principles in mind," he says, "as we begin this first effort to integrate Newberry into McCrory with one initial goal—we wish to avoid the wrenchings and agonies of previous McCrory merge-ins. To the extent that we can accomplish that, gentlemen, we may have the type of painless merger that will create much sympathy and good-will for us not only among the 15,000 Newberry employes but also in the entire retailing business."

They all nod. He nods, emphatically. "How will we do it?" Neaman asks. "As we always do things—the same way that has made us the talk of the retail world. We will use all our normal talents to help each other. The thirty-second largest merchandising company on the Fortune 500 list of all companies will absorb the forty-second largest so that we will automatically push ourselves ten levels up on the list. A big, new land mass emerges between the great continents. Am I melodramatic, gentlemen? I can see it on your faces. No—because if we can forget the bottom-line consideration for just a moment—we will again create waves in the variety-store business and in American business in general. Instead of chopping heads, hands, hearts, we will help more average people with average talents to exceed themselves. It is beautiful. Imagine, people whose efforts previously led only to bringing a major American company to the brink of bankruptcy will soon, by means of our approach, become successful and fulfilled only because they will have the opportunity to use properly their natural abilities and traits. . . ."

He trails off, his round face drained by the purity of his emotion and his long, thin nose tight. He stares into space.

At the other end of the table, Stanley Kunsberg stirs. The

senior member of the five under Sam, he feels it is incumbent on him to react first. "It's wonderful, Sam," he says in a confident, resonant tone. "I think I can speak for all of us and say once more that it's a great privilege to be associated with you in this thing. And in all the company's endeavors. Who says that American business is cold-hearted? Look what you've done for so many people."

Neaman's eyes drift back to those around the table. They have stopped eating, although not finished. The moment, he realizes, is beyond food, beyond the needs of the body but belongs perhaps to the heart, to the soul. "Thank you," he says, hoarsely. "Thank you, gentlemen. Now, let us proceed." But he stares challengingly at each one. It is as if to say, as always, when will you—each of you—contribute to this exercise in positive thinking? Kunsberg, his president, who came to him from another division. Norman Mallor, an efficient financial vice-president albeit without any chemistry for people. Frank Patchen, president of his variety-stores division, probably one of the most conscientious followers in recent American history but always a best man, never a groom. Harold Hughes, his own administrative assistant and vice-president, whose belief in Neaman is often an embarrassing thing. And Steve Jackel, his department-store operations vice-president, who really wasn't too involved in the Newberry acquisition but whose talents and problems are of such dimensions that Sam gives him unprecedented attention, exposure, and criticism.

Some weeks later, Neaman was asked by an interviewer how he worked with people, particularly executives. He replied:

"It isn't a simple matter. You work with them for a lifetime, and you still don't know. 'People' is a plural, don't forget, not a singular. Each case is different. Some people need you to lean on. Some people don't want to see you. They only want to know that you are on the horizon, in case you're needed so they can run to you. Some people don't want you to exist.

"The important thing is to be lucky enough to find a young man who has a certain amount of talent who gets a kick out of exploiting his talent and not out of exploiting the money that his talent earns for him. And that's the big thing. Because most people will work very hard to reach a certain position of earnings. But the day they come home and say, 'Honey, I'm a vice-president and I'm making $35,000 a year as of this morning,' his wife says, 'And when are we going to live? Let's join the club. Let's invite some people. I backed you up to now, so let's enjoy it.'

"So now, instead of being ready to recognize that the compensation he got is not for past performance but is an inducement for future performance, he and his family want—and I don't blame them—to use the fruits of what they think is their past performance. And so he's got to invite people and they invite him back and he comes to the office with rings under his eyes because he can't be out entertaining or being entertained or going to the theater—important as it is to the culture—until midnight and then travel for an hour and a half from that new house that she wanted for the kids to be in the office and take the pressure. In no time, he's tired. If you're tired, your brain doesn't work as good as when you're not tired. When your interests are scattered and you're still worried about did you say the right thing last night or why did so-and-so not get along with you or what wonderful impressions you made on someone, your mind is on the entertainment part of your life and not on your business.

"The society of today and the psychologists and the sociologists keep talking about the diversion needed and the rest and the fact that you have to release your tensions. Therefore, all the emphasis is put on your responsibility to your wife, to your family, to your social life, to community, to everything except to one thing. Your responsibility to your job or to your business or to your function outside the home. And management is a very tough taskmaster; it's a very tough mistress. It's all or nothing. If you don't give all, you won't get anything."

Sam's hard stare has run its course. The others relax.

"Yes, a painless merger," he tells them, "but our real, real goal is something else, of course. I hope in my heart that all of you understand it. We would be foolish if we did not capitalize on the opportunities this merger offers. We have done well up to now—our turnaround from an $18 million loss to an $8 million profit in one year and our ability to stay in the black ever since shows what people can do when they truly work together. But we still need a place under the sun between the giants. We need to find a place where the public needs us, and we have only started to find it."

Kunsberg, the one man besides Steve Jackel who can stand up to Neaman, asks, "Sam, we can't handle all the people that Newberry has, can we? We have to face up to the fact that we are going to have to terminate a lot of them."

Neaman nods. "True, but that comes later. First, there are a few things we have to do. One of them is to set up a merger committee of which this group will be the nucleus. Another that has an even greater priority is a program of communications, which we have to generate among the Newberry people and the industry. It will have a double purpose. One will be to head off all the rumors about head-cutting and discrimination that were so damaging in our other mergers. The second will be to get a jump on implanting our philosophy among the Newberry layers of command even before anybody comes on board."

Jackel asks, "How do you propose that we should do that, Sam?" The youngest in the group, Steve has a voice with a youthful, virile quality that seems to be out-of-place in the tone of discussion. The group's talks, as always, have an elder statesman connotation. And, as always, Neaman suspects that Steve Jackel enjoys injecting his thirty-one-year-old personality and timbre into it, almost like a sexual presence.

"I'm sure," Sam replies, "that you, Mister Hip-Shooter, could have thought of it yourself if you didn't always talk first and think later." Steve's neat head snaps back in surprise but his constant, slightly insolent smile remains. And then, as always, Sam smiles warmly at him, as if he were after all only a fond father chastising an immature but well-loved son. "All right," Neaman resumes, "this is how. We will make up a list of about 200 Mc-Crory executives and managers who know their counterparts in the Newberry stores and others in the industry, and you will suggest to them to call all those that they know and spread the word along these lines—how paternal and brotherly we are in this company, how we function as a team of many teams to get the job done, and how the Newberry people will benefit from it."

He pauses, drains a tall glass of milk at his elbow, and adds, "According to my calculation, if 200 of our people each make five phone calls in the next week and if only half the 1,000 people they reach will each phone five people and they will phone five people and so on, it is not mathematically inconceivable that within two weeks as many as 250,000 phone calls can be made in our behalf. Think of it, gentlemen, a veritable communications avalanche. And who will be the beneficiary? We will."

His eyes are gleaming. Again Kunsberg feels it is necessary for him to say it for all. "Sam, it sounds great. The numbers are fantastic. What a productive way to break the ice! One of us should have thought of it. But you're always a step or two ahead of everybody."

Neaman shakes it off graciously. "It's nothing—but thank you, Stanley," he says.

Margit removes the plates. She is agile, quick, and efficient in this as she is in her regular work as Neaman's executive secretary. She has, in spite of her stockiness, a pure, blond attractiveness without hardness. "Sweet-cream soft," Steve Jackel tells himself, admitting later to Kunsberg that he had felt an impulse as she bent near him to stroke her firm flank but happily had resisted it. Neaman would have been repelled, being known to dislike any sort of sexual demonstration.

"All right, enough," Neaman says, running an impatient hand across his expanse of bald scalp. "We are spending too much time on preliminaries. Tell us, Frank, about the plans for the meetings."

Frank Patchen, quiet up to this point, glances quickly at a typed sheet before him and says, "Of course, Sam." He is in his late fifties, resembles in manner and appearance a long-time history teacher or economics teacher, and has an extreme pallidness which almost shocks those who meet him for the first time. His voice is soft and well-modulated. "Sam and I have mapped two meetings in which we will officially greet the Newberry family," he says. "The first will be held in the Fontainebleau in

Miami Beach. It will combine our annual awards-giving dinner with a meeting in which about 1,000 McCrory and Newberry managers—the number is fluid at this point—and their families will meet socially. The point will be to hail the birth of the newly merged company as the third largest general-merchandise and variety-store chain in America. That meeting will be held in about four months."

"How much will it cost?" asks Kunsberg.

Patchen hesitates, and Neaman replies, "I estimate upward of $250,000. And well worth it, let me add."

"What about the Federal Trade Commission?" This from Steve Jackel. He stares at the top of the table rather than at either Neaman or Patchen.

A big vein expands in Sam's scalp. He answers slowly, carefully controlling himself. "That is irrelevant to the discussion. But since it has been raised, it is not necessary to worry. We have expensive attorneys who have checked into it. The Commission will not oppose the merger since the F.T.C. has, starting in the 1958 recession, recognized the principle of economics in mergers. If a company is on the brink, the Commission will not oppose its merger into another, more successful business. Sometimes, the government makes sense. This is such a time."

Patchen resumes, his smooth resonance easing the tension that flows from Neaman to Jackel. "The second official meeting will come three weeks later at a fashionable hostelry in the Maryland suburbs. All of my top team from the McCrory variety division will be there along with a similar group of Newberry executives. Straus of Newberry will sit with Sam as he holds the first of about twenty-five rounds of private talks with the combined staffs. The objective will be to explain personally why the merger should succeed and why and how all will benefit. The concept of having Straus sitting at the head table with Sam is to symbolize the synergistic approach. Straus himself will hold forth as much as anyone. Sam feels—and I can only agree—that there is no credibility quite as convincing as the local chief advocating the benefits of tribal marriage."

"Sam, how will we charge the $300,000 or thereabouts that these meetings will cost?" Norman Mallor, McCrory's corporate financial vice-president, speaks almost in a monotone. Large, heavy, a seasoned controller, apolitical and unemotional, he never volunteers an opinion unless invited. "Normally, since the Newberry acquisition into a McCrory division mostly involves a division, we should charge the cost to the division. But some Newberry stores, being department stores, will go into our department-store division. Do you want to charge it against the corporation?"

Neaman nods. "Yes, of course," he says. "We could split it up. But frankly I still prefer to have the variety division's high profits to remain the jewel in our crown. We bought a badly troubled chain when we acquired our department stores. Everyone gives us license, time to demonstrate our magic there. So charge the whole company. Not everybody will like it but it will be our policy decision."

"What's next, Sam?" asks Kunsberg. "Do you want me to proceed—or would you rather carry on?"

"Please."

"Fine," Kunsberg says. "After the second meeting, Sam and I will tour the country making personal calls at as many Newberry stores as we can. Each of us will take a different route, criss-crossing the states so we can maximize the number of stores we get to. In three weeks, we estimate we can personally talk to about fifty-five percent of all the Newberry managers. But in the final few days, we will hold mass meetings with managers in the regional and district offices so that we can reach that percentage. Don't forget, there are almost 750 Newberry stores. Our meetings will begin at 7 A.M. and continue as late as midnight. There's a hell of a lot of ground to cover."

"If I can take some of the load off your shoulders," Patchen says.

Sam shakes his head. "Thank you, Frank. That is just like you. But you will have enough to do in the next six months just holding the fort and planning everything. The cross-country travel is mine and Stanley's. We are thinking of letting Straus travel, too. But to be brutally honest, I don't quite trust him on his own. He'll be reliable if one of us is there with him. So I am reluctant to let him go by himself—"

Steve, feeling a need to demonstrate some solid support, interjects, "Sam, I agree. I've had some talks with Straus. I think he feels lousy inside about everything. After all, only a couple of years ago he was bragging to all the Wall Street analysts about his great expansion program and what it would do for Newberry. Now, they're flat on their ass, and only we can save it. No, you can't trust him to go around on his own. He could sabotage us."

Sam seems grateful, but he remains reserved toward Steve, only nodding slightly in response.

"Meanwhile," Kunsberg continues, "we will have an ongoing process of McCrory's executives contacting Newberry's. Our people will work to reassure their counterparts in Newberry that they won't be lost in the shuffle, that we need them, that they need us, and that they will be treated like equal partners with us. We expect the continuing one-to-one communications to work wonders."

Sam arises briskly and goes into his office. The meeting has obviously come to an intermission. After the chairman completes several phone calls, he orders in soft drinks, nuts, and raisins. He is opposed to hard drinks during working hours but never comments on after-hour drinking practices. He himself has never been known to drink liquor. Margit comes in with trays of Coke, Pepsi, Seven-Up, Dr. Brown's black cherry soda, the nuts, and the raisins, and the meeting resumes.

"All right, so much for the communications phase of the integration," says Neaman, sipping and burping Pepsi bubbles. He clears his throat. "Now—to the most important part of our discussion—what will the integration itself demand from us? Our job will be fivefold. We have to blend the merchandise needs and ordering procedures of the two companies and to make them more compatible. We have to determine how to handle the movement of merchandise from all the various warehouses. We have to design a store-reporting system so we know what is selling and what isn't so we can develop our inventory control system around all the stores, including the new ones. Then we will have to separate the company into individual units. And we will develop an operating table-of-organization that will work."

Sam explains that the latter should flow naturally from a breakdown that he, Kunsberg, and Patchen have already made. This will divide the combined two companies into six, each accounting for about $100 million in annual sales. Figured on a roughly equal basis on productivity, says Neaman, it would not be difficult to arrive at an adequate staff allocation.

"That brings us back to my original question," Kunsberg says. "How can we handle all 15,000 Newberry employes when about twenty-five percent of all the stores aren't making a dime?"

Neaman shrugs. "What can we do? Many will have to go. But who will be better off if the company continues on its disaster path and all lose their jobs?"

"Sam, they'll blame losing their jobs on the Jews that run this business," Kunsberg says bitterly.

"Of course," Sam agrees. He is not much interested in the point.

"One thing you can be certain of," volunteers Patchen, as he straightens up from a stooped position. "My team is keeping up its constant contacts with the Newberry people to dispel that notion. I've said it many times—we've never had any problems of racial discrimination since Sam Neaman became chief executive of this company, either going up or coming down, and we're not going to stand for any charges in that now or for any anti-Semitism. The Neaman record speaks clearly for itself. No one person in this industry has done so much for so many."

"Thank you," Neaman says. He swallows some of his soda and asks, "Frank, would you please speak a little bit now on the restructuring? I think you have a lot of interesting things to tell us."

Patchen spells it out pontifically and in a scholarly fashion. He explains that there will be in the new McCrory corporate lineup a sort of General Motors arrangement of six divisions. "Instead of adhering to the traditional method in mergers of having a surviving and a nonsurviving company," he tells them, "we will have a totally new entity. There will be six companies, five buying divisions, and separate administrative and service groups. It will be, if you will permit me my hyperbole, the harvest of the Neaman philosophy of people with normal talents helping and supporting other people with normal talents.

"But—in one of those strange quirks of fate that bless everyone—the entire synergistic process will mean that many people in the resulting organization will be doing things differently and better than they have ever done them before," says Patchen. The cross-breeding will mean an interchange of systems, he emphasizes, a scrapping of old, unproductive ways and the creation of new tools and procedures that are vital in operating a thoroughly modern company."

"Who will assume the direction of the six divisions within-a-division?" someone asks. Most of these presidents will come from outside, Patchen replies. One or two may come from within. But as for the rest, an additional cross-fertilization is the goal. Hopefully, he adds, the outsiders will help to engender a broader outlook.

Already, Sam informs them, he has been getting a flurry of applications from people in companies even larger than McCrory to fill the divisional presidencies.

The meeting begins breaking up on a strong, positive note. But Steve Jackel, who pathologically must every so often step to the edge, cannot resist being the devil's advocate one last time. "Sam," he asks, "what do you think Riklis will say about that $250,000 party at the Fontainebleau?"

To Neaman, it is like a slap in the face. Caught in the process of getting up from his chair and holding up his glass to finish the Pepsi, Sam almost begins to choke with the effrontery of the question. He stands straight after clearing his throat of the phlegm and asks Steve, "Who did you say?"

"Riklis."

"Who is he?"

"Who is he? You must be kidding, Sam. He's only the guy that owns this company. He—"

"I know *who* he is. But who *is* he?"

"Well—"

"As far as I am concerned, he is no one. I run this company the way I want to. He has nothing to do with us. Don't ever let me hear you mention his name."

Steve's stare dies. "Sorry, Sam," he says.

The room empties. Almost but not quite. One remains, the only one of the six who has not uttered a single word. Harold Hughes, Neaman's administrative vice-president, is a tall, sad-faced man about forty-five years old with big, round, wide eyes and a hesitant manner. His function is to be Neaman's memory and right and left arms. Later, he will meet with the chairman and go over the meeting and analyze what was said and what the reactions were. Even though Neaman has had a tape recorder running throughout on a nearby table as always, he trusts Harold Hughes' memory and infallible tone-true instinct much more and will soon summon him for the recap. But Hughes does not move. Neaman has had such a seminal effect on his life that Hughes could not fail but act as a Neaman alter-ego during the meeting. Though his impassive face and reserved stance completely withheld it, his emotions and nerves had bristled at Steve Jackel's youthfully brash interjections, quailed at Kunsberg's insistence on knowing how many Newberry employes would be lopped off, objected to Norman Mallor's question on how to charge off the cost of the two meetings, and had almost convulsed at Steve Jackel's insufferable question about Riklis.

All this left him drained. It was as if he were a raw nerve end in Neaman's body, suffering in greater degree the slings and arrows delivered to Neaman, however subtly, more than any of Neaman's own nerves. A devout Catholic, a devoted family man, an otherwise balanced professional executive, he loved Neaman in spite of Neaman's differences: his style, his puritanical demands, his startling celibacy, his egocentricity, his megalomania, his occasional brutality, and his Jewishness. Before Neaman, Hughes had had little hope, only the certainty of ever-growing frustration over a once promising career going down the drain. Neaman had given him a new life—a reason to hope and to breathe deeply once again—and he would never forget it.

As the expected summons comes from the other room, Hughes straightens his shoulders, cleanses his system of its bitterness toward the others, and jumps toward the chairman's office—all in one fluid motion.

3. Patience as a Virtue

Mergers in business were a way of life in the United States between 1962 and 1972. Although their number has since dropped sharply, there were about 30,000 during the decade. They were the third wave of consolidations which created a major change in the structure of the country's commerce and industry. The first wave, occurring about the turn of the century, involved tidal movements within certain industries which led to the rise of the first American corporate colossi. Each was aimed, often openly, at dominating a market. Such firms were Standard Oil of New Jersey, General Electric Company, and the United States Steel Corporation.

The second wave rolled up in the 1920s. Financial holding companies invested an increasing portion of their assets in various related concerns. Eventually assuming control, they formed umbrella corporations which had sufficient assets and share-of-market to become dominant operators in their fields. All the thunder of President Theodore Roosevelt's blasts against big business and the exercise of the Sherman Antitrust Law, which had cut back the number of large business mergers, became only echoes of the recent past. Such newly emerging market giants were the Radio Corporation of America, American Cyanamid, and the General Foods Corporation.

The newest wave came in the 1960s and early 1970s. At first, the trend after World War II did not appear very pervasive. In 1920, only two years after World War I ended, there were only 206 mergers. In 1950, five years after World War II ended, there were still only 219 mergers. Even in the decade after each war the trends were similar: in 1930, there were 799 mergers; in 1960, there were 844. But, starting in 1962, the annual rate of mergers doubled and tripled, turning that decade into the most prolific for corporate marriages in American history.

Fed by a frenetic stock market, indulged by an Administration that savored the backstop of an immense military–industrial complex, financed by investment bankers always on the lookout for some new star on which to hang lush price-earnings multiples, mergers grew—there were 2,400 in 1966, 3,000 in 1967, 4,500 in 1968, and 6,100 in 1969. It was the decade of the conglomerates: loosely held, loosely financed, loosely operated combines whose common denominator was neither a homogeneous product mixture or related markets. The common thread was a thirst for earnings expansion. It was a new thing on the world scene, grab bags of sundry products and services. The innocuous-sounding multiname designations were at first hard to swallow, but what a resounding ring they soon achieved: Ling–Temco–Vought, Gulf + Western, Rapid–American, National General, Bangor Punta. And behind each, a swashbuckler good at figures, better at *chutzpah*, best at bounce. No temporary disaster was too traumatic, too debilitating at the bottom-line, too corrosive of the reputation.

Agape at the wildly successful antics of the conglomerators, the traditional companies rallied, belatedly no doubt but with gusto. Their moves were as often as not defensive measures, buying into other companies, either product-related or not, so that the conglomerate raider would not find them passive, a sitting duck.

And so if the 1960s produced the most widespread merger movement in American history, its stimuli nonetheless encompassed all the previous trends: industrial agglomeration, market domination, financial leverage, earnings expansion mechanisms. And providing the fuel for all of it was a hyperactive stock market, with 30 million American investors shuttling from one high-flyer to another in a daily search for a windfall that might mean capturing the American dream: early retirement, high fixed income, two cars in the garage, and maybe a trim cabin cruiser at the dock, with recourse to the capital-gains loophole at will.

A few caught the golden ring. But, to the many who didn't, it didn't much matter. Money was plentiful, supply and demand were high, and if the average man envied the twenty-eight-year-old who had made $1 million before he was thirty, he recognized that such were the whims of fate. The but-for-him-there-would-be-I rationale remained part of the national penchant for hero worship. The bitterness of the seventies recession was still a few years away. The sixties, at any rate the early portion, had the effect of instant nostalgia on many, even as they lived through its happy and not-so-happy excesses.

It was a giddy time, with more than a few paradoxes to delight the conglomerate makers. The Wall Street bankers, after acting as the financiers and company-finders for the conglomerates, ostracized them. In the colleges, economics scholars published thick treatises scorning the diversified companies and then published newer ones hailing them under the label of "multinational" companies, singularly fit to grapple with Japan and West Germany for world trade domination. Washington did its own type of flip-flop. The Justice Department version was to warn the country's top 200 companies that it would oppose mergers among them, but it let off the International Telephone and Telegraph Company when it acquired the Hartford Fire Insurance Company, a merger very much in the rarified strata of the top 200. The Federal Trade Commission, two years after releasing a much-heralded report expressing fears on the economic effect of conglomerate mergers, circulated a second report finding no discernible adverse effect on the economy from the same mergers. In 1967 and 1969, two blue-ribbon presidential task forces were named to look into the need for changes in the antitrust laws. They rendered reports calling for some sweeping new legislation and new federal policy. Both studies were consigned to deep White House drawers.

Many old-line companies were absorbed by the conglomerates. Some were squeezed dry of their potential, not to mention their existing assets, and cast on the dump-heap of outlived corporations. Others already moribund had the breath of life pumped into them and thrived in spite of themselves. Others, still alive but static, were going nowhere and were taken over by fast-footed men going somewhere.

McCrory Corporation was one of these static companies, and Meshulam Riklis was one of those fast-footed men.

The company and the man came into each other's orbit in 1956. Much had happened to both by then but in totally different ways. McCrory had already been involved in several mergers, its directions and fortunes rocketing this way and that, reflecting the skills and inclinations of the men who took it over. Since companies are run by people, not by themselves, after more than half a century McCrory, one of the oldest variety-store companies in America, was not a very exciting or highly successful business, which told volumes about its various operators in the 1940s and 1950s. They were, perhaps, too close to the business, too inbred, too conservative, too crony-oriented.

Riklis was another matter. By that time—he was only thirty-five—the short, bustling, moon-faced maker of company marriages had in little more than seven years run through a dozen mergers. Each had been built on the framework of the previous one, erecting a skein of sundry firms. As he added more or traded one for another, he kept widening the circle of his power and wealth. But these were not his only drives. Equally important were his zeal to expand his scope and a restless energy that compelled him to juggle a handful of deals at once.

Some years after he took control of McCrory, he carefully enunciated his three basic creeds in putting businesses together.

One was a conviction that every acquisition must create enough cash or produce its equivalent in credit or borrowing power to equal its purchase price. This yielded funds or credit to make other acquisitions.

A second was that no merger would ever be consummated unless both sides were satisfied with the terms. In a strong sense, he would say, it's like a couple who can only really enjoy the love act if they feel totally equal to each other. "Less equal would make it a rape," he would add, grinning widely.

The third was to ensure that as much capital as possible was retained in the business. Rather than deplete his cash reserves, he would prefer to borrow when he could. This gave him his base. And, in his own manner, he would explain that neither a friend nor a banker would hesitate to lend him $10 if he knew that Riklis had $100 in the bank. But if the lender knew that Riklis had "pissed away" the $100, he might not even lend him $1.

By the time he became aware of McCrory, Riklis had already become the subject of notoriety and controversy. To the Establishment, which meant Wall Street and the big, conventional companies, he seemed out of time and out of place. His bag of tricks—the clever exercise of leverage, buying one company by pledging the assets of another and by continuously floating new versions of securities—worried them. At least James J. Ling of Ling–Temco–Vought had had an electronics background and an engineering instinct, and Charles B. Thornton of Litton Industries had had an aircraft background and a scientific bent—but what did Riklis have? Only a mathematics degree and a security analyst's experience. Yet, he had combined both to organize investment syndicates, using a $25,000 kitty from his own and friends' pockets to move into a variety of companies. Within five years, he had organized from a welter of deals his own conglomerate, the Rapid–American Corporation, a nonentity designation if there ever was one but which he openly bragged would become the nameplate of a $1 billion empire. Would it be built on the emaciated bodies of undervalued companies? he was often asked. He would reply with a fine smile and a humble demurral. He had his own good secret, he gave the impression, and there was friendliness, if not good-will, at its base.

Riklis, in fact, had a peculiar kind of protective coloration. Even then, and especially later, it blunted most of the criticism hurled at him. It was an open amiability, a pleasant, smiling mien with soft brown eyes and wavy, brown-golden hair that belied any charges of deviousness and chicanery. Inside, he writhed under the verbal spitballs, displays of anti-Semitism, and ridicule. Outwardly, he took it all with a grin and a shrug.

It helped in a more important way, too. Not long after he had set up Rapid–American and brought in some old and some new friends to form a management team, he sat with a pair of men who operated a Midwest-based retail chain and said, "I want to buy your company. How about $25 million?"

They studied him and then one another. "How do you intend to pay for it, young man?" asked one of the owners who meant to humor the short, boyish stranger.

"In cash," he replied. "What else?"

And a week later he did pay cash, which was unusual, by selling off one of his companies. But the disarming smile that sealed the deal may have fooled the wily pair of sellers. By spending $25 million to obtain fifty-one percent of the new company, he was obtaining control of more than $35 million in assets.

Less than two years later, already known far and wide as a

company-trader, he was offered $50 million for the retail chain. He quickly accepted. But he showed his real mettle, his sensitive financial acumen, in that transaction. After discussing it with his colleagues, his lawyer, and a financial advisor, he reasoned that if Rapid–American were to sell the chain in which it held a controlling interest, Rapid would receive only a proportionate fifty-one percent of the purchase price. However, if Rapid sold all the chain's assets—stores, warehouses, and inventory—on an individual basis and then sold the retail corporation as a going business, it would cop the entire $50 million and maybe more. They agreed that it was the only thing to do.

In those closing months of 1959, Riklis found himself eager to complete the deal. The reason was that he had waited almost three years to acquire another, bigger retail company that had floated into his orbit but had eluded him: McCrory Corporation.

At the moment, McCrory was in difficulty. If business corporations have a work ethic and a spirituality—at least on the basis that a business that survives represents all the toil, aspirations, and devotion of all the people who have ever worked for it—then McCrory didn't deserve its lot at that point. Too many had put too much into it over the previous seventy years for the company to have fallen onto such hard times.

But, unpredictably, it had happened. It was one of those capricious ironies that sometimes cause man to despair of his fellows and psychiatrists to wonder fruitlessly why when two men are confronted by the same set of circumstances one will steal and one will not. McCrory had almost agreed to a merger with a company run by a convicted embezzler. It had been a near miss for McCrory. The possibility of having tied up with such a man shocked the company to its roots, not only because nothing of such potentially disastrous proportions had happened in all the previous years but also because McCrory was the type of company least prepared for it. Perhaps this was because its origins were imbedded in the rock of Quakerism and in the stern morality of a small Pennsylvania town. And it had never strayed from those basic roots.

In 1882, a twenty-two-year-old grocery-store clerk borrowed $550 from an uncle in a nearby town and opened a tiny variety store in his own community, which was less than 100 miles from Philadelphia. John G. McCrory candidly told one and all that his store would be based on the model of Frank W. Woolworth's store, started only three years earlier just fifty miles away in Lancaster and already a rousing success. Not unlike Frank Woolworth, who had been born on a farm in upper New York State and was about the same age as he was, McCrory was enterprising. Certainly, he was enough so to know a good idea when he saw one, even if it might not be his own.

He became one of several young entrepreneurs, such as Woolworth and Sebastian S. Kresge—the latter for a time a partner of McCrory's—who pioneered the variety-store concept of mass display, low cost, and high volume in an expansion across the country. Perhaps because of his Quaker upbringing, John McCrory never quite jumped as high or reached as far as the other two. But his business, through the opening of more stores first in the small towns and cities and then in the larger urban centers, grew apace in the twentieth century, aided by the country's population boom, the increasing popularity of home sewing, and the impact of the self-service concept.

Wandering into a typical Woolworth, Kresge, W. T. Grant, McCrory, or S. H. Kress variety store without first looking at the store's name, the casual shopper would have had difficulty knowing which one he was in. But it didn't matter. The McCrory stores filled an important need as did their competition. By 1946, when McCrory engaged in its first merger with a smaller, similar chain, it operated almost 215 stores yielding annual sales of $112 million and profits of over $5 million. By acquiring the 235-store McLellan group, McCrory immediately increased its annual sales by $60 million and its profits by another million.

But, one by one, the variety chain founders, including John McCrory, passed away. McCrory's company in turn was acquired in 1956 by a holding company which was itself controlled by a financial syndicate. Absentee ownership and a leadership vacuum (caused in part by management's diverse business interests) robbed McCrory of any dynamism it still retained. Rumors that the syndicate was anxious to sell soon drifted across Riklis's sensitive antennae. Another holding company, however, got there first and took control. The bouncy, affable Riklis was frustrated. But since he was at the time in the process of selling his own Midwest retail chain for a $15 million profit, he could afford to be philosophical about his disappointment.

About a year and half later, the new owners of McCrory, disturbed by its profit drift and its vague direction, decided to accept an offer from an interested Southern retailer. The deal fell through and the circumstances which ultimately prevented it proved that the merger would have been a disaster.

Only thirty-one years old, Maurice E. Olen had recently been greeted as a boy wonder in retail circles. He had a natural talent for making the cash register ring and keep ringing, and if a certain mystical intensity seemed at times to burn in his eyes, it was understandable in the light of his great achievement.

His father, the founder of the small, Midsouth variety chain, had stunned many seven years earlier by turning it over while he was still hale and hearty to his twenty-four-year-old son. But after only those few years of stewardship, Maurice had expanded the number of stores fivefold to ninety and the amount of sales tenfold with commensurate profits. The feat had attracted so much attention that the much larger, better-known H. L. Green variety chain agreed to a merger with the Olen Stores if Maurice would become chairman-of-the-board of the combined company of 450 stores. Maurice and his father eagerly accepted.

And, as if that were not enough of an empire for him to rule, Maurice soon after proposed a merger with McCrory, which also had 450 stores. The offer from the "merchant's merchant" could not have come at a more opportune time for the disenchanted McCrory owners. The slight, myopic Maurice prepared to move triumphantly to New York.

But his elation proved short-lived as trouble developed in his own company. The country was deep into the 1958–59 recession and the newly expanded company seemed unable to improve its reduced profit margins. For a year, he tried every device and technique he knew, but nothing seemed to work. Then, one day, the outside auditing firm that handled McCrory's books telephoned the company's auditing committee and asked for an urgent meeting. The discussion had been under way only a short time when the committee summoned the youthful chairman of the company. A shortage of about $2 million in the Olen Stores' inventories had been discovered. A week later, amid cannonades of sensational stories in the press, the board of directors requested Maurice Olen's resignation. He was in prison before the year ended.

More than a decade later, Olen spoke to this writer and still, despite the passage of time, stoutly defended his honesty. He said he had been "framed." Afterward, the stigma of the sensational court case had fastened itself on him, he said, and had prevented him from going back into business again. No banker would lend him any funds to start over. In addition, his family's assets had been depleted, he said, in an effort to make good on the accounts' discrepancy. All he could do in the intervening years, he insisted, was to obtain occasional assignments as a merchandising consultant and to make sure that his name was kept out of the press.

But he neglected to say that he had been indicted once again during the ten-year period for embezzlement involving securities and had been put on a five-year probation. About two years after our talk, he was indicted for a third time on federal fraud charges.

Between its near disaster with Olen and its own drift, the McCrory board was in a state of confusion. Sensing that his opportunity was coming, Riklis continued to wait. He allowed some rumors to be leaked to the directors that he might be interested, but he made no direct contact with them. It only took a few more days for his long patience to be rewarded in the most gratifying way. He was invited to indicate if he might "care to make an offer."

With $50 million now burning in his pockets from the sale of his own chain, he arranged it so that all he needed to obtain a working control in McCrory was $7 million in cash. It was an unbelievably small amount for such a large company, but the owners were unduly anxious to sell. So now he had both McCrory and over $40 million with which to buy other companies and to obtain a foothold in the H. L. Green stores so he could later merge them into McCrory. He was poised to expand his empire quickly and to activate some long-standing plans.

But its cornerstone would be McCrory. With his purchase,

it was now in its fifth merger or ownership change. It had floundered for more than a decade and had fallen behind its competitors in many ways. If there is an ebb and flow in the life of a business, the company had some good times coming.

Appearing before the McCrory board, the new owner spoke in his eager, candid manner. "This company can be one of America's great companies," he said. "We are going to help you reach that goal, and we are also going to show our confidence in it by buying more and more McCrory shares on the open market. It's already the fourth-biggest chain after Woolworth, Kresge, and W. T. Grant. Does anyone here know any reason why the hell it can't be Number One?"

The meeting broke up as the happy directors rallied around Riklis, pumping his hand and patting him on the back.

4. Who Will Pick Up the Pieces?

It was no surprise to anyone who knew him, however, that as Meshulam Riklis took steps to set McCrory on a straighter course, he was busy on many other fronts. While buying more McCrory and Green shares, he also bought three more retail chains in about two years, adding them to the McCrory fold. But he had even more ambitious aspirations. He told everyone very openly that he had always dreamed of a $1 billion empire. But he told only his closest associates that he really wanted two $1 billion empires. The first would be erected on the McCrory framework. The other, he confided, would be built on the dollars generated from McCrory, dollars which would grow proportionately as Rapid–American increased its financial interest in its retailing subsidiary to far more than the forty percent it now owned.

So it became as clear to his closest associates as it was to him. McCrory would be a funnel. A smooth funnel through which dollars would flow. And the only way to make the funnel flow would be to ensure that the mechanism for which the funnel was only the outlet would be efficient, operative, and well-lubricated.

Always sensitive to the criticism that he was now deeply involved in retailing but knew nothing about it, he appointed merchants to both the top McCrory corporate and variety-store posts. He hired them from within, and he hired them from without. As the variety division added all the Green stores, its multiplied sales expanded those of the McCrory Corporation so that the retailing conglomerate—now the repository of about nine mergers—became a formidable company. As such, it attracted ambitious executives from other companies. Riklis did not hesitate to hire whom he considered the best, paying them top salaries.

In the late 1950s and the early 1960s, there were about six different teams variously running McCrory corporate and the division. None stayed more than a year or two. Few seemed able to adapt themselves to the vicious competition of the new discount stores, whose inroads began to hurt the variety more than the department stores.

Riklis's lavish offices in Manhattan became a turnstile for any who felt that they had the credentials. Despite the frenetic nature of his days, he found time to interview many. He was cordial, frank, and explicit. But he hurt no one's feelings, and all went away with the conviction that they were about to be hired at salaries well above the market. But while he talked to many, he hired few.

And those he hired disappointed him.

His inability to seat the right man—or men—in the key McCrory jobs put his entire $1.5 billion conglomerate into jeopardy in 1962 and 1963. It was an unexpected situation that became so traumatic that it etched wrinkles into his smooth, moon face.

From varied causes, such as a convergence of acquisitions in non-McCrory entities and poor performance from some older companies directly under the Rapid–American umbrella, Rapid had to face up to a sharp decline in its net income in 1962. Yet McCrory, still unconsolidated into Rapid's balance sheet because it was only about forty-five percent owned, gave evidence of topping off the year with record earnings. But, Riklis realized, if he could quickly increase Rapid's holdings in McCrory to fifty-one percent, he could still pull it out. The increased percentage of the subsidiary's earnings could be funnelled into Rapid's and the looming decline could be flattened out or even entirely removed.

Late in the year, he made his move. Committing his own cash reserves, making additional borrowings from banks, and laying on the line his holdings in McCrory as collateral, he spent $15 million for some 700,000 McCrory shares. He began to smile again but it was too soon.

McCrory was not doing nearly as well as he had been led to believe. Too many merchandise categories had not had the inventory turnover rate expected, and the markdowns were heavy. In addition, several new stores opened at high costs had not delivered their hoped-for sales. For these and other reasons clearly stamped "Bad Management," net income at McCrory was sixty percent lower than it was supposed to be. When the news was released, McCrory's stock dropped within weeks from twenty-five to under ten. It was a tremendous blow to many who had extended credit to Riklis and his two companies. Creditors became jittery. Some demanded more collateral for their unpaid loans. Suppliers had their lawyers call. Banks were silent but huddled nervously with each other. Some financial columnists began running rumors of a pending probe by the Securities and Exchange Commission. Riklis had the telephone company change both numbers in his Manhattan town house to unlisted ones.

Night after night, he huddled with Isidore Becker, Rapid's financial vice-president, seeking some way out.

Everything appeared to be foreclosed, however. Even Riklis's standard ploy of countering charges that he was over-leveraged by saying, "Maybe I don't have any cash but my rich subsidiary's got plenty," wouldn't work. The fact was that McCrory was cash-poor in 1963. It had built up large inventories on anticipated high sales to come from both improved merchandise assortments and some new, big stores. Seeking to shift some dividend dollars from shareholders to its own treasury, it had on Riklis's own instruction bought several hundred thousand shares of its own stock for almost $11 million. He winced at the recollection that he had insisted on the purchase. Those millions could have helped. How they could have helped!

Days passed. "Rik, the banks won't wait a hell of a lot longer," Becker told him. "We just gotta do something."

Riklis nodded slowly. His reaction process was malfunctioning. He had lost twenty pounds in addition to much of his credibility. He felt that he was only a rattling shell of himself both mentally and physically. But, staring at Becker, who more than anyone else in his organization was close to the bankers, he saw the harsh reality of the situation in Becker's pinched face and angry, frantic eyebrows.

"Right," he told Becker. "Absotively, posilutely right." He smiled weakly.

Within the next weeks and months, many drastic steps were taken. Riklis sold almost all of Rapid's operating properties to raise cash. He summarily dismissed the latest of McCrory's merchant chiefs. In their place, he installed another top executive from a competitive chain who had come highly recommended and instructed him to "just butcher" inventories. Unprofitable and borderline stores in all McCrory divisions were closed.

A few months later, cash generated by all the moves ran to almost $60 million. Past-due supplier bills were paid. Bank loan payments were brought up to date. A program of meetings with creditors ended in warm exchanges of good wishes. The crisis was over.

Riklis and Becker sat in the former's office late one night talking it over. This time they were relaxed, or relatively so. "We got problems yet, Rik," said Becker. "We scared off the wolves. But you gotta face it, people got memories like elephants."

"Like elephants."

Becker studied him. The wrinkles were not quite as deeply etched on the face as before. But there was something about the eyes—a wariness, an extreme alertness, perhaps a harassed underlayer—that was different. Riklis would never be quite the same. He would never forget how close he had come to complete financial disaster. But, Becker sensed, Riklis would be the better man for it, sharper and more hard-nosed.

"One thing we have to do soon—the sooner the better—is to find somebody to pick up the pieces at McCrory," Riklis said. "It's still our base. Our rock and our foundation."

"Nelson doesn't have it," Becker said. Gene Nelson was the merchant Riklis had recently hired to oversee the belt-tightening process.

Riklis grinned and shrugged. "I know," he said. "He's okay on taking orders and carrying them out. But what we need bad is a self-starter, somebody lean and mean, like they say, who can operate without us worrying about it. Frankly, I don't think it much matters who the hell runs McCrory. What we need is a top man to run the variety stores—that's where the big money and the big drain is. The other divisions are doing fine just running by themselves."

It was almost eleven o'clock. They knew their wives would be angry. Things, after all, had eased up. The crisis was over, at least temporarily. But there was something perverse and yet right in not wanting to run home. They had spent too many nights commiserating about their inability to straighten things out. Now the relief was a luxury, like a hot searing Turkish bath that seeps through the pores and cleanses away all the impurities. No, they would not leave for a little while yet. Sitting here in relative peace of mind was a joy. A joy.

After they discussed some of their potential problems, particularly the matter of market reaction to their plan to sell off another major McCrory division to raise more cash, Riklis stretched his short arms over his head. "Yeah," he said with a sigh, "I think we got our grip on just about everything. Except one big thing. Who's going to pick up the pieces in the variety stores?"

As Becker gave him his tight smile of empathy, there was a brief, decorous knocking on the opened door. Riklis looked up and saw a short, stocky, bald man standing there. It was one of Rapid's corporate vice-presidents. "Hello," he said. "What are you doing around here so late?"

"Rik, can I talk to you for a few minutes, maybe?"

Riklis nodded. The man came in.

It was Sam Neaman.

Two THE SUCCESS

5. Neaman Speaks

"It was Labor Day, 1963. Everybody was gloomy and worried. We had gotten a reprieve from the electric chair, but we knew that we were still in trouble. Obviously, the head of McCrory Corporation would not welcome any outsiders butting in, especially from a parent company. But there was a long weekend ahead of me, so I found some figures that were available in the office and took them home. I didn't know what I was looking for, but I was gonna read the figures and see if I could find something, anything.

"And I worked on them, reading the figures and starting to line them up in a different form, and I got more and more fascinated. I sensed something. There was something that was starting to make sense in the way I put the figures in line.

"I spent all four days of that long weekend working on them, sleeping two hours a night and working around the clock. Twenty-two hours a day, four days. I really felt there was something there. I was afraid of the simplicity of the thing. I made my task much more difficult because I was afraid of what was going through my mind. It was simple. It was absolutely too simple. I copied figures and put them in one way and then in another way. The sum total of it was that by the time I was ready to go back to the office after the Labor Day weekend there was no doubt in my mind. There it was, black on white."

He speaks easily but earnestly. Occasionally, he glares at the microphone and the cassette recorder as though it is a silly thing. A new crutch for mankind, which already leans on too many things. He relives the events with no difficulty in recall. He has an excellent memory, it becomes obvious. Why did he involve himself in McCrory's troubles in the first place when he wasn't asked to? Yes, he nods firmly. A reasonable question.

"My job at that time was administrative vice-president of Rapid, which I had just helped to liquidate almost all of its operating units to raise cash without noise, without getting into the papers, which allowed it for the first time in its life to do something quietly. So McCrory really wasn't my territory, and I wasn't even privileged to any information about it. Nobody talked to me about it or about retailing, as I had never been in the retail business.

"But there were perhaps two reasons why I involved myself that long weekend. First, the atmosphere in the home office of Rapid was so worried, so gloomy, like they were expecting the other shoe to fall. And like in all such situations, people like to point a finger and find somebody that they can accuse of being the culprit. It really doesn't change a thing, but they love to do it; it makes one feel good. And everyone was pointing a finger at the current president of the McCrory variety division. But they should know as I do that such troubles do not begin with just one man, especially one who didn't have the job more than a year or so.

"The other reason is that I had nothing much to do. With all the operating divisions of Rapid sold and only the partly owned subsidiary companies left, I really had nothing to do. Since I am not a crybaby by nature, I started looking for something I should get into. So I decided that I was going to have a look at this variety-store company by myself. I'm not going to ask anybody. I'm going to have a look at what that business is."

He draws three parallel lines on a sheet of paper to show what he found that long weekend. The McCrory variety chain had hundreds of profitable stores and hundreds of unprofitable stores. The big losses came mainly from a small number of stores which were very unprofitable, as well as from a more numerous group in which the individual losses were puny. These small losses amounted to $1,300, $2,000, $2,500 a year. It was interesting, maybe significant, that so many stores were operating at a near profit, while others had huge profits and still others were doing well.

Why? he kept asking himself. Working on the lists, he broke down the gross expenses and compared them with those in each group. How much of a cost does it take to arrive at a fair gross profit? Totally unfamiliar with the logistics of the retail trade, he proceeded to work out some projections of his own. If he cut expenses by so much percent and improved sales by so much percent; if he closed so many big-loss stores; if he reduced costs proportionately based on each one's profit or losses—where would it take him? So he worked out a series of projections—a program, in effect—to bring the troubled variety chain back to its normal profits within one year.

But, he recalls with a rueful smile, it was all theoretical. He had no one to talk to about it, and he knew nothing about the industry. It was all just a lot of figures. A lot of numerical theory.

"I presented my plan to a few people, and of course it was laughed at. It was too simple. Where did I get my *chutzpah?* With all the high-priced experts at McCrory, why did they need me to tell them what to do at retail? Much as my standing was high at Rapid, nobody took me seriously. But I persisted. I said, 'What have you got to lose? You fired the two top guys there; you just hired a new man. Let me help.'

"I kept at this for months, refining my figures, and obviously I couldn't get all the information I wanted because the McCrory management would have objected. They said that the new man was cooperating well, but I knew he was just a me-tooer. Finally, four months after I walked in on Riklis and told him what I had learned on my long weekend, he and his closest people gave in. They allowed me to go look at a McCrory store on Long Island. Maybe they thought I would get lost there.

"Early the next morning, I walked into that little store and introduced myself to the manager. It was a small unit doing about $300,000 in sales a year. I told him that I wanted to understand the working of a store and therefore would he mind forgetting that I'm a vice-president and just hire me by the day for his assistant? Of course, he found that a little amusing and unorthodox. But he was a nice guy. He said okay. I said, 'All right, if you hired a new assistant, what would you tell him to do?' He said, 'Okay, go and unload the truck. There is a truck outside, unload it.' And I went and helped unload it. The merchandise went from the truck to the basement, which was a stockroom. When I finished unloading, I went upstairs and said, 'What now?'

" 'Now, fill in the counters,' he said. 'You see, there are missing items on this counter, so go downstairs where you received the merchandise from the truck and bring up merchandise to fill in the items.'

"And that was the beginning of my education, because the first question that went through my mind as I was doing it was —why do they have to have the stock in the basement? Why didn't I take it straight from the truck to the bins? Why do I need the space, why do I need the electricity, why do I need the extra labor?

"I was still there in March, and it was the year that Passover came in March, unusually early. A woman came in for some crockery, but there was none. I asked the manager, 'Why don't we have crockery?' He got angry. 'You know,' he said, 'I'm in a Jewish neighborhood and Passover is almost here, and I should have double my usual stock of crockery but I don't have any. The buyer doesn't want to give it to me.'

"I picked up the phone and called the general merchandise manager of the McCrory stores. I told him I happened to be in that Long Island store and the manager told me about his crockery problem. An hour later, the G.M.M. called me back and said that it was an oversight. That made me ask myself another question. If it's an oversight in one store, how many oversights are there in the 700 stores?

"As I was standing there thinking about it, I hear the cashier ringing the call-bell for the manager. I followed him because I wanted to know why she was ringing the bell for him. She needed change. He said fine. He went upstairs to a little office where he had a safe. The clerk who worked there wasn't in. There was no answer to his knock. He said, 'Oh, God, she went to an early lunch or she had some shopping to do.' He went downstairs to his desk to get a second key. Then he came back to the office, opened the safe, locked it, and went down to the cashier. A customer had been waiting there all that time. Of course, it raised more questions in my mind. In the next two months that I spent in that Long Island district, questions popped in my mind like firecrackers and I made a lot of notes. The point was: what do I see and what are the problems?

"When the chairman-of-the-board heard that I was spending so much time in the district, he called me and told me that he would like to have a report on my findings in that district. He would like to learn from me what I had learned. Maybe, I thought, I was now getting somewhere.

"And those store managers were hungry for someone to talk to. Here was a guy who comes in without a tie—he is informal— and by now I know one thing about store managers. Next to A.T.&T., they are the biggest telephone company in the world. They tell each other about the vice-president from the parent company who is unloading trucks, working in stockrooms, working with cashiers, and working every day from opening to closing. Then, I started working with the district manager, traveling with him every day, and I saw that the whole thing was not as terrible as it might strike you when you come unprepared to it. Every store manager has the same problems in each store, and if you have solved them in one place, you have solved them everywhere.

"In the weeks that I worked in that district, I dutifully reported to the chairman about the progress being made and what I had been doing. Then one day I told him, 'Now that you are a great district manager, Mr. Chairman, and your district is starting to improve and sales are beginning to increase, why don't you learn about an entire region, one that would include about eight or nine districts?' He said, 'Sure, why not?'

"So I asked for a region in the Midwest. After all, I knew Long Island, but the Midwest was something different. The region I went to was based in Dayton, Ohio. I started traveling with the regional manager, going from store to store. One afternoon, he looked at his watch and said, 'Well, it's five o'clock, we'll go and have dinner and then go to Nashville tomorrow morning.' I said, 'Why tomorrow morning? Let's find out what the plane schedule is.' So he checked. We couldn't get a plane to Nashville until 7:30. So I said, 'Fine, we'll be better off. Let's make our reservations, we'll have dinner, and then we'll get on the plane.' I told him to call the store manager and tell him to wait for us. He said, 'You know, the store closes at six.' I said, 'I know, but he can go and have dinner. Tell the manager we'll be in the store about 10 P.M. It's only a short flight, and we're not going to ask him to do this every night.'

"We got in there about ten and the whole downtown was closed up. Everybody's gone home but here we are. We are in the store and soon it is past midnight. I asked the store manager to tell me his problems. And by now I was able to suggest the same things that I suggested and saw in other places, bringing him some hope. I also drew out of him complaints, some of them unjustified and some of them worthwhile.

"I said to the store manager, 'Tell me, do you know how much you spend a year? If you got a figure, take some paper, write down the total amount you spend a year on everything so we know what the total cost is a year of running your store. Now, how many square feet do you have of selling space? Now, divide the annual cost you gave me by the number of square feet and you'll find what you spend each year by square foot to run your store. Now, how many working days do we have in a year—300? Divide the square-foot figure by 300. Okay? Now, you find that you are spending, let us say, $1 per square foot a day. How much merchandise do you have on this small fixture here, which is about one square foot? About $100 worth. Fine. What is your markup on it? Forty percent? So, that means that if you spend $1 to operate this fixture, you'll make 40 cents on each $1 after your sales cover the expense? Yes? If so, that means that you need sales of at least $2.50 each day from this little space to cover your expenses and make your forty percent markup and maybe a little more, doesn't it?'

"This store manager stared at me. 'I never looked at it that way,' he said. Now, he couldn't care if it was midnight or 2 A.M. The regional manager, who said very little while I talked, looked excited, too. I said to the store manager, 'Tell me, did you sell $2.50 off this today?' He said he didn't know.

" 'Why don't you accept an assignment?' I said. 'I'll be in this part of Tennessee for the next three days. Watch sales at all counters; count the merchandise as you sell it. Bear in mind that in variety stores the ends of the counters are the most important spaces. That's where the traffic is, where there is the most exposure. Now in every counter when you see that a certain area or product doesn't cover your expenses, move the goods to a subsidiary place. Put your best-selling products on the counter-ends. Replace the slow-selling goods with something else. But keep testing until you get the best sales productivity you can from the counter-ends and the better, more prominent parts of each counter.'

"I'm getting ahead of my story—but that started the game of square footage at McCrory, which later on became quite a game. Everyone has been playing the calculation of cost and profit by square foot, by hour, by day, even by minute. The name of the game is a long one: find the cost of doing business by square foot and the gross profit by square foot and therefore the profit or the loss by square foot.

"So there I was in Nashville, the people getting sold on me, trusting me. I left there early that morning and took the regional manager to my motel room and explained the whole thing to him again. The next morning, I was fresh and ready to move, and I was no chick. I was fifty-one years old. At 7:30, I visited the store in Birmingham, then went to Northport, and then to another town, working with each manager on all his problems. I came back to Birmingham, had dinner about nine o'clock, and suddenly who is there? John King, a vice-president from McCrory's home office. He said he had heard so much about what I was doing that he decided to come and join me. I said, 'Fine, let's go and visit the Montgomery store.'

" 'Now?' asked King. 'It's almost eleven o'clock.'

" 'So maybe you should go and call the manager,' I said.

He did and I heard him talking: 'He'll be there tonight. I don't know how or when we'll get there, especially since it's so foggy. But we'll probably drive and you'd better wait for him. Sure, I know what time it is!'

"We reached Montgomery about three in the morning. The store manager was there and so was his assistant. They didn't seem angry. I guess they had gotten into the spirit of the thing. They even had a good cup of coffee for us. We spent three hours going through the store and it helped them. King and I left at six, when it was already getting light.

"And that's the way it was. When the people in the field saw how I worked, that this was no play and that there was only one thing—we were going to solve the problems of this company—they reacted the right way. They realized that the visit was not a check-up on them, it wasn't to point a finger and tell them what's wrong with them. Instead, they realized, the visit was to sit with you, to talk with you, and to ask what the problems were. And as they talk, I and the person with me write it down and I tell the manager, 'You will get action on it.'

"I visited hundreds of stores and I didn't see my wife for weeks. And that's why my relationship with the typical store manager is so close even today. Eight solid months of traveling, traveling, traveling, being with them, helping them to help themselves.

"By that time—I was still in that same region all those months —I still had no official status in regard to McCrory. But all of a sudden, the chairman-of-the-board started to feel that maybe I had a point. The information that was coming back to him from all the places I'd spent time was that things were improving there, there was a different spirit and things are starting to happen. So he called me and told me I was officially allowed to go to McCrory's home office and have some space there. I was not allowed to see Nelson, the president of McCrory's variety division, but I was allowed to talk to the other executives there as the emissary of the chairman-of-the-board of the parent company.

"My place was on the sixth floor, the floor below Nelson. Actually, I had no desk, only a chair next to the desk of a vice-president. The idea was that I should not look like I was interfering; I was not doing anything. Everything that I do, the chairman-of-the-board is doing. I am nonexistent. I'm a cloud. I'm a shadow. But now I started to look around the home office, what it was, how it operated. At the same time, I spent very little time there. I was back again traveling in the Long Island district and back again in the Midwest.

"After all that time, I started seeing some things more clearly. Every store that I visited was so different from the other one. There was no uniformity. Now, maybe that's the variety-store business. You can't have complete duplication, but you should have a certain common denominator between stores that are handling more or less the same price points and merchandise.

"I found all this a little difficult to comprehend. But, after asking some store managers, I found that they hadn't been told what to do, and every one was using his own imagination or was following the verbal guidance of his district manager. And the district manager recommended things that he had learned from another district manager. So what we had was a conglomeration of teachings of different individuals. We didn't have a company. All we had was the United Stores of God-knows-who. And you couldn't tell which was a good store or a bad store. They had no method of evaluating profits because they didn't know their expenses.

"Of course, they had a store operating statement, a sort of balance sheet. But it was a reflection of the store only up to a point, because administrative expenses charged at the home office were not really administrative expenses but a reflection of the mood of management. Sometimes, an item went into the A.E. and sometimes it didn't. There was no way of knowing if the manager in Store A was better than the guy in Store B; which system was better or what teaching we should follow. On top of it all, there was a mixture of the McCrory, McLellan, and Green stores, of all the mergers the company had been in. And each group within themselves had different methods and different ways and different rules. Like: You will not put merchandise above the eyeline of the customer; when you walk into a store you are to see the store; hang the merchandise from

the ceiling; don't put anything under the counter; or put everything under the counter, or almost everything so that the store
looks neat.

"One reason for all this confusion was that there was really
no curriculum in retailing. There was no theory—at least not in
the spring of 1964. It is the experience of the individual that is
the theory, and the stronger the individual the higher he gets
in the hierarchy and he imposes his approach without any need
to prove whether he is right or wrong. He imposes his approach
on his subordinates and that's a mess. So I saw that there was
no teaching, no curriculum, no uniformity, nothing. We had to
do something, and we had to do it fast. We had to find what was
the best that this group of people can produce.

"And then—like a thunderbolt that you don't expect!—something very important happened. It happened so unexpectedly
that I didn't realize at the time what it would mean to McCrory
and to my career. To my life.

"I was in Indianapolis visiting a store with John King. We
walked around, and I put myself into the shoes of a customer.
I'm looking for something to buy my wife and I asked questions about how come I didn't find this or that, where was the
right size. And then we went to the mezzanine where the manager had his office and I said to him, 'Look, the history of your
store is that of loss. But what amazes me is that there is a sort of
strange pattern. One year, you are losing about $130,000 and
the next year about $80,000. Between those years, there is a
fluctuation of about $50,000 a year. And then the cycle begins
again. It's been that way for eight or nine years. How come?'

"Well, he got upset and said, 'If you don't like it, you know
what you can do with it. I've been with this company for ten or
twelve years, and you should pay me for my efforts because if
it weren't for me, you would lose twice as much money here.'

"I looked at him with amazement. Here was a man who had
lost the company some $800,000 to $900,000 and I had to pay
him extra? John King was very embarrassed, and he couldn't
contain himself and did something that normally he should not
have done. He told the manager, 'Give me your keys to the
store,' and he fired him on the spot. Well, usually, I don't like
to throw away my dirty water until I have clean water. But

there we were without a manager. I said, 'Okay, John, now there's nothing else you can do. You'll have to run it yourself until we get another man. Somebody will have to close the store tonight.'

Now, you understand, I still had no authority, I was still sort of incognito. I was speaking in the voice of the master. John and I went to the motel that evening and an idea dawned on me. Here was an opportunity, I told myself, here was a store that had lost so much money. And it became obvious while we were both talking and thinking out loud that the young man had been playing around with the store's figures because he was getting a bonus based on improvement.

In other words, if he lost $130,000 one year and the next year only $80,000, he had an improvement of $50,000. By lessening the losses, he got a bonus. So next year, he tried to get as high as possible in his losses so that the year after, he would go low. That was his big yo-yo game, and he averaged his income over a two-year period.

And, finally, it dawned on me that here was my story, here was my opportunity. I wanted to know how good we were and what it took to make a good store. So I said to John, 'Look, we are going to bring into this store a group of people, a team, and you'll be the quarterback. You and they will go and visit all stores—all the competition in town—and write up what you find. You will check our merchandise and its history in the store and write it up. Every evening you will hold classes with a blackboard and we will have a consultation with everyone present. What did we find out and what is it that we ought to do? And through these evening sessions and during the daily visits, you will come up with a plan. How would we do, what would we do with this store to turn it around and make it profitable? And in addition, I'm gonna bring in the regional manager, the merchandisers, the buyers, other stores' managers, people from trainees to district managers. I want to know the sum total of the know-how of this company by taking a sampling of what a whole group of people dedicated to finding out what they can and then thinking together can do. We will see what will happen.'

"And that's what we did.

"For weeks they studied the store. They replanned it. Then they remodeled it. No outside manpower was used. It was all done by people from the McCrory, McLellan, and Green stores. They had a tough time agreeing with each other, but they did. I kept traveling back and forth to see what was happening. The spirit was sky-high; the excitement was beyond description. Why? Because for the first time, they were given a chance to express themselves both as individuals and as a group, each one giving the best that he knew. If one of them knew more about lingerie, he concentrated on lingerie counters. Another might know more about restaurants and a third more about hard goods. Some had good taste for presentation of merchandise; others had a knowledge of carpentry so that they knew how to take all the counters, cut them, paint them, and put them together. They created fixtures to suit the merchandise. We were doing it without expense. Not a nickel was spent since every change was made from what we had in the store. Merchandise was taken out and other merchandise was brought in. Floors were changed, aisles widened, walls painted. It was a new store, a pleasure to the eye. For the customer, it seemed to me, we had made a store that was very appealing.

"What put that store across? When you give people guidelines as I did, things happen. They knew they had to visit all the competition and then look at our store with a cold eye. They understood that I wanted a store that sold merchandise. So they applied what they learned. Up till then, they had to look at the eyeballs of the boss and guess what it was he wanted. All I did was ask them to use their senses and their heads, and I got a damn good store. Over the next two years, it reduced its losses, broke even, and then started making money.

"After all the hustle-bustle of the task force and when the Indianapolis store began functioning successfully, the whole company became aware of it. Next thing we knew, Riklis, the chairman of the parent company, and his whole entourage came running to see what was happening, what were all the vibrations about. And now everybody jumped on the bandwagon. Now everybody wanted a district—every vice-president, the executive vice-president, even the chairman. They all wanted to do what I had done. Yes, sir, everybody wanted to do what I had done.

"What had I done? I had shown them a way. In the midst of all the trouble that McCrory (the subsidiary) and Rapid (the parent) were having, I had come up with a way."

6. Who Is Neaman?

As he trails off, his huskiness betrays the emotion he feels in the recalling. There is a pause in the procedure as he takes a few calls. Of the five short conversations, he mostly speaks English but occasionally Yiddish and Hebrew. He is deft and cryptic but decisive. When the interviewer says, "You know, we've been talking a lot, but I really know very little about you. Some people say you're a mystery man. Who are you, Sam? Where did you come from?" he answers first with a shrug.

"What difference does it make where I came from?" he asks. "The important thing is that I'm here."

But the interviewer is insistent and so he gives in, slowly at first and then quickly and in detail. "It was a different world," he begins. "It will sound strange. But, I suppose I should tell you, because in order to explain what I did, to understand what I mean, you should know a man's background. The background I came out of doesn't exist anymore."

He was born in a tiny village in Galilee in Palestine, before it became Israel. His father was a Hebrew teacher. His mother died when he was three. There was another child, a boy two years younger. As the two motherless boys grew up, the younger one displayed musical talent almost from the moment he could utter a sound. But Sam exhibited no propensities, no inclination until he went to agricultural school. Then, as his brother developed into a promising musical student and later became a famous violinist in Europe, Sam finally displayed an ability. He became a skilled farmer.

Whether he was milking cows, mastering horses or mules, or

making a clump of the stubborn Palestinian earth fruitful, he was at ease. It was actually the only occupation he ever formally learned. And considering what he accomplished later, it was singular that he hadn't the slightest interest in owning a farm. He was content just to be a hired hand.

Throughout his career, which carried him to many countries and gave him the responsibilities for perhaps a dozen different businesses, he never felt the urge to own any. It was enough for him, he decided long ago, to devise ways to make them function well.

His brother's talents were such that their father, acting on his own judgment and those of friends, became convinced that the young violinist needed more professional and perhaps more classical training. Leaving Sam behind in agricultural school, the Neamans moved to Paris, where an application was made for the younger boy's admission to a prominent conservatory. But the father found that he had been idealistic about his own prospects. Coming to a foreign country where he did not know the language, it soon became apparent that his Hebrew teaching experience wouldn't help much. Within a few months, he was in financial difficulty.

With the help of some friends, the elder Neaman opened a plant for the manufacture of women's sweaters, borrowing money so he could rent some knitting machines. Meanwhile, the boy passed the selection board and was admitted to the conservatory. It was a high honor for such a youth, and the father pitched into his business with renewed hope. But he quickly found that while he was an experienced Hebrew teacher, his skills as a businessman were inadequate. Contemplating eventual bankruptcy and financial ruin, he saw that there was only one thing to do. He sent for his other son.

By then, Sam had finished agricultural school and was at work on a farm. His education had been interrupted by his being conscripted. But since there was no actual military force in the Palestine of the 1930s which nationals could enter, he and many other youths were allowed to volunteer for the police force. For civilians, it was a paramilitary service, and Sam was posted as a mounted policeman in the Dead Sea area.

His father's call came about that time, and it presented many problems. First, Sam knew only Hebrew and Arabic and not any English, or for that matter, French. Second, how does one get from Jaffa to Paris without any funds? And third, what did he know about business and sweater manufacturing? But, in what may have been one of his first experiences in reducing big problems to their components and working doggedly on them, Sam borrowed money from some relatives, bought books on the French language, and took a plane to Paris. It was the first time that he had been out of Palestine.

The factory dismayed him, and its business dismayed him even more. In the midst of the regality of the French capital, there were many shabby back streets, and the Neaman plant was in a back loft of the most shabby. His father had managed to lease two Doublet machines, brand-new ones of the most modern type, and to employ a pair of Swiss operators whose salaries plus the machine and loft rentals were quickly putting the struggling manufacturer out of business. The 2,000-square-foot loft, with only its two machines and its puny piles of yarn and finished goods, was much too large. One of Sam's first decisions was that greater productivity was needed, and at a much lower cost. The obvious solution was to operate a second shift.

Sam became very friendly with the Swiss workers. He chatted much with them, stood by them as they worked, and after several weeks, attempted when they left work to operate the machines. For a week after that, he watched them even more closely and learned why he was making mistakes. Shortly afterward, he became the successful second shift in the factory, producing almost another 30 percent of sweaters at no additional labor cost.

In addition, he visited jobbers during the day, closely determining their needs, and returned to advise his father of additional opportunities before he settled down to operate the second shift. The combination of the two efforts seemed to make the difference, and the tiny company's fortunes improved. Soon, the elder Neaman was able to hire a third worker to man the second shift. A year after he had arrived in Paris, Sam felt that things were going sufficiently well for him to return to the farm in Palestine. As far as he knew, his business career was over.

Two years later, however, his father wrote that things had

gone badly again. Once more, Sam pulled up stakes and joined his father and younger brother.

When he arrived, Sam found that his father had given up the Paris loft and had moved to a suburb. On the advice of several wholesalers, Mr. Neaman had returned his Doublet machines and replaced them with circular knitting machines to make men's underwear. But the market competition was intense. A newcomer could hardly battle the established companies without overextending himself. Sam again tried the technique of increasing output at a minus labor rate by learning how to operate the new machines—this time on a third shift. He tried it for weeks, working from ten at night until six or seven in the morning. But the only result was a buildup in the unmoving inventory.

Studying the problem, he realized that the market for cheap men's furnishings was so glutted that his father's products were making no impact whatsoever. Men's underwear was sold to wholesalers in dozen lots wrapped in cellophane packages, and the resale through retailers was on a commodity rather than on a style or brand basis. Sam suggested to his father that they study the competitive merchandise, issue an improved quality, and package their goods individually rather than in bulk. He also suggested that they give the underwear its own brand name and spend a little money on advertising, even if they had to borrow it.

The changes were good ones. For several years, the elder Neaman's business held its own. But by 1938 the certainty of war increased and the family had to make its decision. Sam would either have to join the French army or return to Palestine. Closing the business, the father, his younger son, and his son's new wife (a Jewish Frenchwoman) left for London where the father had a number of relatives. Sam departed for Jaffa.

He volunteered in 1940 to serve in the British army. Starting as a private, he served first in Palestine, then in Africa and Italy. Within four years, he was a major. Everything he had ever done —on the farm, in the police force, in business—seemed to find practical use in the military. There was much about the army life that he liked but not everything. The application of all the available men, machines, and systems toward a common objective appealed greatly to him as a matter of principle. But, it seemed to him during the experience (and especially so in retrospect) that the rigid command hierarchy and investment of strategically important functions in incompetent specialists created an inflexibility that sometimes appeared bent on self-destruction. Nonetheless, the six-year military experience became a seminal one.

In 1946, he rejoined his family and with money received from his discharge opened a blouse manufacturing business in London. It grew in a few years to be a modest but successful company. Traveling in Europe and later to South America, he stopped off in France to see the smiling Cecelia, whom he had met earlier through his stepmother. The twenty-year-old Cecelia came from an Orthodox Jewish family. She had been born in Switzerland but had grown up in the east of France. Plump, blond, placid, she had been attracted to Sam, his dominant, confident ways, and his gentlemanly demeanor from the first glance. He, in turn, found her warm personality appealing and did not recall when any young woman had ever before regarded him with such a clear, searching although shy expression. How could that be? he asked himself, intrigued. They were married shortly after his second visit.

They returned to London but traveled often to the Continent and other countries. Sam was happy and could have stayed close to his family and his business indefinitely. "Yes, I was all right, happy in a sort of loose cocoon," he recalled. "My aspiration was never for big wealth. Why? Money—especially the way it is meant these days—is applied to many dollars. Of course, then as today, it means the comforts of life, but that does not mean millions. My joys, my kicks have never come from knowing that I have one zero more or one zero less. My kicks come out of doing what I am doing, and what I like doing more than anything else is to take something that is failing and make it work. And that means being creative in my working relationship with people."

But in 1956 he lost this careful perspective. His reluctance to involve himself in ownership was forgotten in the interest of a challenge delivered by a friend. Yet the resulting experience, unhappy though it was, led directly to the most important opportunity of his life.

During his travels, he had met a Mexican Jew. The man, who

owned a small bank and a steel-distributing company, would call on Sam in London and they sometimes met in Paris. Over the years, they had become good friends. One evening as their wives engaged in small talk, the Mexican took Sam aside and offered him a proposition. He wanted Neaman to come to Mexico and enter business with him. They would establish a steel-importing company bringing in raw steel, rails, and scrap for Mexican steel mills. Sam had picked up several languages over the years, he was familiar with the economy of different countries, and above all, he had a sound business instinct. He, the Mexican, knew the steel industry and Mexico, a land of untapped opportunity. This was how his friend spelled it out to Neaman. Of course, it would require a fairly substantial investment on Sam's part, but his partner would provide a greater portion. Together they would constitute a strong team, which would capitalize on a golden potential.

Whether it was because Sam felt the need for a new challenge or whether he himself wondered if he could succeed in a completely new milieu, he accepted. Leaving Cecelia behind for the time being, he joined his friend in the new country and they set up the importing business. Within six weeks, Sam lost all his money.

Neaman was crushed. But his partner guaranteed to make good on all their losses. Obtaining a loan based on the Mexican's strong reputation, they started again with a second importing business. This time they avoided their previous mistakes. The firm prospered after taking its second breath and began to make good profits. Some months later, the partners had an opportunity to buy a small rolling mill. They did so. It gave Sam a chance to learn more about steel and about how to supervise the operation of a mill. A year later, one of Mexico's largest mills became available for sale. The principal owner, who was a major supplier of the partner's company, wanted to retire and offered them his business for what they considered a very fair price. Sam's partner said it would be a blow to them if they lost the big mill as an important supply source. Besides, as he told Sam in both Yiddish and Spanish, the only two languages in which each half understood the other, "You already know the steel business, but I still know Mexico. Together, we can handle such a risk."

Neaman became chief executive of the sprawling mill complex with participation in the profits. But there were no profits. When they took it over, the mill was losing about $1 million a year. But a year later, after they had made many changes, it earned almost $2 million. From ladies' blouses to a large, integrated steel mill? How could he bridge the two types of businesses and yet turn around a $1 million a year loser?

The question brought a smile to Neaman's face. "I changed everything," he said, "as I do everywhere. Policies, buying habits, selling habits, and especially the way people worked."

One measure he took was to invite five young Mexican engineers to his office. They had never been given a chance to show what they were really capable of under the former owner. He explained to them that the mill was losing money and defeating its own purpose as a business because it was apparently unable to master its technological problems. Could they individually and collectively develop a program to reverse the losses through better technology? he asked. Answering for them, he told them that he was certain they could.

Another measure was to set an example in diligence to the workers. Neaman decided to make it dramatic in order to save time and lost motion. Since steel mills are usually operated twenty-four hours a day, he realized, it would be necessary to impress each shift. So at six in the morning, he was at the gate to say *buenos días* to the arriving shift and *adiós* to the departing shift. At the 2 P.M. shift, he did the same and likewise at the last shift. In itself, it was a telling gesture. It was a pleasant surprise for the Mexican labor to find a gringo owner standing there at all hours, greeting them variously with a good morning, a good afternoon, or a good night. It was, in fact, unheard of.

After three years, the Mexican Government purchased the big mill, and Neaman retired in 1960 with more money than he had ever had in his life. He traveled with Cecelia, spending much time in the United States, particularly in Miami and New York. In the latter city, he was introduced to Meshulam Riklis, who was then beginning to make bigger and bigger headlines with his financial activities, his manifold mergers. Having heard of Sam's Mexican success, Riklis wired and phoned Neaman at least a half-dozen times over the next few years to come and work for him. But, after a few brief consulting assignments,

Neaman decided that he liked retirement. Casting about for a likely quiet place for himself and Cecelia, he chose Palm Springs. Six placid months drifted by. But Sam found himself restless. Cecelia couldn't understand him. He had made his choice. He had enough money that he wouldn't have to work again, but he was not happy. He found that while he had no great craving for lots of money, his yearning for a comfortable life was an illusion.

"I felt that I might find something to interest me in retirement," he said. "But, instead, I discovered that my interest is work, that's all. I had to find myself once again. I found out that I cannot play the piano, I cannot paint, I cannot write, I cannot do anything but work with people. That's all I know and that's all I am good for."

When Meshulam Riklis called once more and said, "Sam, I need management. I need guys to help me run this big structure that I'm building. Come with me and name your own price," Neaman replied, "Maybe, it's not so far from ladies' blouses to a steel mill to a conglomerate. They all use people, don't they?"

7. Do Me an Indianapolis

For a few moments, Sam has nothing to say. Drinking some milk, taking a few more phone calls, he appears bemused. Have the time frames separated either by just a few years or by several decades come together and caused an eclipse in Neaman? No, not really. He looks up with an eager smile and observes, "Show the people a way. . . . Now that I did that, I even had a place to send everyone. Indianapolis. . . ."

"And that's where I sent them. 'Go to Indianapolis in Indiana,' I told them. 'Go there, look at that store and learn. It was put together by people like you, using spit and polish and only their own normal talents. Look what they turned out.'

"A little while later when I was in the home office, I changed the pattern a little. To a variety-chain vice-president who was in charge of buying, I said, 'All right, Joe, you don't have to go to the Midwest. Do me an Indianapolis right here in New York. You have seen what can be done. So go do an Indianapolis in Flushing. But I don't want you to copy it. We'll keep Indianapolis as a sort of school and anyone who spends time there, who applies himself with study, he's a graduate. You're a graduate and now you're the teacher.' I told him to give me his version of a good variety store in Flushing. Only this time, instead of a group of people giving it their combined treatment, I wanted his treatment. He would be one of my teachers. The reason for that was that he had always been on the buying and merchandising end. He gave the stores what he thought they ought to have. Now, I was putting him in their shoes after I gave him the benefit of going to school—to Indianapolis.

"Of course, I didn't restrict him in his use of people. Whoever he needed, he got. But it was to be his version. Well, several weeks later, he invited me to that store and I found one of the most beautiful retail stores I have ever seen. I immediately invited a few others to see it. After all, I'm not a retailer. Everyone had the same praise. The store manager there got a new life. He never would have believed that his horrible store would be the attraction of the neighborhood and the jewel of the company. Sales began rising right away, and that store became one of our best in New York.

"But what it also did was to challenge the other home-office executives to go out and 'Do an Indianapolis.' You know how that vice-president of buying did it? He worked in the office all day and then went to the Flushing store in the evening. He had almost no home life for six or seven weeks. But look at what he accomplished—for himself and for the company. Never again would he send any managers what he thought they should have without finding out first. He did such a beautiful job in Flushing that I made him take district and regional managers there to see it. Sometimes I would go there with him and admire it.

"As the parent company began to brag more and more about what I had done, I expanded the variations. For example, I used the idea of the Indianapolis store as a visual aid. This meant devising a system of selecting one unit for improvement, getting the people to bring it into shape, then bringing others to see what they did so they could learn from it. This became a substitute for writing memos or giving instructions on the phone, which most people never understand or want to follow. Instead, I said to them, 'Come and look and see. This is the new company—nothing else is—this is it!'

"Then I instructed every district—a district has between ten and fifteen stores—that it must have its own model store. That was a signal to every district manager that he would have to reflect all his knowledge and all his professionalism in one store and from that 'Indianapolis' improve all the stores in his district. It would be his model, his managers' model, and the model for everyone who would look at it.

"The idea caught on like wildfire. For a year, we spent hardly any money on remodeling with outside people, but the store managers used to join together to improve each other's stores. They did it evenings, Sundays, holidays. The Sundays became big shindigs with beer and food provided by the store's restaurant manager, who got it from supply for free. They had the year of their life getting the chain in shape, all forty-seven districts.

"So that's how it works, that's what it comes down to. It's taking your people and encouraging them to do the best that they have. That's the maximum you have in any organization —the sum total of your best and your normal talents. You put it all to work in one place in a concentrated form and let them produce a finished product so that they can enjoy the fruit of their action. Then use that as a model for others. People will copy it because you've got more copyists than originators in any organization. In other words, not too many people can be original, but if you give people something to copy, most have the capacity to copy. And as long as the model's good, what can be bad?

"By then, of course, my presence started being felt. Strange as it might seem, Nelson, the president of the whole McCrory business, acted as though nothing was happening. Or, maybe he just tolerated me and what I was doing. Certainly, he never had an angry word, but it's probably because he knew that the parent company chairman was excited about what I was doing in the field and in the home office.

"Things almost came to a head in Houston. The way it was, I walked into the regional office there for the first time, and I bumped into the representative of Mr. Nelson in the process of firing the regional manager. I asked the others in the office what had happened. They said that the New York man came in off the plane, walked into the office, and told the regional manager, 'You're fired!' What bothered me was that the regional manager had served the company for thirty years, and after that you don't just fire a man even if you have proof he is not very effective. And you have to have real proof, and you can't do it single-handed through one man's decision.

"I asked Nelson's man to come into a separate room and asked him what happened. 'He's no good,' he said.

" 'Who's gonna replace him?' I asked.

" 'We don't really need anyone.'

" 'With things as bad as they are,' I said, 'how can this region not have a head to keep an eye on things? And how will you in the home office know what is going on here without a regional manager?'

" 'No, we'll get along,' Nelson's man insisted. 'We don't need him.'

" 'I'll tell you what,' I said. 'As of this minute, your function in this building and in this region is terminated. Now, I can't fire you, but I can tell you what you should do. Get yourself out of here and don't come back for at least a year, or even better, never. Or, if you wish, you can take the next plane and go back to New York and complain that I have told you to get the hell out of here.'

"Maybe I was ready for a fight or maybe I wasn't. I just felt that that method was not gonna get us anywhere, and it might as well come to a head. I was beginning to have a feel of things. The company had good people who were willing to work. They needed a normal environment. But the strange thing was that after the man went back to New York I didn't hear a word about it. Not even a single phone call. I just went on traveling around, doing my job, and nobody questioned what I was doing, which maybe was an indication of how things were.

"Between going out in the field and working in the home office, I got another idea. It was easier now for me to do things, even though Nelson was ignoring me. Riklis continued to be intrigued with the things I had generated, and so I went one step further.

"I still had a growing feeling that the people in the home office—the buyers, the merchandise managers—didn't know much about the stores out in the field. They had no way of knowing what was happening there, what was selling. The buyer, of course, buys goods and the merchandiser gives him his plans and between them they decide what goes into what stores. From sitting in a central place, they decide what to ship without much information. I wondered how it was possible for those merchandisers to plan what goods go where or when and in what quantities just by being in New York. So I came up with a revolutionary idea: why not put merchandising at the store level? I got permission from Riklis to assign five merchandisers, or one each, to each region. And what they should do was what I did—travel to the stores, see and talk to each district manager, find out what is selling and what is not selling, and pass that information on back to the buyers.

"Now, I said that was revolutionary and I'll explain why. There was never any love lost between the store managers and the buyers. The merchandiser and the buyer had the attitude that the manager was a bum, that if this bum had a little bit higher I.Q. he could make a truck driver. And the manager felt that the buyer and merchandiser were crooks who were being invited by the New York suppliers to lunches and dinners at the Four Seasons; they were receiving tickets to all the ball games and money, too. And because of that influence, they were buying goods that wouldn't sell and at the same time expecting the managers to bail them out.

"So I felt besides giving the home-office guys a better on-the-site knowledge by putting the merchandisers in the field, I would also be establishing a relationship of brothers. In other words, the manager could look at the merchandiser now working alongside him in the field and say, 'It's an exiled brother I have here—poor Joe!—they put him out to Siberia. He was demoted. I got to help him out.'

"That's what happened. There was better cooperation between the home office and the stores in shipping the right merchandise. Of course, those who were exiled to Siberia hoped that it would only be temporary. But I knew that in time they would reconcile themselves to it, and I hoped that eventually they wouldn't want to dream that there would be anything but that arrangement.

"These experiences encouraged me to practice a few pet ideas of my own on people.

"In a Texas city, I visited one of our stores with a young district manager. The store manager, an old-timer, had been sent there by an earlier division president to run that store and he showed us around, explaining why things couldn't happen. I don't even remember the reasons, but he said that the store could not be cleaned properly, the prices couldn't be displayed like they should be, the merchandise couldn't be folded right, and so on. But every time we walked around some corner, I saw the young district manager, Bill, doing something there, bending, tidying up, working with his hands. I made a mental note: here is a man who is doing the work when he should be telling the store manager what to do.

"At one point, I asked the store manager, 'What do you think of Bill, your district manager?'

" 'Oh, he's great. Whenever he comes here, he sets up the stockroom for me, he straightens out the notions counter, he does everything.'

"I said, 'Tell me, what do you do?'

"He smiled at me. 'I take care of the store, and I've been doing that for the company for a long time, since the president sent me down here.'

" 'So why does your store lose $250,000 a year for the last ten years?'

"He shrugged. And then I heard a familiar answer, one that I first heard in Indianapolis before we changed things. 'This is a loss store. But you're lucky I'm here. If it was somebody else, you would lose more.'

"He told me this at his desk in his big, fancy office. Maybe it should have been a big office since his store was a big one with sales of about $4 million a year even though it was losing a lot of money. I said, 'Would you please excuse me for a minute?'

"I went outside to where the young district manager was working on a nearby counter. I said, 'Bill, do you like retailing? You do? Well, what is the thing that would give you the greatest pleasure? What is your dream?'

"The eyes of this young man got big. Here he was only about thirty-two years old with already about fifteen years' service behind him, and he was a big success. His father had been a store manager before him for forty years. 'What do you mean, Mr. Neaman?' he asked me.

"I repeated the question. Taking a deep breath, he said, 'Give me this store and I'll give you my right arm.'

" 'All right, Bill. You just come in with me and you'll see something.'

"We went back into the store manager's office, and I told him, 'Mr. Store Manager, we are very grateful for the effort you have made. Now, as of this minute, you are no longer the store manager. Bill will take over. But now that we are changing guards, you can go back to New York. The company will pay for your ticket. And you don't have to worry about your future assignments at McCrory because there won't be any.'

"Well, I don't like to fire people. That was my first and last firing. I'd rather they resigned. I don't say that I don't cause them to resign, but I don't like to fire people and in that way block them in the future from getting a job.

"But this fellow Bill who took over was something to talk about. And I did talk to him plenty—sometimes on later visits and sometimes by phone. Within two years after he became manager, the store was bringing us $500,000 a year in profits. It was a strange case: by demoting a man, I made him happier and more productive. He was a born store manager but as a district manager he didn't have it. And he never would.

"The experience of those two so-called managers in Indianapolis and the Texas city made me wonder how many other managers were working at cross-purposes to the company. I spent a little time on this, and I must tell you that I was horrified. It was worth the detective work because I uncovered two flagrant situations, which I resolved by getting the news to Nelson so that he had to fire the individuals involved.

"One was a store manager who had developed a unique mer-

chandising idea. It was to me unbelievable. In one of the towns
of this beautiful country, this store manager decided to make
a fortune by appealing to the sex instincts of his customers. With
a big inventory of television, furniture, and appliances to sell, he
rented an empty apartment and put several televisions in it,
furniture, carpets, and a couple of girls. A little brothel of his
own. Once you had a drink and a girl, you were sold some major appliances. You signed a contract. And so, from his store,
he would send in contracts of customers who later on we mostly
couldn't find. We would not get paid but meanwhile he got his
commissions for appliances and who knows what else.

"And the other got himself an even better deal. Why should
he do things regular when he could do things irregular? He was
a district manager in charge of about ten stores. He made sure
when the truck came into the warehouse with merchandise,
fifty percent went out to the stores but fifty percent stayed in
the warehouse. All the books on shipments were kept in the
warehouse, not in the stores. He sold the warehouse inventory
to other retailers. He made himself a fortune.

"Now, you have to ask how it was possible for both these
men to do what they wanted and get away with it? The answer became an important lesson to me. They got away with
their deeds because information came directly from them
through channels. Everything that came in from the store or the
district managers was *it*. Nobody could check up on them. And
what it taught me pretty early in the game was to talk to everybody up and down in the structure of the organization.

"Soon, I realized that we needed information about our own
people. What did we know about our store managers, our buyers, our district and regional men? Oh, sure, we had personnel
files, but they were basic and revealed very little. So I suggested
that we set up a separate file on all the thousands of people who
worked in the variety stores. We wanted a balance-sheet of our
manpower, and to get it we needed a record updated on every
executive and worker—their date of employment; their education, their parents; how many stores they worked in; what
was the store's productivity, the profit, sales, loss, whatever.
This would give us a rundown on every executive, and we could
use it quickly for reassignment. But I was surprised to learn

that some of the best people had left the company. They had lost heart.

"More than a year after I involved myself in the variety stores, things changed for me. Even Nelson, the division president, seemed to accept me. I got a large office in the division home office and forgot that I still had an office in the parent company. And I no longer had to do anything under the guise of Riklis. I was allowed to come in and discuss things with Nelson and to attend division executive meetings. I felt frankly that I was poised for maybe the biggest step, whatever that could be. I was very excited.

"You see, my new acceptance by the formal structure of the company showed me that essentially there is no difference between one business 'and another. Business is business. The fundamentals are the same.

"What is management? It's logic and common sense. But above all, it is using people's knowledge and talent and specialties. Management is nothing more than putting the right person in the right place and giving him guidelines so we all move together toward the same objective. I call it a guided autonomy. And it's no paradox, either.

"In its simplest form, it is like this. I say to my people, 'Gentlemen, we are going to have a meeting in Los Angeles on Tuesday at 8:55 A.M. at the Such-and-So Hotel. Please make sure you are there promptly.'

"One will go via the North Pole, and after spending his weekend in an igloo, he will appear at 8:55 A.M. in Los Angeles. Another will start walking and after two days get tired and then take a plane from Trenton, New Jersey, to Los Angeles. A third will go to Miami first and then to the Coast. A fourth will go directly to L.A. and spend the weekend there and be ready first. But, at 8:55, we had all better be sitting there. That's guided autonomy—get to the goal your own way. I am not telling you to put the left foot forward or the right foot forward. But get there and on time, and we'll all be ready to work."

8. The Confrontation

Neaman fixes the interviewer with a curious stare. "Tell me," he says, a tiny tic under his left eye providing a warning, "do you know what an auction, what a bazaar, is in business?" Puzzled, I ask him, "Are you referring to a bargain sale of merchandise or what?" The question annoys him. "People, I mean people," he replies. "I told you that I consider people the everything of business, of any endeavor, and I don't care what that endeavor is."

He draws a deep breath. There is a strain of anger in it, and it is evident that he is keeping a rein on himself. Impatiently preparing to narrate his denouement, nonetheless it seems that he must clarify first one or two more points. "Let me tell you about the auction and the bazaar matters," he says, "so you will begin to understand why I finally did what I had to do . . ."

"Executives in the home office were talking about an 'auction' for weeks and looking forward to it like it was a great event. I didn't know what it was or why until I sat in and then I was, to be frank about it, horrified.

"Every season, Nelson called a meeting of the large store managers and the district and regional managers so the buyers could show them new merchandise. Fifty to sixty people came in from all over the country. The buyers came in and showed their goods. I remember the toy buyer showing Scotty dogs, one black and the other white. He held them up above his head, and like an auctioneer he shouted, 'Now, who wants to order Scotties at the cheapest price that we ever sold them for?'

"A regional manager near me said, 'I'll take 2,000.' Another man yelled, '500 here!' A third man said, 'I'll have 1,500.'

"I turned to the regional manager sitting near me and asked, 'Tell me, what made you decide to take 2,000 Scotties?'

"'Oh, that's nothing,' he said. 'You know, you got to help

the buyer. The president is sitting there and the buyer's got to make a show. What does it matter how much I order?'

" 'Yes,' I said, 'but the buyer is writing down all the numbers and from that he'll place his order.'

" 'That doesn't matter. At least he'll come out of here smelling like a rose.'

"Well, that shook me up. Here they paid for all the people to come to New York to tell the home office what they will need for the next season in certain departments, but it was all meaningless if the buyer took them all seriously. But, I discovered later, he didn't. Otherwise, he might have cornered the whole Scotties' market. But everyone played it for the gallery, and the only one who got fooled was the president, Nelson. The whole thing disgusted me. So that was the auction.

"Now for the bazaar.

"I would notice every February or March, after the fiscal year ended, that there was a line outside Nelson's office, sometimes dozens of people. What were they doing there? They were asking for raises. And I overheard some of these conversations because my office was nearby. 'Sir, I didn't get a raise for five years.' Or 'I didn't get a raise for three years.' The president would consult a sheet with his figures and say, 'Okay, I'll give you $2,000.' And the man seeking the raise would say, 'What, only $2,000?' And Nelson would reply, 'All right, $2,500.' Or he would say, 'No, you won't get anything.' There was no rhyme, reason, or logic to it. Those he liked he would raise. The rest he wouldn't. That was the bazaar.

"I made two decisions right then and there. If I ever got the command, I would have no auctions and I would have no bazaars. Orders would be based on sales records, and there would be no haggling or bargaining on salaries. It made sense to me on salaries to have a starting base of $6,000 a year for the manager of the smallest store, one doing $75,000 a year in sales. That would be for the first year. It would go up the second and so on. Every $100,000 additional volume would increase the base. And the managers would get a bonus. But before any bonus, they would have to show a profit of four percent before taxes and that would be for earning their salary. And then for every dollar of profit that they would produce over four percent, they would get a bonus of six percent. That would be profit-sharing.

"And that would be the end of the bazaar and the apple-polishing. Those who did well would be advanced to bigger stores, which would mean a bigger base salary. And for producing more profit, they would get a bonus. That would make each man his own master. It was like he would be in business for himself. Finally, when I was able to put that plan into effect, it proved very effective. I don't remember one case where anybody asked me for a raise. I can meet with people and I always know that we'll talk about everything in the world, but I know there is one subject we won't be talking about. Money.

"So you can see that I was having all these experiences in the field and in the home office. And I was making lots of changes and storing up lots of others that would have to be done later.

"I discovered a few other things, all of them leading to a climax.

"There was a room I used to walk by in which a man sat before some bright, shiny equipment. He was surrounded by a lot of paper. I finally walked in on him one day and introduced myself as Mr. Nobody, since despite everything that I had done I still didn't have any title in the division. And then I discovered that we really had a computer. That was what that man was doing in that room, operating a computer, but no one I had ever talked to knew about it or had mentioned it. Certainly, the field people didn't know about it. As the operator told me what the computer could do, I realized how important it could be in taking the guesswork out of the retailing business. I could sense its logic and capacity. Later, we accomplished a great deal with the computer; but there it was all the time, hardly being used—maybe not at all.

"Another thing I discovered was that we had an immense warehouse in York, Pennsylvania, which cost us a fortune to lease. When I say discovered, I am not being either facetious or cynical, because everything I found I had to discover myself. Nobody would tell me what was going on. I was still the outsider. But that warehouse was already a white elephant, two years after it was built. It had been part of a grandiose scheme to have a central distribution center with satellite warehouses in different regions. But because McCrory's profits had been so bad, the plan was dropped; and instead of using the big distribution center as the focal point for the whole system, it was just being used as a warehouse. All the shipments from coast to coast were coming from there instead of any satellites feeding the regions. It was like a great idea that couldn't be put to use because somebody had forgotten to bring a few extra chairs. We could easily, for example, have taken some unprofitable stores around the country and made them the satellite warehouses. But we didn't.

"The more I looked, the more I discovered. I remember attending a meeting of the division's top people. The subject was a recommendation to hire another accountant to set up procedures for control of the merchandise in York. After an hour, no decision had been made. The decision was to have another meeting. Here were people with a total of hundreds of years of experience who couldn't make a decision that should have been made by one man. What especially stunned me was that for two years they had never had an accountant to work down there, although they had spent millions to rent the building. God only knew what accounting horrors were being made in that immense place!

"I walked out of the meeting in a daze. I sat in my office for hours, thinking and brooding about it, and that afternoon I came to a decision. I went out and hired an accountant. I knew that this was one interference that they would not just overlook, as they had overlooked everything else I had done. People are funny that way, you see. They don't mind that you help them and especially if you don't seek credit for it. But try once to take over their authority and the ceiling comes down.

"That's what happened after I hired the accountant. Nelson must have felt humiliated. He had done everything Riklis wanted him to do, but we all knew that unless a lot of things were done the profit situation would return to chaos. And, in the meantime, here was a direct challenge to his authority. He phoned Riklis and I was summoned to the chairman's office.

"The whole incident took about five minutes. Nelson was flushed and upset. And he forgot that you should never give an ultimatum unless you are willing to walk out. He told the chairman, 'I am sick and tired of having this man interfere in the division. He doesn't even have a title in the McCrory organization, but he's been running around giving orders and changing everything. Now, Mr. Riklis, it's either me or him.'

"Riklis smiled at each one of us and told Nelson, 'Okay, you're out.'

"And with that, Rik turned and walked out himself. Nelson and I looked at each other, but we left separately, of course.

"The next day, I saw the chairman again, and he told me how happy he was that this thing had happened. He said that he couldn't make me president of the variety division yet but I would be 'Acting President.' A unique title, I remarked. He said that the reason he wanted to do it all in careful steps was that he had bigger things in mind for me, which he didn't dare to disclose but which I could guess if I tried.

"So there it was—July 1964. I thought, 'Riklis should know next time not to put a nonretailer in as the president—excuse me, acting president—of one of the biggest retail chains in America. But maybe he knows as much his way as I do my way.' And I remember thinking, 'No, he knows what he is doing. I'm already trained. I spent almost a year in many tank towns learning the business and coming up with some pretty good answers. Maybe I can do what is needed to complete the job. If I succeed, look what joy it will be. But what does it matter, like heaven on earth, I have the company to myself, at last.' "

Three A MULTITUDE OF AVERAGES

9. The Trajectory

Between 1964 and 1973, the reputations and prowess of Sam Neaman and the McCrory Corporation soared like missiles. It was difficult to tell which had the greater trajectory. The man and the business became so closely identified that many people referring to "Neaman" meant the multifaceted McCrory and at least as many talking of "McCrory" really meant the complex, admired Neaman. But the superimposing of the two was an evolutionary process, taking up almost five of those nine years. There were perhaps three distinct phases in those early years when the retailing industry, Wall Street, the public, and the press became acquainted with the unusual things that were happening in the fourth largest American variety-store chain.

The initial phase took place in the very first year that he assumed the variety-chain presidency, in fact, in the first six months. As Neaman heaved himself into the president's chair, he found it a hot seat. The division had just reported the expected first-half loss of about $3 million, reinforcing Riklis's fear that he had closed the front door on the wolves only to have them come through the back. "Can you do the *chochma*, Sam?" Riklis said, calling on the first hot July day to offer his best wishes. "If I don't do this *chochma*," Neaman said grimly, "you won't have to fire me. I'll find the Brooklyn Bridge and jump off."

But neither action was necessary. By the end of that fiscal year, or six months later, Neaman had wiped out the first-half deficit and replaced it with a $7.5 million profit. It made all the difference to McCrory, contributing about eighty-seven percent of the year's total corporate profit of $8.6 million. This was against a previous year's profit of only $3.9 million. Riklis began to breathe easily again. He had Izzy Becker talk up the viability of Rapid–American to the bankers and, also incidentally, of its chairman. And he threw Neaman a party at the Plaza.

Other retailers, skeptical about what a nonretailer could do with a troubled, much-merged company, remained skeptical but less so. There was considerable curiosity about Neaman, but he stayed close to the office or his stores, totally ignoring industry functions. The press came after him, but after consulting with Riklis, he decided to be uncommunicative for another year, or at least until he could repeat or preferably better the *chochma*. Nonetheless, he, his division, and the parent company had come under a bright new light.

How had he been able in just six months to give his division the best profit it had had in years? The answers to this question began to leak out despite Neaman's reluctance to disclose them.

Everything he had done the previous year came in handy. But whereas before he had only been able to suggest new ideas, concepts, and practices, now he could implement them. That single difference permitted him to achieve dramatic results. Immediately on taking over, he had adopted the roles of teacher, analyst, and guidance counselor. There was in his earnest, pragmatic demeanor a sense of urgency but it was not blatant. He had already met many of the home-office executives, store managers, district and regional managers, and he had worked with them. He accelerated his plan of putting merchandisers in the field so that they could make their buying plans from first-hand knowledge. With an almost religious zeal, he proselytized the simple store manager, giving him his "freedom."

Neaman prepared a little speech.

"I am giving your store back to you. It was taken away from you by people who sat in a central office in New York and pushed the wrong kind of buttons. Instead of consulting you, instead of honoring your knowledge of your store and your customers, you were ordered to conduct yourself as *they* wished. They forgot that you are the trustee of your store. So now I am taking it away from them and giving it back to you. You will tell me what to do. Now let's see what you and I can do together!"

In the Manhattan division headquarters of the variety stores, the atmosphere changed. Depression and lassitude turned to fear as the new man took over, but it was soon followed by curiosity. What would this stolid, bald man in the expensive suits and flashing eyes do? What could he do? But his reputation had preceded him and his earnestness overcame them. Within a few days of his arrival in the president's office, a small group began gathering in his office at about the hour they normally went home. Curious executives who had not been invited made it their business to troop by and look in. It became obvious that the meeting was open to one and all, and the group grew quickly and voluntarily. Sandwiches and beer were ordered in. Within two weeks, the discussion group had grown to over fifty. Although it lasted only during those early months, it convened almost every evening and endured for several hours. The talk generally started over some matter or issue that had come up that day and spread to other facets. Inevitably, Neaman turned the discussion to general management concepts. A technique he employed was to raise an existing or potential problem and invite solutions from around the room. The variations sometimes grew intense amid the odor of corned beef, mustard, and pickles. It was a Socratic exercise, except that instead of ethics and logic the disciples were being taught the ABC's of management.

Sometimes it proved painful. They listened with thudding pulses as he told them, "You people don't even have a record of what is going on. Why aren't you putting things down in an orderly manner—step #1 is accomplished, step #2, and so on? Because you don't seem to have any, now I have developed a series of operating reports—numbers one to seventeen—which will indicate performance progressively. Now we will be able to see progress, results, a gradual image of what we are accomplishing. Otherwise, we are flying by the seat of our pants like high school boys. Does anybody have a better idea about how we can know how we're doing?"

They found it difficult to contradict him. Fear, of course, was one deterrent. The other, more durable one was that he was almost always right. When he told them of his dismay at the contents of two rooms he had discovered in addition to the computer room, there was nothing they could say. What he found in those two rooms was unbelievable, he told them. One was filled with huge files containing invoices. The other was filled with receipts of merchandise delivered. No payments could be made to suppliers unless the invoices were matched with the receipts so that it could be ascertained that the actual goods ordered had been received. After he had discovered the two rooms, he had asked some people how far behind the matching process was. "Thousands and thousands of hours," was the answer. That, Neaman figured, meant months and months. And that, in turn, he told the nightly group, meant that the name and credit-rating of the division must have deteriorated badly in the market because its accounts payable were long in arrears.

"What do you think should be done about this problem?" he asked them.

Some suggested letters expressing good intentions should be sent to the trade. Others said that the accounting and disbursement processes should be drastically speeded up. Neaman held up a hand and told them it was already done. He had put the invoice and receipt offices on a three-shift operation until all bills were paid.

"You know, we've got a computer," someone said. "Why don't we put accounts payable on the computer?"

Sam's face grew round. "Of course," he said, with a smile, "that computer, I can assure you, will become important in our lives around here."

Having given the stores back to their managers, having made the merchandisers honest by relocating them in the field, and having created an "Indianapolis" model in all forty-seven districts, there were two more strategic things he wanted them to do. One was a drastic reduction in inventories, so drastic that every store must risk losing half of all its customers by cutting its stocks at least fifty percent. A list of suggested categories to be reduced would be distributed. But the store manager, now a free man, could make his own choices as long as the value of his inventory was slashed.

The other proposal was that every month buyers would have to produce certain items that could be sold to the public for the price that the company normally paid to the manufacturer. And a fifty percent markup must be provided on each such item. When they heard of this, the buyers couldn't believe they had heard right. Selling the wholesale price at retail at a fifty percent profit? It was impossible. But the new president smilingly described how it could be done. Each buyer would have to select only a few items once or, at the most, twice a year for this project. Buyers should in the process of cutting their inventories also narrow down the number of suppliers which they have traditionally dealt with in order to become more important to each producer. Being more important, the buyer should have no trouble convincing each supplier to reduce occasional items so that the "bargain buys" could be offered to the public.

Meeting with a representative group of buyers to hammer home these points, he asked, "Now, what do you think you might gain from this approach?" No one spoke up. Neaman said, "All right, maybe you need some encouragement." He turned to a grizzled buyer of toasters, percolators, and hot plates and said, "Joe, why don't you take a crack at it? Think out loud for us." Joe arose shakily, a silly but worried grin on his face. "Well, Mr. Neaman, it would for sure make me depend more on my own productivity. The suppliers would get the message—put up or shut up. And the company, it would give us a different look in the market—we would look more demanding and more confident. But most important, it would give us something exciting to sell."

Neaman grinned. "Right you are, Joe," he said. "That's exactly what this will do for us. There isn't a thing I can add to it, gentlemen."

Prodding, challenging, teaching, maintaining a ubiquitous presence in the division offices and in the field, Neaman established numerous one-to-one relationships in the organization. Increasingly, many in the division came to believe that each had a uniquely personal rapport with the new president. Neaman not only thrived on this, he also fostered it and sometimes received heartwarming results from it.

One Sunday in the summer, he visited a McCrory variety store whose manager had suggested an unusual effort. Located in one of the proliferating Long Island shopping centers, the store would open only its restaurant on a Sunday to determine the demand for a fast-food service in such a store. It would not run afoul of the Sunday blue laws, since those ancient statutes did permit drug stores and restaurants to be open. As he approached the otherwise closed store, Neaman noticed a tall man in a black raincoat staring into the window, starting to enter but holding back. Curious, Sam stepped up to him. "Don't you want to go in?" he asked. "The restaurant is open."

"I know," the man said.

"So?" said Neaman. "Go in."

The man turned his gaze away. Obviously interested but shy, his curiosity would only carry him so far. "Why don't you go in?" Sam persisted.

"I work for McCrory. . . ."

"Ah. So do I."

The tall man's eyes widened and he stared a bit wildly at Neaman. Near recognition hovered on his face. "I'm Neaman," Sam announced, with a smile.

"Neaman," the other man repeated. "The new president." His dismay twisted his long face, and he appeared terribly embarrassed. Neaman quickly placed his hand on the taller man's shoulder. "I am most happy to meet you," he said. "What is your name?"

"Hughes. Harold Hughes. I am manager of Store #127, just a few miles from here."

"So why don't you go in," said Neaman, "and see if the restaurant is doing any business?"

Hughes shrugged. "I should," he admitted. But he remained standing in front of Neaman, seemingly far away for a moment or two. Then he glanced again at Sam. "I've got to go back," he said, weakly. "There's some work I must do in my own store. . . ."

"You're here already."

Hughes' body wilted. "Excuse me, please. You see, ever since last year, I haven't been myself. I . . ."

"What happened last year?"

Hughes hesitated, then said, "I was demoted."

"Demoted?"

"I was a district manager. Mr. Nelson demoted several district managers those last few months he was in charge. He thought it might cut the losses if he shook up the organization. But I'm afraid it didn't work out."

"Mr. Hughes, I want a cup of coffee, and I would very much like some company. Would you please join me?"

They went into the store. In the next half-hour, Neaman learned that Hughes had spent twenty-five years at McCrory, having been a department head before becoming a district manager. He was one of the few executives who had graduated from an Ivy League college. Neaman could see that the man's soft-spoken, rather intellectual manner had made him stand out unpleasantly in an environment that had become increasingly mundane, uncreative, and desperate. Hughes was still just under fifty but his life, judging by his bleak, watery eyes and sagging stance, was all but over.

Afterward they visited Hughes' store. It was a small one but with some interesting features. Obviously, the manager had visited the district's "Indianapolis" unit and had incorporated some of its strategic qualities. But Neaman, while pleased by this, the store's neatness, and a generally professional aspect, sensed an absence of dynamism that he had seen in some other stores. An hour later, as Hughes locked the front door, Sam said, "Mr. Hughes, how would you like to come and work with me at the home office? I believe you have a strong capacity for staff work. I need a good administrative assistant. Who knows, it might even work into a vice-presidency."

Hughes' surprise was even greater than Neaman had anticipated. He stiffened and then put a hand to his forehead. "Yes," he said in a muffled tone, "I would like that."

He became an administrative vice-president about five months later. What took other executives four or five hours Hughes could do in an hour or two. His zeal was intense. He had a capacity for listening whereas most people seemed to interrupt with questions while the answers were already being supplied to them. He became what Neaman called "a believer," one of his most devoted, productive men. A follower, no doubt, but an eager, dependable follower.

"A believer?" Neaman was asked. "He's a believer, have no doubt about it," he replied. "You have to know one thing about Catholics, especially those like Harold Hughes. They believe that Jesus went to heaven bodily, but they can be scientists, too. They can know everything but they believe. This is a quality that you can't wipe away. For a man to believe when he wants to believe, he can move mountains with that. They are believers, and he believes."

"Is it because you gave him back his self-respect?"

"It's that but it's not all. The promotion that you give a person doesn't guarantee you loyalty and respect. He's got to believe in you. He's got to see you and for years he saw me. He knows that I make mistakes but that they're unintentional. He knows how dedicated I am to what I am doing. He knows that I'm the hardest man in the world for him. I kick him from pillar to post. But he knows that I worry about his family, his wife and his children; about his health; about his financial condition. But I don't give him money; he doesn't earn more than other people at his level. There are no favorites. But I worry about him and I help morally. I have many hundreds like him in the organization who believe."

The second phase in the evolutionary recognition of McCrory and Neaman came nineteen months after he was appointed division president. In early 1966, Riklis and the directors of Rapid–American elected Neaman president and chief operating officer of McCrory. This put him in full operating charge of the entire corporation, which then had sales of about $550 million. It was a singular recognition of what he had accomplished. In his dual role as chairman-of-the-board of both the parent company and its largest subsidiary, Riklis paid ample tribute to Neaman. "Our confidence in him," he said in the McCrory 1965 annual report, "was fully justified." He gave Neaman permission—in fact, he urged him—to talk to the press and the Wall Street community.

The third phase in the McCrory–Neaman trajectory occurred almost simultaneously with the second. Ever on the prowl for likely acquisitions, Riklis, backed by the financial acumen of Isidore Becker, bought control of about ten companies, increasing either McCrory's or Rapid's holdings in them from 1963 to virtual ownership through 1966, 1967, and 1968. The skepticism generated toward Riklis's digestive ability to accommodate his great appetite waned because whenever it surfaced he pointed to Neaman and his achievements as an answer. It was no mere offhand response. The new McCrory corporate chief truly seemed able to absorb everything Riklis brought to the table to chew on. The conglomerator told everyone that Neaman had about the best metabolism in New York and that, added Riklis, meant anywhere.

10.   The Interlock

But it was much more than that. Although he would only admit it to Izzy Becker and the tight, little group that he had put together to operate Rapid–American, Riklis was frank about it. "Sammy saved my skin," he told them. "If it weren't for him, I'd be flat on my ass, all the lions of Wall Street would be grinding my bones and the wolves in the press would be waiting to suck out my blood."

Becker and some of the others, however, quickly pointed out to Riklis that first he had done the important things to save himself. "Yeah, you're right," he answered, meditatively, "but—"

He recalled how he had lost his bearings in the debacle at McCrory in 1962. The pressure to unseat him and return him to the hustings had been much greater than the press had reported. The outside professional management he had installed at McCrory had exaggerated the profit projections in 1962, the bankers had been staggered by the low figures reported in April 1963, and stockholders had howled for his skin. After ousting the misrepresenters, he had installed Nelson as McCrory's new president and had temporarily shored up the earnings leak. But the bankers seemed no longer to trust him, and a committee had been formed to find a successor to Riklis himself. Only a few supporters with clout at the banks had prevented that from taking place, but the threat had remained since.

On top of all that, Riklis took an action of desperation. Still looking for some avenue to produce substantial cash to quiet the bankers who held his loans and to assure the merchandise creditors to whom he remained worrisome, Riklis decided to dispose of a major subsidiary chain of women's shops, Lerner's. It was a difficult decision because Lerner's was in 1963 transacting record business and was a solid rock in the entire swaying structure of Riklis's empire. But he was convinced that by selling Lerner's for about $60 million in cash Rapid could become more liquid. It would also demonstrate dramatically to the bankers that Rapid was willing to go to any length to meet its financial obligations.

The McCrory shareholders, however, opposed the Lerner sale and defeated the management plan. It was a stunning reversal. Riklis had hung on by a thread. His timing, his judgment, and his instincts all seemed to be seriously in question.

But, suddenly, McCrory had come alive. Neaman's efforts in the field somehow seemed to be creating an outburst of new spirit; his techniques in handling people and in setting up new systems had sent a wave of fresh air and hope through the tired, old organization. And the following year, after he had only been division president six months, Neaman's dramatic reversal of the first-half loss could not have been better timed. The intra-year turnaround had involved a number of achievements. Store stocks had been reduced $8 million. The York, Pennsylvania, warehouse was operating at a lower cost and at greater efficiency. Many loss stores were now breaking even and more surprisingly making money. And while hardly universal, the press had turned from publishing negative stories to publishing positive and even laudatory ones.

And when McCrory's net jumped sixteen percent in 1965 over the already surprising results of 1964, the bankers began to change their attitude completely. Admitting that Riklis was doing better than they had expected, they sat back and waited. It became an invitation for the bustling, little conglomerator to set the next step in his drive to greater personal and corporate growth.

But, for the first time in several years, he relaxed, basking in the sheer joy of having beaten down all his opponents, of having achieved the strategic advantage of his lenders and of having quieted all the skeptics. Looking around his organization, he was grateful to the courage, loyalty, and acumen of the bald, rangy Izzy Becker; to the rocklike devotion of Leonard Lane, the big, florid vice-chairman, who was the in-house trouble-shooter; to Harry Wachtel, the outside counsel who wore his hair long but gave clipped and classic legal advice; and to others. But his greatest gratitude went to Neaman. Early in 1967, when it appeared that net income again would show a gain, although not as great as the year before, Riklis phoned Sam (who sat in his own office about three miles away) and said, "I love you, Sammy. You were the best idea I ever had in my whole life."

"Thank you, Rik."

"What can I do to show you how I feel?"

"Nothing, believe me."

"If you think of something, Sammy—"

"There will be nothing, Rik. Just give me the opportunity to do all the things I need to do without interference."

"That, I don't have to tell you, is the least I can do for you."

When Riklis told Izzy Becker of the conversation, the financial vice-president was skeptical. "You've already done a lot for him, Rik," he said. "You gave him the chance to show what he could do. You put a nonretailer at the head of a big retail chain. That was already recognition plenty—few people have ever gotten in at that level. Don't be too damned grateful."

Riklis cocked a surprised eye at him. He knew, of course, that in any large organization conflicts and jealousies always arose among the executives closest to the top. Insecurity about a possible juxtaposition in the pecking order invariably led to sniping. While he hoped that there would be little of this overtly, he had had so much exposure to corporate life—not only in Rapid but among the businesses he had acquired—that he had long ago concluded that executive in-fighting was impossible to erase. But it could be controlled by the exhibition of strict decorum and lack of favoritism on his part. As a result, it was with a trace of resignation that he asked, "So why shouldn't I be too grateful?"

Becker shrugged his bony shoulders. "Okay, Rik, let me be real frank, maybe brutally, and you'll probably wind up getting sore at me," he said, "but I'll take a chance. There are two things about Sam that worry me. One is that he's such an egotist, maybe worse, an egomaniac. The second is that he's got that smell about him, that force of a fanatic, like an animal. I don't know a hell of a lot about his personal life. You know that he's a hell of a private guy. He never talks about his wife, his family life, or anything like it. That's gotta mean something. I think it means he's got himself entirely involved in his work. It's his whole life. And that's not good because it means that inevitably he's gonna suffer from lack of perspective. I think we're gonna have heartaches with him."

Riklis drummed his short fingers on the shiny mahogany of an immense desk. Becker's comments disturbed him. Izzy could be abrasive and there was no doubt that occasionally, as at this moment, his timing could be terrible. But he knew that the man was honest, as honest as the day and implacably loyal. "You don't get along so hot with Sam, do you?" he asked. There was a clear touch of exasperation in his voice.

Again Becker shrugged. "All right, Rik, I see that you are getting sore at me and I'm sorry. But, I gotta tell you this. I think Neaman is one big pain in the ass. When he was here, he was always going around questioning who was doing this and who was doing that. He was always looking down his nose at people either because they were specialists or performing incremental steps in a process. He's supposed to be great with people but I don't know. He's a rough guy."

"You still didn't answer me directly, Izzy," said Riklis sharply. "You don't get along so hot with him, do you?"

Becker's sallow complexion darkened. "All right, I don't," he said. "He's always kinda knocked what I do. To him finance and control are minor, but operations are the important thing. Once, after you made him a big man, he came up here and looked around, and he told Leonard Lane, 'What's all this but a support function for what we do in McCrory. We pay your salaries because we're on the line of combat.' Now what kind of shit is that, Rik?"

Riklis grinned. "I know all about it, Izzy. Leonard told me about that incident. I guess Sam never forgot his military life. You know something, I'm not so sure that he is wrong. But let's let him think that way, as long as he produces. Okay?"

Becker nodded. "Sure."

Smiling, Riklis said, "Don't worry about Sammy when he knocks you. I got something in mind for you soon. A vice-chairmanship. I need another one besides Leonard. It won't be so easy for Sam to knock a vice-chairman, isn't it so, Izzy?"

Becker arose quickly and pumped Riklis's hand. "You don't have to do it, Rik, but I certainly appreciate it." His radiant expression was such that it appeared he would have laid down his life for Riklis.

Alone at his desk, Riklis thought about Becker's fears, worries, and prejudices toward Neaman. They were a complex brew. He knew that Neaman was hardly popular in Rapid's offices. The man himself was a strange combination of the autocrat and the socialist. His concepts consisted of a set of simplistic principles which in the sum were difficult because they placed emphasis on men achieving their full productivity. He himself, Riklis, had no such illusions about people. Most were lazy, especially mentally, and lacked the imagination to realize how they were undershooting their own fulfillment potential. But Sam was imbued with the opposite philosophy. Sam had something basic and hopeful to sell, and while he, Riklis, didn't believe in it—he believed instead in the root superiority of an individual's mental capability over others—he would hardly interfere as long as the results it produced achieved the goals he sought.

And Neaman had produced results. It was, in fact, a near miracle how he had taken first the division and now the entire McCrory Corporation and given them increased profits and a new direction. There were times that the ecstatic publicity Neaman was getting in the *Times*, the *Wall Street Journal*, *Business Week*, *Women's Wear Daily*, and the other trade journals annoyed him. But, after all, he had given Sam the go-ahead to be exposed in the press. And Neaman, as with everything else he did, achieved maximum potential. Riklis knew that the almost weekly stories about the "greatest nonretailer in retailing" were a particular source of irritation among Rapid's executives. It didn't matter, he told himself. Neaman deserved it and more. He was carrying out Riklis's own plan to make McCrory continue to be the funnel through which cash would flow. What more could he ask?

Indeed, what more could he ask in general? Life had been sweet—and fulfilling. In less than seventeen years, Riklis had accomplished the truly tremendous feat of catapulting himself from being a shaky Palestinian refugee to America, teaching Hebrew in Minneapolis to support his wife and child, to operating one of America's major companies. The journey had been filled with fits and starts—an early career as a junior security analyst in a Minneapolis stockbrokerage followed by the welding of a small syndicate to buy his first company, and never more than a brief period to brood over a disappointment. His goal of erecting a vast financial empire that he could control without much interference from the banks was never long out of sight, so that his failures were soon shoved aside. A mathematics prodigy, shortly after emigrating to the United States he had put his philosophy of corporate escalation to paper in diagram form. It consisted of a trio of circles. The first was the toehold company, the initial one he would acquire. The second one would mean that two companies were working to achieve the goal, two firms generating the cash and credit to buy another. And the third circle, considerably larger than the others, would represent the sum total of all the acquisitions and mergers that he would make over the years, a massive structure built on piles and piles of leverage. And, as time drew on and he achieved his goal, more than twenty companies with annual sales ranging from a few million dollars to several hundreds of millions of dollars had been absorbed within those circles.

He knew that in addition to having the dream, the concept, the skill, and, of course, the *chutzpah*, he had been lucky, too. Even during his attack on the early targets—Marion Power Shovel, American Balcrank, Smith-Corona, Gruen Watch, Butler Brothers, American Colortype, Rapid Colortype, and United Stores—he had been fortunate enough to attract either the backing of financiers he had impressed or the eagerness of colleagues who were easily awed by him. Two of these had become his closest associates.

Five years after his first acquisition, he had organized Rapid—

American as the holding company for a half-dozen heterogeneous divisions. But while he knew that he was on the threshold of much greater adventures, more ambitious in scope, he knew too that he would need additional credibility with New York's leading bankers to climb the next rung. It would take a lot more than just his stunning ability to scan a balance-sheet and quickly detect hidden assets or liabilities. It would take a capacity to engage trust. He spoke of the problem while at the offices of a certified public accounting firm that his new company was using.

"The banks?" asked the senior CPA partner. "Yes, they can be a hell of a problem, especially for a Jew on the rise and trying to buck the Establishment. You know, we have a guy on our staff who's had a lot of success working with the banks. He talks their language. Let me call him in here. His name is Izzy Becker."

The other colleague-to-be was Leonard Lane, the owner of a pair of New York correspondence schools and a friend of Harry Wachtel, Riklis's outside attorney. Lane was a massive man with a thick mustache and wide, staring eyes who had taken Wachtel's recommendations about Riklis and had bought heavily into Rapid's stock. When Riklis and Lane finally met, there was a quick rapport, perhaps because Riklis's facile people insight immediately recognized that Lane's deep awe might make him a very loyal associate in addition to an experienced administrator. Both Becker and Lane had turned out over the years to be staunch pillars, often taking the brickbats intended for Riklis himself.

And so it had gone all these years. Dwelling on the matter, Riklis wondered of all the strategic people who had cropped up in his life how many came from just plain good luck, how many from sheer coincidence, how many from natural response to his basic affability? If he wanted to cut it even finer, there was always someone in all the twenty mergers or more in which he had been involved in his career who had risen from below the surface and helped to seal the marriage or help turn it in a more advantageous direction. Why? Who knew? Maybe the strategic ones were always there, lying in wait for the dynamic incident or the promising opening?

Neaman, Riklis knew, was such a one. It amazed him in retrospect that Sam had been there all that time, those years from 1960 to 1963 when McCrory was going to hell. And the one—the answer in terms of the one stolid, intellectually curious, and determined investigator who could solve the problem—had been sitting there all the time, working on some routine dispositions. Riklis recalled that he had been amused and irked when Neaman had interrupted that meeting with Becker one night and had first come in with the suggestion that he involve himself in McCrory's problems. Shaking his head with a mixture of regret and amazement, he asked himself, what if he hadn't given Sam that half-interested, half-resentful approval? The alternative—pure, unadulterated disaster—made him shudder down to his toes.

He knew Neaman was in the process of creating his own empire. New executives, new specialists, new generalists, even a bunch of MBA's were coming in, attracted by McCrory's new, golden reputation. Neaman was building his own exciting world of people, systems, divisional and interdivisional structures. As an operating company, its size, number of employes, network of facilities, and scope of systems were already larger than were his own Rapid's, and based on what Neaman was doing bid to grow much larger. It would, in other words, become such a funnel that its yawning mouth could conceivably someday swallow the parent company, Riklis mused. And then he shook his head in self-reproof. Let Neaman empire-build. If it would produce correspondingly better profits, it would all accrue to Rapid, which owned fifty-one percent of McCrory and would be constantly buying more shares.

He got up from his chair and half-turned to the right wall where a twelve- by fifteen-inch portrait showed the two of them, Riklis and Neaman, shaking hands. It had been painted from a photograph taken right after the board meeting when Sam had been elected corporate president of McCrory. Studying the oil painting, Riklis smiled and raised an imaginary toast.

"We're locked together, Sammy. You and I. For better or worse, except that it had better be better and better. Less than that—"

His voice trailed off, and he lowered the invisible glass. He had never had more confidence in any one person than in Neaman, and any doubts that had infiltrated into it had been raised by Izzy Becker. Rather crossly, Riklis moved to the door and yelled up the hall, "Come on, Izzy, you sonofabitch, let's go to lunch! This time you buy!"

11.   The Concept Is Refined

Within a year after becoming division president, Sam Neaman had formulated his full management philosophy as it pertained to the variety-store division. After several million words of verbal guidance to the executives in the division office and in the field, he decided that he needed something formal to "express the composition of my lifelong experience in managing people."

He wanted something, a credo perhaps, that he could show to the executives around him as an aid, as a set of guides to remind them of the shortest road to success. It was something that they could either carry around in their pockets or post on the wall over their desks where they could see it every day.

After intense, concentrated effort, he completed it. He had several thousand copies printed. He dispatched them, suitably framed along with a photograph of himself to over 3,000 division executives. Executives in other McCrory divisions heard about it and phoned to ask Margit Bergklint for complimentary copies. Suppliers learning of it also wrote or phoned for copies. The 126-word statement read as follows:

Our Credo

We believe in the effectivenes of the multitude—a great many normal people with normal talents working together supporting and compensating for each other.

We believe in guided autonomy—individuals using their initiative, having authority to act upon it, and looking to fellow executives for guidance in fields of their specialty.

We try to break our big problems into small segments and assign each to an individual who is totally dedicated to solving it.

Our operating systems and procedures are designed to provide for individual as well as corporate success. In the long
run, the two are inseparable.

Finally, we believe in a continuous reexamination of everything we do in the light of new experience. This is the only
way we can maintain our progress.

The credo had a curious reception. When it was first circulated along with Neaman's photo, there was a generally
negative reaction among the McCrory executives. Despite his
dramatic success in turning around McCrory, it seemed presumptuous to many for him to express his business philosophy
on a formal document with his round, smiling face beaming from
it. It smacked to them of egotism, of self-indulgence. As far as its
ideological substance, to others it smacked of the *kibbutz* men-
tality, of a socialistic approach to achievement. To at least half
of those who verbalized their reaction, the framed document
posted on every wall ("Why not in the john, too?" some asked)
had the semblance of a regimentation, of a Big Brother attitude.
For more than a year, the credo drew ridicule.

And then attitudes seemed to change. As Neaman's achievements accumulated, the sneering glances at the framed credo
turned to thoughtful stares and to a slow rereading of the text.
The words, the phrases, the sentence structure had a slowness,
a ponderousness which, when weighed against the reality of the
company's improvement, appeared to have acquired a solid ring
of truth. Of course, everyone began to admit, it was a dogmatic
exercise to set down a credo on paper and then distribute it to
several thousand executives who took it as a tacit order that it
must appear on their walls, above their desks, within reading
view of even the most astigmatic. But then, Neaman was dogmatic. He was a formalist. He was an ultrapragmatist. He believed only in what could be seen, in what could be done, and in
conscientious follow-through. In that sense, many said, it was
better that he was dogmatic. There was never any question as
to where you stood with him because you always knew what
he wanted.

That, at least, was the attitude of the average employe among
the multitude that Neaman believed in. Yet among the more
sophisticated and the more talented, who believed that Neaman

in his credo and in his behavior spurned them, there was never any surrender of their conviction that he and his statement were awkward and dull. He was not quite American in his management style, rhetoric, or behavior. Nor was he quite European or even Israeli. His metier was somewhere in-between, and it was not smooth or graceful but crude.

During this evolutionary process of reaction, Neaman was asked by this interviewer to explain his credo. He did it this way:

"Every idea here supports the existence of the small man within the big corporation. Accept this as a world that is going toward big corporations—there is just nothing you can do about it. The cost of research, the cost of computer services, the cost of everything is so great that the small corporation can't maintain those costs and be efficient. You need big corporations. But within them you will have to learn to create small units of operations to accommodate the efforts of the average man and allow him to see that his contribution benefits the total company. We are not geniuses—there are very few geniuses!—and it appears that every time we get people who try to be geniuses or act like that, all we get is a business that within a few years is going to be destroyed. They cannot work within a team and it is only teamwork that can cope with the problems and burdens of the big company."

"How can you be sure," he was asked, "that your tactics aren't putting down the people who have more than average talents? What about the man who isn't a genius but has above-normal talents? Aren't you putting a cap on him?"

"It could be," he said, "but I think that every man puts forth his best when he is asked to give his utmost, even if he should be in the midst of mediocrity. I see my job as a teacher—a teacher who shows other people how they can rise above themselves."

He lapsed into silence but his eyes grew wide, filling with a radiance that bespoke deep personal satisfaction. "Let me tell you about a man," he resumed, "and maybe you will understand what I am doing."

When he assumed the division's command, one of the New York store managers with whom he was most dissatisfied was a fifty-four-year-old McCrory employe who had spent thirty years with the company. His store's performance was poor, with sales gains of a negligible percentage and annual losses continuing without let-up. After several visits to the store, Neaman sat with the manager and told him that after thirty years of merchandising the manager obviously had more knowledge than he showed in the selection and presentation of his merchandise. His stockrooms were not arranged to permit easy access or exit. Would he be willing to look at the store with new eyes and make changes as though it were his first managership, instead of possibly his last? Would he also do something about the shabby, dirty look of his restaurant so that people would not be afraid to eat there? And, also, would he get "a new pair of glasses" so that he could really see how uninviting his display windows were?

Stung by all this and by the implicit criticism of all he had learned in more than three decades, the man swallowed and slowly nodded. "I've never felt so lousy in my life," he told Neaman. "You make me sound as though I don't know a damned thing. But then you're the first president who ever came into my store. Sure, let's try it."

They worked together every time Neaman had a chance to come downtown; this was supplemented by frequent telephone conversations. Sometimes they met on Sundays and went through the store. Spurred by Neaman's criticism and interest, the manager found within himself the capacity to change things he had done for years and to look around him with new eyes. Many changes were made; there were numerous misjudgments, but gradually the old store began to take on a new life. Within three years, it was producing record sales and new, if minimal, profits. It was in the black for the first time in a decade.

After the second year of profits, the manager called to invite Neaman to the store. "What is it?" Sam asked. "You'll see when you get here," said the manager. "Believe me, you'll be surprised."

When he arrived, Neaman was surprised indeed. A large, swaying cloth hung over the windows from which a ten-foot sign was posted reading, "Help Our Store Celebrate Its Golden Anniversary." As he entered, he saw a variety of similar notices, bouquets from other managers, and all the sales personnel wearing replicas of early 1900 clothes. When the saleswomen saw him, they left their customers and thronged around him. Most were not young, having worked in the same store for twenty-five or thirty years. They kissed Neaman and handed him such gifts as a large cardboard key, paper flowers, peanuts, candy. Customers, curious and smiling, clustered around the group in the center of which was an astonished Sam Neaman.

The manager approached with his young assistant, both wearing tight sackcloth suits, high celluloid collars, and straw hats, circa 1914. "Sam, you are going to have lunch in our restaurant," the manager said, grinning widely. "It's the cleanest place in town—that is, if we can find a seat."

Neaman thoroughly enjoyed the simple lunch. He ate flanked by the manager and the assistant manager and faced half-a-dozen of the aging but happy saleswomen. As he glanced at his watch and began making his farewells, Neaman was asked by the manager if he had noticed the main, outside display window. "No, I didn't," he said. "Did I miss another surprise?"

The group ushered him outside. He stood before the window and soon felt his pulse pounding so heavily that he experienced a moment or two of faintness.

Neaman paused in his narrative but the interviewer prodded, "What was in the window that excited you so much?"

"I looked in that window," he related, "and couldn't believe what I saw. It consisted of a display that took up its entire contents. There was my picture in it with the credo. Then there was the plaque that the manager had won the year before for the best improvement in performance in the district. Then there was a photostatic copy of his bonus check. And the entire window, the largest of all the front windows, was filled with mementos, including a very beautiful white strip of bristol cardboard on which was written in Hebrew—in Hebrew!—the words, 'All this I owe to one man—all this I owe to this man,' with an arrow running from the cardboard to my picture and underneath there was an English translation of the Hebrew words. This was his tribute as a non-Jew to me as a Jew and as his boss. He had gone to a local rabbi and obtained from him the words that he gave to a sign painter.

"As we looked at the window, we were both trembling with

emotion and excitement, this manager and I. And do you know what he said to me? He said, 'Sam, I didn't know if you could read Hebrew, so I had it translated as much for you as for my customers, but I wanted them to know it, too. But I can see that you can understand the words because I know it means so much more in the original. Thank you for everything, my dear friend.' "

Shortly after relating this incident and explaining his credo, Neaman told me that he was going one step further. Each of his 3,000 executives would soon receive a card listing among other things the "Keys to Successful Management." The reverse of the card would contain the credo. The neat plasticized cards were currently being printed, he said, and would be on their way in a matter of days.

The "keys" were "facts, plans, execution, and supervision." In addition, the remaining space on the noncredo side would contain his "Directives for Supervisors—Detect, Correct, Prevent."

He regarded the interviewer with a distinct measure of pride. "Now, aren't you gonna ask me," he said, "what this will do to the man with the above-average talents?"

"Actually, no. But I was beginning to wonder, though, if you won't be hounding all your people with the framed credo and now these cards—"

Neaman shrugged. "Anyone who feels he is being hounded could come and talk to me," he said. "This doesn't even enter into the question. What is important is that we have to protect ourselves. I am giving them the means. Facts. Plans. Execution. Supervision. And if they've got the reminder in their pockets, on their walls, or sitting on their desks, maybe they will remember. The main thing is you don't plan to do anything if you don't first have the facts. It's that old military axiom: 'Time spent on reconnaissance is never wasted.' If Napoleon knew about the weather in Moscow in the winter, he never would have attacked. No. He would never have gone there, and he would never have had his testicles frozen. If he had known the facts, he might have waited awhile instead of going in at the wrong time of the year, and maybe the whole history of humankind since would be different."

Once the facts are in hand, he added, one can truly move ahead. But obtaining the facts is no simple matter. "You should never accept less than the true situation," Neaman said. "Not the fancy, not the story, not what somebody told you, not second-hand information, but facts. Facts that you can look at, evaluate, authenticate."

"What then?"

"Then the rest is common sense. Using the facts that you have authenticated, you make your plans. Then you execute them. Then you supervise the execution. But if your supervision shows that your execution of plans based on facts is not accurate, then you have unearthed new facts. These will show you that there is a serious flaw in the process, and so you go back over all of it and find which step was wrong. It could be any of them. If execution shows need for changes in plans because of the emergence of new facts, good. That is the cycle of management. The protective process is functioning. So you start all over again, verifying the facts and taking the other steps to achieve your objective."

"It sounds to me that you've refined even those four management 'keys' in the directives—detect, correct, prevent."

"You're learning," he said, smiling. "Even journalists can learn." His eyes were shining, and he shook his head with exaggerated admiration. "That's good."

As I wandered through the McCrory organization in New York, in some of its stores in various cities, and in the York distribution center, I saw the framed credo everywhere. When I asked a man if he were familiar with either the "keys" or the supervisors' "directives" or both, he was apt to reach into his wallet and pull out the card. Often, he would carry it in his breast pocket. In no case during any interview when I asked for it did any executive fail to produce the card. As for the credo with its Neaman photo, it had an even more ubiquitous presence. It hung on every wall.

When Neaman was told of the saturation that his documents had received, he beamed. "I'm a happy man because you can never tell how your methodology will work out," he confessed. "It could be resisted or just accepted in a token way. But I know this is not what is happening. You see, in half the cases, I sent the cards along to the executive with a little note. 'Just in case I'm not always going to be around, here's a little bit of Sam Neaman you can hold onto.' "

"Why did you do that?"

"It seems to me that it would help. There was enough of the note of concern from a father and enough of the *shtip* to make everyone get the message."

"What about the other half who just got the card, not the note?"

"They are already believers. They don't need any *shtip*. They believe in Neaman, and they know Neaman believes in them. They understand that I don't have to send them a little bit of Sam Neaman because they already know that they have all of me, but they also know that I can't be at their beck and call. They know already because we have been through a lot these last few years that the sequence of events in everything we do in management is contained in those four functions called the 'keys.' Any company could learn everything we have done and do it too just from the credo and the card. And the other thing it proves is that it reduces the structure of the big company to just the small man. You don't have to be a big man to be an executive, this is what it all says. You can take a big problem in your teeth, chew it into small bits, and be just as smart and just as effective as any man."

But as he worked on one level to refine his people concept and on another to refine his operational techniques, Neaman found that success added to his burdens. Riklis, who had never really slowed the pace of his acquisitions even when his fate hung on the whim of his bankers, became inspired with Neaman's digestive ability and adroitness in producing profits from all. Between 1964 and 1970, he used McCrory not just as a funnel for cash but as a sort of vacuum cleaner to absorb one company after another. He bought control of Glen Alden Corporation (a New England holding company for mines, real estate, and theaters), and later transferred it to Rapid-American's ownership. The other ten companies he acquired, mostly under the McCrory name, included S. Klein (a pioneer New York department store chain noted for its bargain offerings) and Best & Co. (a prestige, old-established specialty store), as

well as other, lesser-known companies. Riklis had an eye for
J. J. Newberry, a big, diversified but financially troubled chain.
But he decided to wait until it came closer to the brink so that
he could buy it at his price.

Through it all, Neaman structured and restructured, refined
and rerefined. He added to his methodology and availed himself more and more of the computer and of all the complex
communications equipment he maintained in his upper East Side
penthouse to keep in touch with his increasingly farflung network of stores, executives, and store managers. If he groaned
privately about Riklis's greed for profits and power, he restricted it only to Cecelia, his quiet, placid, ever-smiling wife.
As he moved up from division president to corporate president
and geared himself to accommodate the latest acquisitions, he
brought in several outside executives. But some of his choices
were not good, and only a few stayed more than two years or so.

He was, it seemed, at his best with the people he inherited.
One by one, they all appeared to become believers. But there
were others, too, whom he brought in and made into believers.
So the people who remained were a diverse lot, but they were
believers all.

12.   The People and the Prism

A challenge being a challenge, Neaman was never afraid to
take a chance on people. But he was as dogmatic in pushing
them to their inmost core of possibility as he was dogmatic with
methods and systems.

This became obvious in many hours spent with McCrory
executives. He gave demanding new assignments to jaded employes. He accepted others who could not make it in other
firms and gave them more responsibility than they had ever
bargained for. In the process, he separated man from home and
said, "Choose . . . you can't have both until you can prove
yourself and maybe even then. . . ." Hating hopelessness and
negativism, he attacked them with gusto. And he prodded,

goosed, and kicked those who wallowed in them without mercy. "I'll give you guided autonomy, which means I will let you show me all the initiative you've got in you, providing I like it," he told them.

But, in other cases, his appointments were calculated. They were intended as a step that would lead to another step. While these were fewer in number, they made a contribution in reinforcing McCrory's new position vis-à-vis other retail chains and its own parent company.

Yet, regardless of the rationale for their appointments, transfers, promotions, or demotions, everyone wanted to understand Neaman. Few managed to understand him completely, but all admitted that once they came under his influence, their lives seemed to change.

The Buffer-Man

As he basked in his success, Neaman felt that Riklis's offer, "What can I do, Sam, to show you how I feel?" was an open invitation which was impossible to ignore. It may have been rhetorical or sentimental on Riklis's part, but its acceptance fitted into Neaman's concept of how things happen and what follows from them.

From that heady moment in September 1966, when he became corporate president of McCrory, Neaman knew that one more turn would be needed to complete the circle in which McCrory would become his world. It would, of course, be his assumption of the twin posts of chairman-of-the-board and chief executive officer. In that way, though the bouncy conglomerator would still control McCrory through the parent company, Riklis would no longer have any presence either on the McCrory board or in its offices. It was neither necessary nor desirable.

The more Sam Neaman contemplated it, the more sense it made, and it became overwhelmingly important to him. The company would never become an efficiently functioning mechanism if its people were confused about who its head was, both actually and symbolically. It was a matter of discipline and example in equal parts. It would, in other words, scarcely help if they knew that a man whose total consciousness was in financial dealings was their chief. But if he were an administrator, the priorities and the criteria would be very clear. With Neaman as its combined head-of-government and chief-of-state, as it were, there would be no short cuts in which individual responsibility, the reliance on methods, and the efficacy of systems could be glossed over.

There was no question, too, that a hardening of rapport, a sort of rift but perhaps only a cooling, was developing between Riklis and Neaman. It was nothing overt; rather, it was psychological or natural. When there is a stunning success, whether people want to or not, they inevitably draw up a scorecard. Who was really responsible for McCrory's success? Within two years of the variety chain's reorganization, its profit margin on sales had already become the best in the industry. Riklis had created the vehicle for it by putting it together from a rag-tag motley of stores and had engineered a big company from it. But Neaman had rescued it from disaster. Riklis was Neaman's boss, but where would Riklis be without Neaman? But where would Neaman be without Riklis? It was the old theatrical question of who was more important—the impresario or the artist? Could one exist without the other? The top associates of Riklis and Neaman quickly rallied to their own chiefs but avoided publicly endorsing one over the other. Some things are better left unsaid.

Neaman finally took the initiative. In May 1969, after a McCrory board meeting, he approached Stanley Kunsberg, chairman-of-the-board of the Lerner stores division, and asked him to lunch. As they sat in a nearby restaurant, Neaman quickly got to the point. "Stanley," he said, "how would you like to become president of McCrory?"

Kunsberg smiled indulgently. "Of course, I'd love to, Sam. But what will happen to you?"

"I will become chairman-of-the-board."

Kunsberg smiled wider. "What will happen to Riklis?"

"If you came over as president and I became chairman-of-the-board, Riklis would step out."

"Sam," said Kunsberg, "don't mind my asking, but will Riklis go along with you on this?"

"He will. All I have to do is to tell him."

When Neaman called that afternoon and related the plan, Riklis readily agreed. Afterward, when Riklis dropped into Izzy Becker's office next door and told him, Becker exploded.

"Goddamn, what did I tell you! The sonofabitch's got an ego as big as a horse! You're just creating a Frankenstein, Rik! Somewhere along the line, you gotta put him down or we'll all be sorry."

"Maybe," Riklis conceded. "But now's not the time. He wants to run his own show. So we'll let him. In the meantime, I'm glad he picked Kunsberg. He's a solid citizen, and he's got sense. And he knows the retail business."

In that regard, Neaman had pursued a logical course. Sensing that the move would not sit well with some of Riklis's top crew, he knew that one good way of offsetting it would be to choose a proven merchant as McCrory's number-two man. Most of the Rapid brass, he knew, still remained skeptical about a nonretailer running a big retail organization over the long pull, despite what he had already done. So he was in effect throwing a bone to the dogs. They could have their retailer.

Kunsberg, as a matter of fact, was a retailer down to his toes. He was also an executive who knew how to straddle a fence effectively. He knew how to stand between opposing forces and not be mowed down by the cross-fire. After forty-five years in the retail business, when he should have been frayed and faltering, he exuded instead an air of competence, of being able to carry weighty responsibility, and of being the last one to give in to panic or fatigue. He was credited with much of the success of the 400-store Lerner chain and because of it had been named a year earlier to the quasi-honorary post of executive vice-president of McCrory, Lerner's parent company.

Among Neaman's top executives, his announcement the next morning of Kunsberg's impending election generated some highly pertinent speculation. Without question, Kunsberg was an impressive man. He carried his sixty-six years well on a stocky, firm frame topped with a broad brow and bright eyes that made up for his lack of ready articulation. He gave an impression of such quiet, inner strength that he felt it unnecessary to speak except when it meant something. He was a strong man like Neaman but hardly as verbose. It was obvious to the men that he had a totally different management style. But they wondered if his well-known amiability wouldn't clash with Neaman's hard pragmatism. Would he use his tact to smooth over the crevices in Neaman's rough-hewn manner or would he really be Riklis's man sitting next door to Neaman? Was Neaman—and this was the question of questions judging by its unanswerability—actually prepared to share a rule that had been purely his for almost five years?

In his York office, Frank Patchen privately told some of his team that the two would get along well. "I know Kunsberg," he said. "I've had some dealings with him. He's actually much like Sam Neaman but with retail experience. They will complement each other."

The extreme opposite of this view came naturally from Steve Jackel, the *enfant terrible* in Neaman's offices. "Not a damn thing is gonna change," Steve asserted. "Sam will still be the top man and run things any way he pleases. Kunsberg will get the crumbs that fall from the table and be damn well paid for it. And the rest of us will still run our behinds off."

But the question that was difficult to answer because Kunsberg, like Neaman, was a private person was why he should have accepted the new post in the first place. It was a question that begged for some answers.

Born in 1906 in Columbus, Georgia, Kunsberg was the third generation of one of the many Jewish families which emigrated from Europe to the United States but avoided the melting-pot of the North. Instead, they scattered through the Southern states. Some settled in the large cities such as Richmond, Atlanta, Louisville, Chattanooga, and New Orleans. But handfuls cropped up in numerous small cities and towns in the Carolinas, Georgia, Kentucky, and Mississippi.

Most Southern Jews, hemmed in by large Gentile majorities and a narrowly based agri–business economy, did what they had in earlier, similar situations. They became clerks, tradesmen, merchants, or professionals.

Stanley, who grew into a sturdy, barrel-chested, genial young man with a zesty outlook, followed the tradition. He became a shipper in the Lerner Shops at the age of twenty-two with the aim of making a career in that company. For the next forty-one years, he pursued that goal as Lerner's became the country's largest chain of women's and children's apparel shops. But it wasn't until 1955 when he was forty-nine years old that he was elected a corporate vice-president. Lerner's was not a fast-moving company, but what it did was solid and long premeditated. In 1961, Stanley Kunsberg was elected president after thirty-three years with Lerner's.

Yet, despite this tardy although high recognition, his most interesting and challenging stint with the company lay ahead in the next eight years. He was to become the catalyst, the balance-wheel, the interlocutor in a difficult family situation involving both Harold Lane, Sr., and Harold Lane, Jr.

As big, bluff, and domineering as Harold Sr. was, his son (Harold Jr.) was medium-sized, reticent, and self-effacing. The situation was not unique. It seemed that more than a few physically big and successful men tend to grind their heels into their sons, particularly if the son happens to be willing to accept it. When Stanley Kunsberg met Harold Jr. in 1955, he found the younger Lane at thirty-three years old looking as though he were in his fifties. Although the father then was already sixty-four years old, in many ways his erect form, angled but unlined face, and snapping eyes made him seem more vibrant if not younger and more virile than his own son. Junior already had a slight pot, and at times his eyes watered without warning. He had a habit of looking down at his feet often during discussions, as if the answers he sought might lie below rather than above where most people found them. In due course, Kunsberg decided he felt sorry for Junior, but he felt a certain amount of contempt for him, too.

At meetings, Senior would dominate the conversation, frequently ignoring his son and the other officers, and speak directly to Kunsberg. It was as if, Kunsberg gathered, the old man were really speaking to Junior, who had to eventually succeed him because the two had the dominant amount of McCrory stock on the Lerner board, but he didn't think enough of Junior to address him directly.

"I want to see a helluva lot more care given to the tolerance limits on our inventory-control sheets," Senior typically would say, "because while we do allow some tolerances, we don't want to be too tolerant about them. Ha, ha! You understand me, of course." Kunsberg, thus addressed, would nod in a token manner. But Junior sitting next to him would nod his head vigorously. He understood, as always, who was the target of the sharp command and the butt of the cruel humor.

"I'm also goddamned appalled at the reluctance of some of us to get out and visit the boondocks," Senior would tell Kunsberg. "That's what the name of the game is. Do they like us in Dubuque, in Sioux City, or in Calumet City? Or are we afraid we'll be bitten by a customer? Too many guys are getting fat asses around here." And Kunsberg would say nothing, but Junior would quail and look wildly down at the floor.

After he became president, Kunsberg soon found that besides functioning as chief operating officer to Senior's chief executive role, the old tyrant wanted him as a buffer in residence between himself and his son. If he had had to deal directly with Junior, Kunsberg perceived, Senior might have had to resort to mayhem. But how Junior would ever rise to a height where the father considered him worthy of succession was a possibility that Kunsberg couldn't envision.

By 1969 when Neaman offered Kunsberg the McCrory presidency, he had finally come to understand the realities of the situation. Senior honestly believed that he would never have to retire because he would never die. Kunsberg was considered to be vital because he had all the performance and perhaps the character traits so sadly lacking in Junior. And Junior found in Kunsberg the ear and the heart completely lacking in his own father. But what both the Lanes ignored was the fact that the buffer takes his lumps and bruises, too.

So, by then, the situation had begun to pall on Kunsberg. Too much of his time, effort, and energy had to be given to keeping Senior from tearing Junior apart and Junior from jumping out the window. As a result, when Neaman made his offer, all Kunsberg could say was, "I'd love to, Sam."

Three years later when I interviewed him, Kunsberg was able to dispel some of the doubts raised when he was appointed. But he was evasive enough in other respects to confirm that he had developed unusual tact in the Lerner wars so that he would not become a combatant in others.

Asked for his appraisal of Neaman and his management style, Kunsberg said, "I think he's one of the brightest men I've ever known. In the beginning, I had difficulty becoming adjusted to Sam's credo of management. I have always operated on the reverse basis: having strong individual people that I could give responsibility and more important assignments to. But since I came here I have come to agree with Sam's philosophy. How can you argue with something that worked out so well? Sam has another great ability—he knows how to listen—and that's a sign of a good executive. I've seen him many times under pressure listen to stories from people that could really be considered minor compared to the problem at hand."

Asked how he and the chairman divided the duties between them, Kunsberg replied, "Neaman functions as the chief executive in all things. But when it comes to divisions, he spends most of his time with the variety and the department stores. I concentrate on Lerner's and the other divisions. But we operate like a team on all matters. We check with each other two, three, and four times a day and exchange information. Also, Sam does not like to attend outside functions. So I'm the company on the outside."

How long was his employment contract at McCrory? Kunsberg gave me his ready, natural smile. "I never got a contract," he said. "When Sam and I shook hands on our deal, we never even discussed salary, contract, or anything like it. But after I had been there a few months, I asked Neaman to have dinner and told him, 'We've never discussed contract, Sam.' He said, 'That's nothing for me to discuss. You write your own contract and I'll sign it.' Now, I'm reasonably well off, so money doesn't mean so much to me at this stage, but I appreciated Sam's gesture."

As to his current relationship to the Lanes, his smile became rueful. "Senior hasn't talked to me since I left. When I gave him the news that I was going to corporate, he said I was a traitor. Junior, of course, does exactly what his father tells him and so he doesn't talk to me, either. Neaman and I deal with them through other Lerner executives."

"Neaman, too?"

"Oh yes. Senior hates him. He resents Neaman because Sam represents a higher authority in the corporation. Senior doesn't ever want to give up the rule, you see. Strangely enough, he doesn't resent Meshulam Riklis, and he didn't from the minute Rik walked into his office in 1961 and said that he wanted to buy his company."

"Is there an elite or elitist situation here?"

Kunsberg said, "There might be, maybe because Senior founded a very successful company and Neaman came in to run one that was already in business. But I think there is even more eliteness in a guy like Sam who took a company that was in the toilet, like the variety division, and turned it around to where it is the most profitable chain of its kind in the country."

Isn't there a growing resentment between Riklis and Neaman? Kunsberg took time to answer and said, "No, not that you can put your finger on. Sam feels, and rightly so, that he is the chief executive officer of McCrory, and I believe he is saying, 'As long as I do my job I want to be left alone. This is my job, my territory, my turf. Stay out as long as I run it well.' "

"Last question—where is this company heading?"

"Well," he replied after another pause. "I see this company growing from here on in through its own efforts. I don't think that we are going to have to swallow any more mergers for a while. It would give us indigestion. We are pushing for more profitability in those divisions that are not yet achieving a three percent before-tax profit. That means working hard on the Klein's chain and the Newberry Company, the latest acquisition, which used to enjoy a high profitability before it fell on its face. And I think it's do-able, yes, I do."

"Another question has occurred to me. May I ask it?"

When he nodded tolerantly, I said, "Is it possible, Stanley, that by coming to the parent company, what you did was simply transfer your role as buffer from the Lanes to Riklis and Neaman?"

He took his time again and then replied, "No, I don't think so. The problem between Lane Senior and Junior is just that if Junior would ever fight back or stand his ground, Senior would give in. But this situation is entirely different. Riklis and Sam respect each other's rights and prerogatives.. Maybe they don't like each other's lifestyle, but they respect each other's accomplishments. Besides, Neaman is a fighter and Riklis is no bully. No, it's a different situation. I'm comfortable."

Second Chance

After acquiring a new president and succeeding to the chairmanship, Neaman moved quickly to reinforce McCrory's newly emerging individuality. Its financial controls, accounting, billing, and payables procedures still emanated from Rapid's uptown offices, however. Seeing this as a patently remaining vestige of Rapid's ownership, he proposed that they be separated and housed as their own unit in McCrory's offices. Again Riklis agreed, much to Izzy Becker's dissatisfaction. Neaman immediately set about appointing his own financial controls group and instructed Stanley Kunsberg to find a top controller.

Within a matter of weeks, Kunsberg asked Neaman to meet several men whom he considered prime candidates. These were soon narrowed down to one.

At fifty-two, Norman Mallor was involved in probably the most difficult period of his life. After twenty-eight years with the Macy's organization, he had been discharged by an angry divisional chairman-of-the-board because of a large, unexpected inventory shortage in furniture. It was obvious after a physical check of the stock that it was all mainly due to a paper error, a discrepancy in the records. But one of the features of a control system was to avoid paper errors. Investigation showed that the fault lay in the failure of several people within the computerized controls system to perform their jobs properly.

Since he was the division's senior vice-president in charge of financial controls, Mallor was responsible for their mistakes, especially if the chairman chose to make it so. And so, on June 1, 1970, having been the chairman's "fair-haired boy" for years and having recently bought an expensive new home in New Jersey, Norman Mallor was fired.

When an executive recruiter sent him to meet Stanley Kunsberg, Mallor was uncertain and confused. A chunky, self-contained looking and deliberate man, he had, however, a fortunate trait. Unlike most people in such a situation, he did not exhibit his real anxiety, his overeagerness and nervousness. Obviously he needed a job. But he had developed a calm disposition and a reserved personality during his many years as a CPA and corporate controller. He had learned long ago that people respected equanimity and self-assurance in a man who handled money matters.

Fortunately, his effort to achieve a stoic self-assurance as a professional earmark was bolstered by many years of personal success. Circumstance, devotion, and skill had combined to propel him into one of the most important jobs in his field. But they didn't help him much when the axe fell.

Growing up in Newark, he had worked as a messenger and junior clerk for a small firm of accountants while in high school. Acclimated to accountancy, he majored in it at New York University, continuing at the same concern and going to school at night. In May 1941, he received his accounting certificate while still with the CPA firm. When he found himself about to be drafted into the armed services in 1942, he gave the company his notice. But he was rejected from military service on an eyesight disability.

Norman decided that he had spent enough years with a small firm and began making the rounds of local, large accountancy companies. Living in his own rooms in the center of the city, he often used the facilities of the nearby Young Men's Hebrew Association, playing handball and availing himself of its steamroom. While sitting in the Y's *schwitz* one evening, he discovered that the man huddled next to him was an accountant, too. When Norman announced that he was one, the man asked him where he was working. "I'm looking," Norman said. "I know where there's a job open for an accountant," the man said. "My brother-in-law's an accountant, too, and he's just been promoted. He has to find his own replacement. Would you like to work for Bamberger's, the Macy division in New Jersey?"

Norman was hired as a junior accountant and stayed with the large department store chain for almost three decades. He rose to the top controller's post, swept along with the success and momentum of the division's chairman, a temperamental but brilliant merchant who had an immense drive. But Norman found that temperament can be a two-edged sword. It can propel associates to the pinnacle and then blithely drop them over the cliff.

"Oh, I basically admired the chairman," Mallor recalled, "for his push and his general capabilities. We put together a pretty good system and I had a pretty good team of my own. Most of the changes that I proposed were damned good because we were successful. But there was the one systems change which turned out to be a Vietnam for me.

"I had been responsible for instituting the data processing operation in our division from the outset. We were already well advanced in all areas of data processing as it applied to department stores. I had probably one of the best operations of its kind in the country. And, as part of it, I had begun planning a complete system which meant involving not only the controller's office but also the people on the selling floor, the warehouse and delivery men, the whole works of tying in customer service in a furniture business. But this part of it didn't go, even though I had been successful in every part of the program of implementation up till then. Some of the reasons for the failure could be laid at my door, some at other people's doors. It wasn't the program necessarily that defeated us; it was the inability to get people to do the things they had to do to make the system really work. As it turned out, we had a horrendous inventory shortage on furniture."

The shortage developed at a bad time. There was a mini-recession that started in the fall of 1969 and lasted through spring 1970. Much money had already been expended on the new EDP system and more was on the line. Delivery agents were being changed with consequent disruptions in the information flow. And perhaps nothing was more disturbing to the intensely motivated as expectations not met.

"In some ways, the chairman saw the difficult period coming, the recession," Mallor related, "so the fact that we were having these difficulties with the furniture inventory didn't help. It was a constant problem that we just couldn't seem to get resolved to my satisfaction or his. Then when we finally realized the extent of the shortage, I guess that made up his mind that it was time for a change."

With a wife, two teen-aged daughters, a new house, and age

creeping up on him, Mallor told himself that he was not "going to sit back and take my good time looking for a good job." He promptly went to two executive recruiters, contacted friends in the industry, and within a few weeks was sitting in Kunsberg's office. He returned for several more interviews during which he met Sam Neaman. Norman knew that he was being seriously considered by McCrory.

Realizing, however, that he really knew very little about the company, Norman spent some hours at the main branch of the New York Public Library on Fifth Avenue and read a number of periodicals which had carried pieces on McCrory, Neaman, Rapid–American and Riklis. He left with a conviction that McCrory, while not as sound or consistent a performer as Macy's or Federated Department Stores, was nonetheless a company with strong possibilities. He confirmed this the next day with acquaintances in the trade. They spoke in glowing terms about the concern's achievements under Neaman.

Kunsberg impressed him as a "nice" person. Neaman appeared to him as "quite forthright." But the second time he met Neaman—the first time had been "a simple hello and a visual sighting"—the McCrory chairman leaned forward, stared piercingly into Norman's face, and asked, "How, Mr. Mallor, can we be sure that you are right for us? After working for one company for twenty-eight years, I am not convinced that you could make the transition in mental attitude toward our company. Could you give the same kind of devotion the second time around as you gave the first time?"

He assured Neaman and Kunsberg that he was capable of showing both the right mental attitude and the devotion. At that point, he was asked to come back for one more interview at which time, Kunsberg told him, "We'll give you our final decision."

The next time, Neaman took over the interview. And after a series of additional questions obviously designed to further probe his behavioristic traits and business philosophy, Norman was hired as controller. But, as he added much later, "I learned in that last interview that Neaman apparently had all kinds of sources of information. Apparently he had gotten a pretty good feedback on me."

"I'll take a good chance on you," Neaman told him. "Any man who stays in that company for twenty-eight years must have a lot of guts and a hard head. Here, there's a lot of back-breaking work ahead, but if things go right the future could be good for you. Congratulations. And now, what do you drink?" In a few moments, Margit, his secretary, brought in whisky, bourbon, and ice. Neaman, Kunsberg, and Mallor drank a toast to a "promising association."

At their suggestion, Mallor made a month's tour of some of McCrory's most important facilities, as well as the various divisions. When he returned, he hired five people as part of the new corporate controls team. One was a former associate from the Macy operation; another was a girl whom Neaman had highly recommended; and the rest came from outside. But when he wanted to visit Rapid's offices to see the facility that his unit would replace, Neaman flatly told him to stay away and didn't explain why. Mallor surmised that Neaman wanted a complete break, but didn't refuse him later when the new controller decided to hire a few people from the original controls unit.

As he devoted himself to his new responsibilities, Mallor found that they were totally different and more encompassing than his last ones. At Macy's, his function was that of senior controller, overseeing the day-by-day supervision of such things as accounts receivable and accounts payable, sales audit, payroll, cashiering, data processing, and the like. But at McCrory, in addition to all that, he had to concern himself with controlling cash, its availability and its flow (as a treasurer or financial vice-president would). The difference was essentially that of a controller for a division and a controller for a public corporation.

Since a major part of his new job involved cash-flow responsibility, a phase that he was unfamiliar with despite his long experience, it was obvious to Mallor and others that Neaman had given him more than just a second chance. He was, in effect, taking a gamble on Mallor in the hope that the new controller would use not only his knowledge but also his intelligence, his instincts, and possibly his subconscious to grow into a job that was more important and more challenging than any he had ever had.

Was there also the fact that Neaman savored the prestige of

having a top financial controller on his staff who had been with
the highly regarded Bamberger's? When he was asked this,
Norman Mallor said he couldn't respond. The impression he
gave was that if it was not quite a valid question, it also had little
relevance to him. He had needed a job at a hazardous period in
his life. One learned to disabuse oneself of the more abstract
considerations at a time when pure practicality was vital. Too
much analysis at the wrong time, in other words, can hurt.

The fact was, however, that the three—Neaman, Kunsberg,
and Mallor—were all learning at the same time. Neaman was extending himself from the daily operating supervision to acquire
a long-term overview. Kunsberg was obviously busy trying to
adapt himself to Neaman and to keep an open conduit to Rapid.
Mallor was grappling with the unusual financial leverage of Mc-
Crory, which, unlike Macy's one-half to one-third debt to
equity, had three times the amount of debt to stockholders'
equity. And all three were jointly filling the role of financial
vice-president until Norman could assume it.

Assume it he did within two years. Like many other Neaman appointments, he became a success because he measured up
to the challenge. As Neaman showed more and more interest
in the possibilities of using the computer to remove the unexpected from retailing, Mallor put much effort into budgeting
and reducing the amount of short-term debt that McCrory
needed. Although the company had a $70 million line of credit,
better money management enabled McCrory to use correspondingly less each year, thus reducing the debt load an average of
about fifteen percent annually.

In a large but almost bare office in which several pieces of contemporary furniture were placed without any attempt at balance, Mallor was more affable and open than his words were revealing or informative. He had found a place for himself again;
he was the slide-rule man on a new, big team and he wasn't
about to create any ripples. This was the impression he gave
and related to it was the implication that he had learned something from his previous experience. He would make no mistakes
that would create the havoc in his life that the last one did.

Our interview concluded with a discussion of the company's
financial policies.

Question: "Why is McCrory so highly leveraged—having so much debt?"

Answer: "It's leveraged, you might say, by the design of things because this has been the expansion policy of Rapid–American."

Question: "Would the management like it to be less leveraged? How could that be done?"

Answer: "I'm sure if it were in the cards most people would like it the other way. . . . Changing it would require an influx of additional capital. We have been getting ours from banks or by using debentures, but we have primarily been using other people's money. That has been Riklis's policy all along, and it has allowed him to expand greatly. But it gives Rapid and McCrory quite a debt obligation on a continuing basis."

Question: "Would you describe McCrory now as a healthy company financially?"

Answer: "Yes, we are. We're making money. Eight years in a row, we've increased our profits. And when you have a company like McCrory that can return twenty percent or better on an investment and do it fairly consistently, it is an indication of health. I don't think there's any question of that."

Courage Revisited

On November 30, 1964, a short, intense man named Charley Gass was hired by Sam Neaman in an undefined capacity. Twenty years earlier, in a disputed bridgehead on the Seine River, the same man, then an infantry sergeant, had taken a personal stand which later exerted a major force in his career.

Within eight years after joining McCrory, Gass had become one of Neaman's several alter-egos. He also became vice-president for internal audit and vice-president of two divisions, holding all three posts simultaneously. But, most importantly, perhaps, he was to function as McCrory's in-house inspector general and save the company many millions of dollars.

In an interview that lasted an entire morning on a spring day, it became increasingly obvious that he was pouring forth a personal rhapsody of an unusual nature. Anguish alternated with exhilaration. Articulation fought with personal pathos. His comments rushed forth in an unchecked torrent, mostly defying the interviewer's attempts to control it.

"I'll be happy to tell you what internal auditing is," he said. "It's just about everything.

"But mainly it's an examination of inventory and finances to make sure that theft, bookkeeping, and human errors are discovered, or better yet, prevented before they get very far.

"I was formerly with a big retail company that was going bankrupt. I had to find another job. Mr. Neaman had just been appointed president of the variety division. In the other company, I had been in charge of the accounting and control office, but when Mr. Neaman hired me it was through the back door. That means he had no definite job for me.

"I was born fifty-three years ago in Mount Sinai Hospital, in Manhattan, and I lived in the Bronx all my life. So I'm a product of New York City. My father was a foreman in a place that made the canvas that goes into the shoulders of jackets. I went to DeWitt Clinton High School and then to the College of the City of New York, where I majored in accounting. And after that, of course, when I graduated I went into the U.S. Army Infantry, the European Theater of Operations. I was in infantry communications, that is, stringing wire. I have been decorated with the Silver Star Medal, the Bronze Star Medal, the Purple Heart, and a Presidential Citation.

"Why did I get the Silver Star? We had made a bridgehead on the other side of the Seine River, and the enemy launched a counterattack and the Jerries threw everything they could at us and knocked out all our communications lines. The battalion commander had no idea as to the disposition of his companies, and we were in danger of being completely overrun. I was the staff sergeant in charge of the communications platoon, and without orders from anybody, I asked for one volunteer and he joined me and through the shell-fire and the machine-gun fire and everything else we physically found the broken communication wires and held them together with our hands while the other one cranked. This allowed the battalion commander to communicate with his frontline companies and to find out what the hell was happening. I don't know why I did it, but I have found out about myself that I take responsibility seriously. I was the platoon sergeant, I was the one wearing the stripes, and I couldn't just sit there.

"You know that old Jewish expression about being at war—you can get killed there? I kept telling that to myself the two or three more times we did that, the two of us, and we were sitting ducks. The citation said that we were completely exposed to the enemy. How they didn't hit us as the tanks were approaching is beyond me. They were maybe twenty-five or thirty yards away, and we had this wonderful luck on our side.

"After the war, I was well prepared for retailing because retailing is kind of like combat. It is, even though we all wear the same kind of suits. It's a very, very competitive business. You're always living with yesterday's numbers and it's the kind of business where people can only make their mark by showing improved performance and a sort of ruthlessness sets in. It's what Macy's, Korvettes and Gimbels are doing and all the rest.

"I got a job as an accounting clerk with that first big retail chain in 1946, and by 1964 when they started going out of business, I was the controller there. I was also very much involved with administration, and when all the difficulties started to take place, I was the one who relayed it to the market and to the creditors. The heads of the business locked themselves up in their offices and didn't answer their phones.

"After I joined Mr. Neaman, he said he wanted me to find my own level. But he really amazed me with my first big assignment after just telling me to give him a report on this and this, and it was to take charge of the physical inventory-taking of all the 600 variety stores. Now, this is only two to three weeks after I started. I know very little about the company, and he is entrusting this complete kit and kaboodle, which can naturally mean so much to the year-end statement, to my hands. That's where your meat and potatoes are. Inventory is the biggest account in retailing. And then on top of that, he says, 'Charley, I want the results of every one of those 600 stores no

later than two weeks after the taking of the physical inventory.'
Two weeks after the taking of it would have brought us to
February 15, 1965, which was a Sunday night.

"Well, I managed to get three girls to help me. I visited all
the regional offices and introduced myself, and then I held a session on the coming physical inventory and went over the instructions. I came back from this trip and Mr. Neaman knew
every move I had made. He knows everything that's going on.
He keeps track on new men, on what's being said, and he likes
to get feedback on presentations. This was my first knowledge
of how thoroughly Mr. Neaman went into any subject or how
thoroughly he went into finding out about people. He was very
pleased. I remember very well what he said: 'You handled yourself beautifully.' I was walking on air.

"Now came the task of taking the inventory, recording it,
and then working up the shrinkage or losses in inventory. In
those days, we weren't programmed as we are now. Of course,
we got certain information from the machine like what the book
inventory was. But the important thing we were now doing was
relaying the actual physical inventory to the book which we
got back from all the 600 stores and adding the reserve for shrinkage and everything and getting the shortage figure inserted into it
all. Myself and these three lovely girls worked day and night,
Saturday and Sunday. One night, I slept on a receiving table.
I started feeding Mr. Neaman the results, about thirty stores at
a time.

" 'Charley,' he said to me, 'you call me any time of the day or
night as you get the results of thirty or forty stores. Don't worry
about waking me up.' I called him twice at 4 A.M. because he
imparted to me a sense of urgency and I knew he meant it."

Charley Gass is taken aback at a question the interviewer believes is relevant. "At any point, did you think this was a little
silly? Why couldn't it wait until ten in the morning or, say,
when a third or half the stores were in?"

He shakes his head emphatically. "No, never," he says. "I
might have maybe. But when you think of the effort and the
push Mr. Neaman placed on cutting back inventory to get the

company back to the bottom line, I didn't think what I did was silly at all. And when he picked up the phone on the first ring wide-awake, we had an animated conversation at 4 A.M."

"On February 15, 1965, at 11:40 P.M.—the date is indelibly etched in my mind—I called Mr. Neaman and gave him the results of the last twenty or twenty-five stores, and I said, 'Mr. Neaman, I'm twenty minutes early.' He had said he wanted the results in by midnight of the fifteenth. I looked out and it was snowing. I can't ever forget—you know, if I said to you, 'What were you doing when Pearl Harbor was bombed?' We all remember what we were doing. And if you said to me, 'Charley Gass, what the hell were you doing at 11:40 P.M. on February 15, 1965?' I'd tell you, 'It was snowing out and I had just finished one of the toughest jobs in my whole life—'

"The next morning, I walked into the chairman's office and put all the results on his desk. Two of his top executives came in, I don't even recall exactly who they were, and he said to them, 'In my thirty-one years of being in business, I have never seen a job of this complexity planned and executed with such efficiency.' And of course I felt like a million bucks.

"Well, it was quite a thing. I had had a lot of bitterness in the days with the old company. I'd had a lot of frustrations and no fulfillment in those days, and I knew I had the experience and I knew I had the savvy and the background, but I somehow couldn't reach the people I worked for. But I had the feeling that Mr. Neaman knew when I met him what my depths were and he knew the bitterness and the hostility that was in me. Nevertheless, he gave me an opportunity and a chance that makes me wonder to this day. Because if I'd fallen flat on my face, the whole thing would really have reflected on his choice of me to undertake such a thing as being responsible for the entire physical inventory.

"Let me tell you what happened then. The next month, March 1965, he gave me a book. It's still here on my desk and one of these days I'm going to have Mr. Neaman autograph it. It's called *Management Audit*, and it's written by William P. Leonard. It was obvious when he gave it to me what he was driving at. 'Henry, why don't you read it?' he said. 'We have nothing resembling an audit department within the variety division, and I'd like you to think along those lines.' After I read it, he said, 'I would like your ideas for an audit program for the division because we're wide open; we don't have any kind of deterrent, police force and so on.' I sat down with a member of my staff, and we put together schedules that we called 'Schedules A through O.' This was the schedule of steps an auditor would take when he visited the stores.

"One night in Mr. Neaman's office, we started going over the schedules. We started about 6 P.M. and ended about a quarter to nine and again he amazed me. Whereas most presidents would not want to get into the details of such a program, he insisted on going through every schedule and getting my interpretation of exactly what each one would bring to light. When we finished, he said, 'Charley, go full speed ahead and make us audit-conscious.'

"Since then, we have refined those schedules and made them part of the division manual. We have set up auditors in each division and even in the regional offices. They coordinate with us from the field. Basically, we want the stores to use these audits as a tool for themselves. We said in effect, 'Mr. Store Manager, we're not out to catch you. We're not out to embarrass you. We want to prevent—the idea of auditing is to prevent. Help yourself. Do it yourself. Do your own self-audit. Then when we come in, we'll be more than happy to give you a clean bill of health.'

"We found that we didn't have the systems to prevent the exposures that we discovered, and we started setting them up. We had to cover a lot of ground. People were making up false documents; there was phony ringing up on cash registers; there was a lack of control on money orders; and lots more. Eventually, we cut our inventory shrinkage from three percent of sales to two percent, and that meant several millions of dollars. We had the variety division rolling, and in reducing our shrinkage, we found that we got involved with fraud that ranged from major to minor. We would find a cashier who never passed on mail to the store manager. Where the home office would be writing to the manager about certain cash shortages that they wanted an explanation for, she intercepted the mail and he would be unaware of it.

"They used the cashier in the variety stores as a secretary and a cashier, especially in the small stores. Now this would be similar, I would say, to entrusting my bookkeeper to make disbursements and also trusting her to do the bank reconciliation. So we found money-order thefts, people using money orders to their own advantage. We found stockroom thefts, but what catching these people really did was get the word started that we finally had a tool to act as a deterrent, and that meant we would put people in jail.

"Finding out about internal crime is a complex thing. My feeling about dishonest employes is that they can kill a company. I was away a lot in the field with my staff. The most unusual time was when we went down to the variety-division headquarters in York, Pennsylvania, for a one-day visit, and we ended up staying there for thirteen months, living at a motel. There were many things we had to do with the exposures we found to get them straightened out. For example, the accounts payable department wasn't functioning 100 percent properly, and the accounting department, while it was overstaffed, wasn't doing things it should have. In other words, it wasn't just that people were dishonest but that systems weren't working right. After a discussion with Mr. Neaman, we diverted from just auditing and put on another hat to correct and educate.

"That's why today this office is more or less an information center, too. The auditors, when they get through with a store, end up with a book. This is an enema for the store. A complete flushing out of the facts. It tells the store manager and the chairman-of-the-board everything. A few examples of what we found in one typical store: refunds weren't being handled right, which was causing unnecessary losses; there were thefts in layaway sales; and there were cash register shortages. You would think that a manager would know everything that goes on in his store? Forget it. The small-store guy might know more because he's operating in a tighter world. But when you are dealing with a Klein's store, some of which are huge with 300,000 square feet, the manager is dependent upon what his people tell him. And let's not kid ourselves. People will tell you what they want you to hear if their own behavior and perform-ance are involved. But in this office we will tell management things that no one else tells them.

"One Monday morning when I was getting ready to go down to York again, Mr. Neaman's secretary came in and said he wanted to see me. 'Charley,' he said, 'forget going to York, things are pretty settled in that division. You've got to involve yourself immediately with the Klein's accounts payable depart-ment. We got *tzuras* there. Something is rotten in accounts payable, not so much a question of money but of paying their invoices and recording them.'

"We found everything at Klein's that we shouldn't find in an accounts payable department—duplicate payments, prema-ture payments, everything. Things were so fouled up that the more we looked, the more we were appalled. We found that there is a gentleman who makes a living going into retail firms, into the accounts payable department, and saying to the man-ager, 'Look, fifty percent of the duplicate payments I find go to me, fifty percent go to you, okay?' It's a good deal for an or-ganization because without this guy they lose even more money. He's a sort of auditor. Whatever he finds, he's got a joint ven-ture with the company. An independent guy, and this is how he makes his living.

"So you can see what we were up against. This involved us with the accounts payable department for about a year. In fact, nobody really knew my identity. I was introduced to the Klein's staff as their new accounts payable manager. But, let me tell you, I had something good going for me: the suppliers in the industry. They knew me from the days with the old retail company, the one that went bankrupt, because I was the guy they came to, if you remember, and I worked out what we could do about paying them what we owed them. So I had the advantage of calling up big vendors in the industry or factors, the money lenders, and I asked them, 'Look, from your point of view, tell me: what is wrong with Klein's accounts pay-able?' I wanted to get an outside feel for it rather than just ask people from the inside. Anyway, with the help of others and my staff, which I had stationed at different points in the A.P. department, we eventually turned it around.

"Then we started an audit program for the Klein's stores, as we had for the variety stores. Again with Mr. Neaman's 100 percent backing, we went to work at it at Klein's, which never knew from auditing programs. But we were working with much bigger stores and the response of the people was not so good. In the beginning, at least, I had the impression that the last thing in the world they wanted was controls. It became obvious from the amount of people there that we had to let go because of dishonesty. About a hundred or so among the executives, and if I were to estimate how many down to the rank-and-file, the clerks and cashiers or the ilk of that, I just can't estimate how many.

"How many were prosecuted? Plenty. We more and more now throw the book at people, because with the shrinkage problem what it is, with the economy what it is, we go all out. We let it be known that we will go all out. Most of the people got suspended sentences and some got jailed, but that's up to the judge. But we let the people in the organization know who the crook is—pardon me, I should say was.

"You see, the days of operating on the q.t. are over. I have two doors in this office, and they're always open. I have them closed only once in a while when something very unusual is going on, like this interview. This door over here is more or less for Mr. Neaman's convenience, and it is always open. And I want people to know that they can go through channels, but if they are rebuffed and they feel that the company is exposed, if they know that their supervisor is doing nothing to help a certain problem, they can with impunity call this office. I challenge anyone to take umbrage with anybody calling or visiting this office. Mr. Neaman often refers to this office as an adjunct to his office and he comes in here anywhere from one to six times a day for briefings. He wants to be brought up to date as to what is happening. He has this really wonderful power of retention, numbers or facts, either one. And I keep a book over here, by the way. I don't trust my memory because so much takes place. I get on the average of 100 calls a day from the divisions, not just on audit but on anything. If we have to get involved with restructuring an area and hold the fort while we do it with one hand and interview people with the other and then slowly build it up as we did with the A.P. department and then slowly extract ourselves, we'll do that, too. We're the troubleshooters of top management. I report directly to Mr. Neaman, by the way, not to the president, the financial vice-president, or the controller.

"You asked me before about my personal life—I am married and have two sons. I never take my wife with me when I go out into the field. I'm very outspoken about this with her, and I think Mr. Neaman has an inkling of it. I don't want to be distracted by her saying to me, 'It's six o'clock and I'd like to go to dinner.' Once I'm involved with something, there is no such thing as hours. I'm in my office before eight in the morning, every morning, and I usually make the 7:05 home from Grand Central so that I get home a little before eight o'clock. My sons are twenty-five and twenty-two; the older one's a teacher at a private school and the younger's a student at Brandeis.

"We're pretty well set up now in our department. One day, Mr. Neaman came into this office and said, 'I'm gonna give you the names of X amount of people, Charley. They are not working out in the original jobs assigned to them. However, they are sincere people. Maybe you can use them in building your loss-prevention team. They're rejects, but maybe we can rehabilitate them.' Well, I already had enough people, but our job kept getting bigger all the time. Mr. Neaman even started asking me to attend merchandising meetings, even though I wouldn't know a good dress from a bad dress. So I said, 'Mr. Neaman, I'd like to have these people rather than have them terminated. I'd like to have a crack at them, and let's see if we can make retail auditors out of them.'

"There were five of them, and to put it in a nutshell, these people walk ten feet tall now. They knew they had fouled up and they felt terrible. And now, after a while, they have a wherewithal in their field and they also are used as educators. When we get new people into the company, this office does the educating. Someday it will be performed in the personnel department, where it should be, but we give them the tools. It was all Mr. Neaman's idea, and we are implementing it.

"Earlier, you asked me about my advancement. I became a

divisional vice-president of the variety store on May 5, 1966. About a year later, I was also made a vice-president of Klein's. And on May 25, 1971, Mr. Neaman made me a corporate vice-president of McCrory. No, I don't draw three salaries but I'm now making about three and a half times what I started at. I'm very active on all three levels, but I only draw one salary. The three titles weren't so much to give me stature as to provide a direct line to produce results.

"Security reports to this office. We have security forces in all our divisions, but I think when Mr. Neaman came in, he put a much greater stress on this than the previous management did. Let me tell you this, what he has created here: if you can picture ten fingers reaching out to all facets of the company, feeding into this office over here, which in turn feeds in the information to Mr. Neaman. Remember, as busy as he is, he comes in here at his convenience. He's right across the hall. He runs in here and sits down; he might have ten minutes between appointments and he'll spend it here.

"Once, in defining his job, he said to me, 'Charley, as chairman-of-the-board, my responsibility is to the stockholders. And the other facet of my job is to stimulate and provoke.' He has passed this on to me. I have never met a man as stimulating, as invigorating as he is. He's a hard taskmaster; he's all business. He's working seven days a week. Sundays he is on the phone all day. He used to call me, too, on Sundays. But now since I see him probably more than anyone else, probably between fifteen and twenty times a week, he doesn't call me Sunday. Sometimes when he is eating lunch, he calls me into his office and says, 'Charley, sit down with me and if you don't mind what I'm eating—if it doesn't bother you, my melba toast and cottage cheese—please brief me while I eat.' "

As Charley Gass pauses to take a phone call, his short, pudgy body straightens up and his face muscles vibrate slightly. Apparently, it is an important call; he is quickly and intensively taking notes. Over his head on the wall is an eighteen-inch replica of a papier-mâché telephone, which he later explains was given to him by a group of McCrory buyers to note the fact that "Mr. Internal Audit," as he is called, gets about 100 phone calls a day in connection with his duties. He has the "Big Telephone," in other words.

On the other side of the wall behind his desk is the inevitable framed Neaman credo and photograph. And nearby, hanging from a large calendar, is a sign in red ink reading:

BULLETIN!
Let's Burn the Word
ASSUME
from the McCrory
Vocabulary

The word "Assume" is enveloped in flames.

"You asked me about computers. From the moment I met the chairman, the word computer was emphasized. He firmly feels, and he has passed it on to me, that anything that can be computerized and taken out of the human hand should be computerized. That is the machine's purpose and essence. A computer is supposed to spit out knowledgeable information that the management can use in everyday operations. Mr. Neaman is a great believer. In fact, he's always thinking of ways to enhance the computer setup in order to give us more information.

"We use it a lot in this office. We say, 'Mr. Computer, we would like you to program for us a run so that, when we make two or more payments, the following characteristics are checked: invoice number, amount, vendor.' If they are the same, we have discovered an overpayment. What a tremendous tool!

"I was talking about human rejects before. I can never forget that Mr. Neaman took a chance on a reject and you're looking at one right now. He is the only man I have ever met that has truly acknowledged me. I worked just as hard for the other company. But if there's one thing that I learned from those people, it was how not to do things. I felt very much the part of failure in a failing company. Why would Mr. Neaman want to get involved with me? I asked him only a year ago, when he gave me another big assignment, why he had entrusted such a big job as the taking of physical inventory to a new man and he said, 'Charley, I know people and at that time I wasn't afraid to entrust it to you.' He has acknowledged me in many ways, not just by title and salary. He shows it by the way he relates to me, by the way he talks about me to others, by his confidence and trust in the information I give him. And I reciprocate by never embarrassing him. In eight years, he has never been embarrassed by acting on the findings of this office. Now that's a lot of information and facts. But I'll tell you this—I don't think I'll meet another fellow like him in my lifetime.

"You know what Mr. Neaman calls our marriage? A Catholic marriage. No divorce. Other people have come and gone. He knows I won't ever leave.

"You see, I had a different kind of life in the other company. Mr. Neaman doesn't operate behind closed doors, but I've seen top executives who were unapproachable, who hid behind closed doors. Do you know that when that other company started going *mahula* and top management was hiding, I had creditors visit my home. They found out where I lived, and they came looking for me on weekends because they couldn't get any information. It got so bad that my wife and I went to a motel to get away. And yet, when I came here, those same creditors gave me a tremendous vote of confidence. They spoke to Mr. Neaman about me. Imagine creditors who got screwed by my old employer endorsing me! I wouldn't trade these contacts for anything in the world.

"When I tried to work things out with those angry creditors, my former bosses said, 'What the hell are you gonna get out of talking to those shits?' They only had contempt for those vendors. But my girls in accounts payable in that company were being abused by the vendors and the girls complained to me. You know, it was a little like the Silver Star. I said to the girls, 'You tell them to call me.' Soon, there were lines in the hall waiting to see me, but the principals of the company wouldn't come out of their offices. You know, some of these dress houses are operated by the Mafia, and some used to call me up and say they were worried about my health. My health! Other times, it wasn't so subtle. I was threatened bodily with some anonymous phone calls, but one dress manufacturer who heard about it called and offered to pay for my protection.

"Sure, Mr. Neaman drives. Sure, he doesn't know from the clock. And he passes on his drive and his awful hours to his subordinates. He makes family life second, but with him I'm a fulfilled guy. My wife tells me I'm only happy under pressure. Maybe so. I'll admit something to you. I went to group therapy. I went there the first few years I was with McCrory.

"I went to group therapy for two reasons, maybe three. I was troubled by my experiences at the other company. I was troubled by the sudden death of an uncle of mine. But I was really troubled most by what it was in me that continuously made me expose myself. Why, for instance, did I take on the responsibility of being the spokesman for a dying company to the creditors? What made me do this? You know what I found out? That I'm more or less the kind of guy who looks to pressure conditions that I feel practically nobody else can survive in. In other words, if something is almost impossible for most people to do, that's a place where I want to make my presence felt. It's like I want to say, 'See, I can do it. Everyone else is afraid.'

"What made me expose myself to the Germans? I don't know, but it had to be that I gotta live or die by my stripes. You're gonna laugh at me, but look, I was scared to death but I felt very keenly about the fact that I was the platoon sergeant. Scared as I was, I didn't want to be a coward in the eyes of my men. I really didn't. I didn't want to be unworthy of the responsibility. I didn't want to be unworthy of being the office manager when the bosses were ducking out. And I don't want to be unworthy of my job here. I guess maybe you can never forget it when you are once a platoon sergeant."

Once upon a Computer

There was little doubt in Neaman's mind that he was beginning to fill his principal people needs.

He had his buffer man. He had his financial man. He had his inspector-general. But the one man he didn't have could prove to be the most crucial. As he came to respect and even thrill to the possibilities of the computer, he realized that he needed a computer expert who would be unrelated to and untrammeled by the feeble efforts of the previous regimes to use electronic data processing properly.

As his victories became more than a taste on his tongue and he moved boldly from people triumphs to systems triumphs, he would sometimes stand out in the hallway by the computer room and hungrily glance in. The low hum, the electronically antiseptic air, and the cold temperature made him breathe deeply. But his conversations with the EDP man he had inherited from the Nelson regime left him dissatisfied and frustrated. The man, a sallow but well-dressed holdover named Reaves, had the air of the cloister about him, as if the IBM 7070 system which he administered with the aid of two assistants was too pure for this world. Perhaps it was his aloof manner, just this side of frigidity, that angered Neaman when they spoke together. In simple terms, the fact was that Reaves seemed to regard the primary purpose of the IBM 7070 as theoretical science while Neaman saw it as applied science.

Although he was able at times to jar and shove the aggrieved Reaves into some manner of applying the IBM to his purposes, Neaman knew rather quickly that he urgently needed someone else to oversee the computer. In his mind's eye, he promptly drew a profile of the man: he must be young, be familiar with at least two generations of the major computer families, understand the computer's technology and its applications, and preferably have a little retail experience. Such a proficient young man, Neaman hoped, would have the advantages without the prejudices of a newborn baby who entered the world at the mental age of twenty-five.

Neaman knew he wouldn't be happy until he found the man who could flesh out that profile.

A Depression child, Marvin Shenfeld literally grew up in sneakers and sweatshirts. He was one of those seemingly countless youths in a Bronx highrise without any unusual prospects or life-direction. Both his working parents left early in the morning, leaving him and a younger brother to make their own breakfast and take care of themselves until the evening.

But between the year of his birth, 1931, and 1948, when he

graduated from high school, Marvin developed two talents. They gave him both prospects and a direction. Lithe and graceful, he displayed an athletic ability and became a proficient basketball player. The speed and the fine reflexes that he demonstrated on the basketball court also denoted a quickness of mind. He soon showed a facility for mathematics, too, and he majored in it at college.

However, like many youths born to immigrants, he could get little guidance from his harassed, weary parents. His father worked on a production line in a handbag factory and knew little about life outside the plant. His mother, who studied English and secretarial work in night school, obtained clerical work and spoke vaguely of wanting her older son to become a doctor. But she died when he was a high school junior and his father followed within two years.

Medical studies were out. But while the lanky, serious-faced boy could hardly cash in as yet on his mathematics proficiency, he could on his athletic prowess. On graduation day in June 1948 at Stuyvesant High School, he was informed that he would get a basketball scholarship to Tufts College in Medford, Massachusetts.

Still retaining a link with his mother's ambition for him, he worked into his curriculum enough premedical requisites to cover him in case he eventually went into medicine. But mathematics remained his major. By the time he graduated in 1952 with a Bachelor of Science in mathematics, he was anxious to start his career. The United States Army and the Korean Conflict, however, were waiting for him, and he was drafted instead.

He wound up in West Germany, serving as a lab technician in the Medical Corps, but spent a good portion of his time in that country playing basketball for the post team. It was, he admitted later with a sort of lingering surprise, "a generally and relatively easy army career."

For Marvin, whose growing-up years were difficult and uncertain if not lonely, the athletic scholarship and the army service were the first of a number of fortuitous breaks that changed his personality. Instead of the dour, rather downbeat type that he had been, he smiled more readily, everyone noticed, and he even learned to take a ribbing instead of bristling at it as he used to.

After his 1955 discharge, he lived briefly with his younger brother, who had married, in Forest Hills, and obtained a job at the Univac computer division of Remington Rand. Upon completion of a three-month training course as a programmer, the company sent him to Huntington, West Virginia, to be an on-site programmer for a Univac account, the Chesapeake-Ohio Railroad. While there, he met a Long Island girl who had come to Huntington to visit a college roommate. When she returned to New York, they corresponded. And, in 1959, when the IBM Corporation became attracted to Marvin for his computer experience and hired him, he moved back to New York that same year and married the girl from Long Island.

The IBM job was basically the same as his job at Univac except that IBM called Marvin an "assistant engineer." His work involved helping to install the equipment that IBM sold and assisting in the programming and training function after it was sold. At twenty-nine, while in a field already dominated by the young, Marvin had the distinction of being one of the few with several years of experience in large-scale computers.

His association with the retail business began in 1962, when he left IBM to join a medium-sized discount store chain as the head of its systems and methods department. Although it was a better-paying job, he was dismayed to find out he was the head of a one-man department. After three years, he took a job with a larger, more diversified retail company, where he was one of a team of four specialists operating as "captive consultants" for the various divisions. By then, though expert in both the Univac and IBM computer installations, he had little knowledge of its applications to merchandising.

All this was related in an interview of several hours. Asked why he had kept moving around to new jobs on the average of every three years, Marvin replied with an easy grin, "Money, I guess. That's the usual reason, isn't it?"

Speaking in a slow, relaxed manner, he said, "Of course, it was more than that. First, I changed jobs within the computer field because I wanted to build up a rounded computer experience. Once I achieved that, it began to appear to me that I might have a problem. Here I was a Jew with expertise in a field where Jews would have trouble really moving up. When the retailing jobs came along, I realized that I was in demand and that my Jewishness would be no barrier. The retail business is a field in which a Jewish boy can move up if he has what it takes, and there was no arguing with the accepted facts."

One day in fall of 1968, Marvin sat in the office of a vice-president of McCrory Corporation and discussed his background and whether it would fit into the company which was quickly nearing the $1 billion pinnacle in annual sales.

After a few minutes, a stocky, bald man in a medium-brown suit with extra stitching on the lapels entered without knocking and sank with a sigh into a seat. He was introduced as Sam Neaman, but his function or position was not mentioned.

"I didn't know who he was. I guess I was supposed to know but frankly I didn't," Marvin recalled. "He sat through practically the entire interview and later, when I learned that he was the chairman-of-the-board of the company, I was impressed as hell that he would spend three-quarters of an hour and even talk to me about the whys and wherefores of coming to the corporation. What I didn't realize at the time was that Neaman would probably be the most data-processing-oriented top executive I would ever meet. Maybe that was why he was attaching so much importance to my interview."

Within two years, after prolonged hard work including many twelve- and fourteen-hour days seven days a week, Marvin Shenfeld became vice-president for electronic data processing, succeeding the man who had interviewed him. In retrospect, he realized that only his ten-year exposure to both computer installation and its application to retailing kept him going, for he found the chairman an insatiable user of and experimenter with computers. But after four years with McCrory, Shenfeld told me that he had found the man and the company for whom he had been looking all his working life. "I think I'm most fortunate to be here," he admitted, "for two reasons. First, I think I'm answering an important need here. And, second, I think this company has great potential."

Had the "need" proved itself?

"I think that when you walk out to the elevator through the fourth floor," said Marvin, "you will see one evidence that there was a need for EDP here and that we showed results. You will see a number of empty desks. The work that we've been able to do here with the computer has created savings throughout the company without relative increases in our expenditures in the computer operation. Another example is that when we went into the merchandising of home furnishings, we never had much in the way of reporting systems. Now, with the implementation of electronic cash registers and with a merchandise reporting system based on the input from the registers, we are able to do much hard-goods business with considerably less inventory."

While the retail craft consists of both an art and a science, he observed, the art part is difficult to quantify or formularize. But it is possible that by improving the science ingredient one can at least partially systematize the art ingredient.

"We—Mr. Neaman and I and the others—feel that we can ask a buyer to buy X number of pieces of an item and leave the rest to us. 'You think it's a good item, Mr. Buyer,' we tell him, 'then you go ahead and buy it and leave it to our systems to decide how many size-5 dresses, how many size-7, and how many size-9 dresses are needed. And leave it to us what stores should get what sizes. Are we perfect? Not entirely. I don't think we are ever going to be perfect, but then you know that the human being is not perfect and you need the buyer to supply the art in our business. But I think we can improve on what is human because we are omitting the emotion."

The computer and the overall EDP system have made good progress in controlling the problem of inventory losses or inventory "shrink." Trying to curb his enthusiasm but smiling, he confided, "We've even been able to shrink the shrink. . . ."

He smiles warmly now. The Bronx highrise is far away. So are the uncertainties of prospects and a life-direction. The former basketball star no longer plays, except for an occasional dribbling session with his two young sons in the back of his Long Island home. Despite his largely sedentary work, his body weight has hardly changed from his undergraduate days. "I keep pretty thin just from nervousness or the pressures of lots of calls all day long," he explains.

Considering his new self-assurance, doesn't he sometimes find working with Neaman uncertain? he is asked. Marvin Shenfeld shrugs. As the interviewer leaves, Shenfeld is freed from the questions and turns with a happy, relieved sigh to his computer print-outs. He has not only found a career, it appears, but a key role in a world in which machines will yet improve on man. As for himself, what greater security could a man who runs those machines have? And as for Neaman, he has found his computer man.

Men Wanted

Ordinarily, being the man he was, Sam Neaman might have been compelled to look for new worlds to conquer after his stunning turnaround of the variety-store division and then his consistent profit performance as McCrory's corporate chief. But no such problem existed. Meshulam Riklis, who wasn't happy unless he was juggling at least two or three balls in the air at one time, took care of that. He simply kept buying companies.

In 1965, when McCrory was still enjoying its first profit gain in a decade. Riklis acquired control of the S. Klein department-store chain, one of the New York area's largest and most troubled retailers, and tossed it into McCrory's, or rather, Neaman's lap.

There was no implicit sense of urgency in absorbing the new addition. Although its earnings were puny—less than one percent on sales of $200 million—the sixty-year-old chain was a community fixture, a New York landmark without the official landmark plaque, a sentimental symbol of New York's rich ethnic life. It stood for bargains, for a joyous romp among women eager to tear a smock, a blouse, a girdle, even a mink stole—all greatly marked down, of course!—from the piperacks or from one another. Riklis had bought it cheaply from the estate of the founder, signing the papers with a happy smile, a flourish of his hands, and the offhand comment to Izzy Becker, "We'll keep Sammy busy, right?" The acquisition moved McCrory's volume immediately within a whisker of the $1 billion level, although the added profits were minimal.

What Neaman initially thought about having to absorb Klein's eleven stores, only half of them earning any money, isn't known. He didn't recall it during many hours of later interviews. But the differences and the interdependence between "mergerers and managers," i.e., Riklis and Neaman, were very clear to him. He outlined them in his usual, didactic manner.

"The one of several important things that has to be understood about McCrory Corporation is that it has a strong relationship to the two functions in the world of business," he said. "They have to work in the same environment, but they are distinctly different from each other in methods and in goals. One is ownership and the other one is management. Those are two big rivers that flow parallel, but they have nothing in common except that.

"Ownership is imaginative—it brings businesses together under a common control. The goal is to increase the value of those business units. Management has another goal. It is the productivity of the business unit. Management wants to know how it could increase the quantity of milk that the cow will give. That's it and no more—the cow must give more and more and more milk up to the maximum of her capacity. Ownership wants to know that the price it can sell the cow for will be superior to the price it paid for it. Does ownership care why the price of the cow is higher? No. It could be caused by a famine. It could be caused by a disease that destroyed all but a few herds. Management doesn't need famine, doesn't need the destruction of other herds. What it needs is to develop a method of turning food into milk through a system known as a cow, and therefore it studies the function of producing milk and how it can increase the cow's capacity. Management takes a long-term view; ownership takes a short-term view. That's why ownership can buy so many new companies; management enhances the product, regardless of whether it will be kept or sold at a profit. So management can take only one road—efficiency. Ownership can take many roads, and it often has an inconsistent point-of-view, depending on its financial health at the time.

"When ownership puts its money into a business or a product or buys equipment on good financial terms," he went on, "then management can work in peace. It can go on promoting its long-term development and long-term programs, and each year it can increase its efficiency and therefore its productivity. If ownership is not endowed with the necessary finances and it has periods of tribulations, management suffers. We come back to one fact: management depends on people, and people are emotional and listen to everything that they hear and worry about anything that might hurt them. So if employes of a corporation hear about difficulties of ownership, they naturally mix it up with difficulties of management. Yet the reality of it is that while ownership and management support each other, otherwise they have nothing to do with each other.

"What difference does it make to a store manager in Pascagoula if Rapid–American owns McCrory or if some other company owns it, since he has to run a good store anyway? But unfortunately this is not the way it works. The guy in Pascagoula keeps listening to rumors about the financial position of ownership, and he reacts to it in his management functions on a day-to-day basis. If things are good, he wants a share of the good things whether he did anything in the store or not. If things are bad, he's scared and he starts wondering if he should leave and go elsewhere, even though his store might be doing very well.

"We're locked into each other that way—ownership and management—but sometimes I think it's better if we are not conscious of each other. We would all do a better job. That's why if Meshulam Riklis came into this building, I would call the security guard to throw him out."

Pushing to repeat his success with the S. Klein stores, Neaman assumed the additional post of chairman of that chain and went through a succession of presidents in the first three years after the acquisition. But whether those promotional department stores were a peculiar animal or whether the merchants he appointed as their operating head were bringing the wrong kind of experience to the job, nothing seemed sufficient to jog the big, old stores in the city's core or the big, new ones in the suburbs out of their rut.

He let it be known that he was in the market for a top department-store man. He would pay any price consistent with the performance he received. A procession of newly discharged and not so new retreads passed through his office. He spent hours with each, plumbing their minds and dangling the challenge before them, a challenge literally dripping with dollars. None of them could quite fathom him. Even those who flatly refused walked away not quite sure who had refused whom. There was a definite semantic gap between his, "I think that maybe you could do the job very well" and "so let us both think about it."

In New York's close retailing community, it became a standing joke. "Neaman offered you the job at Klein's yet?" . . . "Who said no first?" . . . "Did he pick your brains right down to the bone?" . . . "I don't think he wants to hire anybody— just wants their opinion about what's wrong." . . . "The salary he's talking about could be the difference between Klein's profit or loss." . . . "He tapes every damned interview—and then calls a senior management meeting to see how many ideas they can use." These were only a few of the quips that reverberated around the market. While much of it represented ridicule and bad-mouthing of Klein's, the rest of it had at least a degree of wishful thinking. Neaman, though a nonretailer, had built an impact for himself and for McCrory which seemed to grow and grow, even spreading a rosy glow of hope over Klein's.

Neaman's campaign to sound out everyone's interest and qualifications led to some strange incidents—some funny, some cruel. A young retail executive who had headed two chains before he was thirty-seven heard that Neaman had a marked Jewish accent. When a recruiter called him and made a date for him to see Neaman, he wasn't much interested but his curiosity convinced him to keep the appointment. But when he found that Neaman's rhetoric and delivery were only faintly ethnic, he responded with a heavy accent. "Vhy deed you chanch your heccent? You shouldn't be hashamed! Be prout vhat you ahr!"

"What?"

"Be your-salf! Be prout! Don't be ah shreenkeeng daisy!"

"Get out—you maniac!"

Another time, the former president of a big New York chain climaxed his interview by advising Neaman that his only salvation lay in changing the name of Klein's to something less prone to invite bigotry. "Call it Marshall's—or Robinson's," he said, "and you'll see how well you'll do." Neaman quickly waved him out.

Finally, in 1968, he came to a decision. He would be both chairman and president of Klein's, in addition to his posts at McCrory, and he would name a team of senior vice-presidents and vice-presidents to help him run Klein's. In characteristic fashion, he promptly made a number of appointments to fill these posts and touched off a series of new moves intended to turn around the troubled chain. Among them was a program of concentrating on the best-selling, most profitable departments and terminating fringe departments; the building of several giant 300,000-square-foot suburban stores; a new information-reporting system like the one used in the variety stores; and a series of new methods of store presentation and display.

Most of his new appointments worked out well; others did not. It became a question not only of how well Neaman took to the new man but also of how well the new man could take Neaman.

Capitalist Ambition

Although just two months shy of his fifty-seventh birthday, Ben Litwak could admit his age without feeling any perceptible twinges of pain or regret. He was "ordinary as hell." What he had achieved by late middle-age was a testimonial to the free-enterprise system, which luckily rewarded people as much for their drive and stick-to-itiveness as for their talents.

He had few enough of those, he conceded with a flash of broad, white teeth, and he had lost any illusions about it long ago. He was ambitious, hard-working, excessively devoted, all those platitudinous attributes that everyone talked about but really patronized. Yet, those qualities had made all the difference for him, a most ordinary guy. And maybe there was something else, too, which had helped him reach his present role as a $50,000-a-year senior vice-president of the Klein's chain. Consistency. Pure consistency. He could always be counted on, and he had been like that all his life.

A tall, beefy man, he sat comfortably, obviously belonging, in a large, rectangular office on McCrory's merchandising and buying floor in mid-Manhattan, an office filled with books and with three framed items on the walls. One was a pale landscape in water-color. Another was the Neaman credo and photo. The third was a small, white sign with the "keys" in capitals: FACTS. PLANS. EXECUTION. SUPERVISION.

It is not difficult to place Litwak in other milieus. About six feet tall, he weighs about 200 pounds, has a thick shock of brown hair with silver strands, and long sideburns. He wears heavy, dark-rimmed glasses. A cigar chomper, he keeps tapping it on an ash tray, even though it's not lit. He has not actually smoked for five years, but he chews his way through six or seven expensive cigars a day. Morally supporting the big inventory of men's double-knit suits that Klein's seems to be constantly advertising at "the lowest, lowest prices in town," he wears one with a salt-and-pepper pattern and accents it with a mauve shirt and a striped purple tie. His hairy right wrist is almost covered by a large, silver watch. He could just as easily be an insurance man, a wholesaler of job lots, a real-estate broker, or a manufacturer. Though soft-spoken, his voice has a brusqueness, breaking firmly at the end of the declarative phrases he is prone to, indicating, to an interviewer at least, that he is accustomed to giving lots of orders and to passing quickly on to the next matter of business.

"Ordinary? You?" he was asked. "I know that's the theme around here, a lot of ordinary people working together, but maybe you're not giving yourself just due."

"Maybe not," he said. "But look, it took me twenty-three years to get where I am today. I'm the same age as the chairman. If I had some special talent, who knows how high I might have climbed? A lot of young guys have made it big in the retail business. But I'm not bitching. Look. I'm lucky."

"Maybe it's luck. Or maybe it's that old fact-of-life—you're the right man in the right place at the right time."

He shrugged, flashed his teeth again and chomped for a moment. "Neaman tapped me," he said. "That's lucky."

Like so many others in the McCrory ranks, he appeared to have had a difficult, even lonely youth. He came from a family of Jewish immigrants in the industrial town of Passaic, New Jersey. In 1929, his father, a builder, went bankrupt. The Litwaks moved to Newark and in the heart of the Depression

Ben's mother, who had had six children, suddenly died. Shortly afterward, the father remarried and left the children. The youngest of the six, Ben quit high school at seventeen to take a job and enrolled for night courses at Pace Institute. The absence of parents hurt. Working at Bamberger's as a truckman's assistant, Ben lived with a married sister in Newark, saw his father occasionally, and came to rely on himself earlier than most youths. Through 1934, he continued to work on the truck and studied marketing, advertising, and salesmanship.

Late that year, he read an advertisement in a local paper. He was, he recalled, fascinated by the blind ad because it "told me about a kind of a dream." The ad sought anyone interested in retailing who was willing to start at the bottom and work his way up to president. He quickly applied, hurried to the appointed interview site, and found fifty young men waiting in line ahead of him. The name of the retail company was the McLellan Stores, later to be absorbed into the McCrory empire.

The applicants were put through a screening process which in three days reduced them to twenty-five and then to five. Ben Litwak was one of the two applicants finally selected. He was hired at $16 a week to be a stockman and third assistant to the manager of one of the McLellan variety stores in Newark. The grizzled, veteran manager sat the young man down and laid out the requirements for success: "I don't care about your educational background, and I don't care much about your personal background. But if you don't mind breaking your back, if you've got common sense, you might make it around here. You might even become a store manager and maybe even president of the company."

Ben took the message seriously. Although he was supposed to work only three nights, he volunteered to come in other nights, too. Healthy, young, and the owner of a strong back, he didn't mind the physically harsh nature of the job. "I had to *shlep* cartons, cases, racks, whatever the manager desired. I guess I had that real zest of youth. I would do anything, try anything because in my mind I was already the president, twenty years later."

The pieces of the dream suddenly came apart. Less than six months after he was hired, an economy cut in force was ordered, and as the last man hired, Ben was laid off. "Well, as a young man who thought he had done a hell of a job, I blew my cork. I told the store manager off. I went over to the New York office to see the personnel manager and blew my cork with him. I told him that I wasn't hired for a part-time job, and I had given up a good job with Bamberger's to come there. I told him they had treated me lousy. And then I guess I just stalked out," he recalled.

But, by the time he got home in Newark, he found a telegram waiting for him, requesting that he report to another McLellan store as head stockman at a salary increase of $2 a week.

The new store was located on Pitkin Avenue in Brooklyn. Ben moved in with another sister, who lived in the borough's Bensonhurst area and pitched into the new job. His sister, who was the most relatively affluent member of the family, refused to accept any room-and-board money from him. "So the $18 a week was really, really velvet," he said. "I loved the job and everything was going just fine until the sitdown strikes started."

Those strikes became identified with the Depression. Across the country, the opposition-with-possession spread like a wild rash. Production lurched to a halt, and management looked on aghast. On Pitkin Avenue, the retail union decided to use the McLellan store as a testing-ground for the launching of a major organizing drive. Three other McLellan stores were struck and rendered inoperative, while pickets paraded outside Pitkin Avenue. Everyone joined the stoppage except the manager—and his head stockman.

"I refused to join the union," Ben related, "and I refused to join the picket line. My philosophy in those days was that I was a capitalist, and it hasn't changed much since. I wanted to be president of the company, so how could I think of joining people who depended upon a union to help their welfare in those days? It was unthinkable."

The strike lasted about a week but the head stockman stubbornly walked through the line every morning and back again every night. He endured the epithets, the spitting, and the hissed, "Dirty Jew." He didn't even mind much when the curses came from fellow Jews. But when the strike was settled, management decided that it would be best if the capitalist stockman

were relocated to another store. The decision was to send him to
a store about ten miles away.

Litwak recalled it and the ensuing events vividly.

"Same position but with $2 more a week. Now I was making
$20 a week. That was great. Oh, boy, still better. And there I
worked for an old ex-Marine who was the store manager, and
he gave me some extra work to do because there wasn't enough
for me to handle in the stockroom. It was a small store, and I
was handling it all with ease where they used to have a full-time
and a part-time man. I started working and had time to spare,
so he taught me how to trim windows, how to do a little floor
work, and how to get into the merchandising concept of a
variety store. We got along great because I absorb quickly and
I guess I satisfied the needs of the job. And it was great. I was
there a year approximately, and then I got promoted to the next
big step. Floor man. That means you can wear a jacket. You
can take care of a section of the store, the old guy told me, and
merchandise it. And here's another couple-bucks increase. From
there, the moves came faster and more furious. I was transferred to other stores and each one was a bigger one with more
responsibility. I became an assistant store manager in Manhattan. I met my wife-to-be there, and I was about to get drafted
so we decided to get married before I shipped out. I spent most
of the war between 1942 and the end of 1945 as a technical sergeant with a troop carrier group in the Army Air Force in the
Pacific. I guess maybe you could say that even in the Air Force
I was a kind of capitalist. I was in charge of a small unit of men,
and we worked hard but we lived well. We lived very well."

Back in New York, he entered McLellan Stores' refresher program for returning veterans, and a year later he reached one
plateau in his ambition. He became a store manager. Within
the next decade, he managed three stores, each one larger than
the other. In 1958, he was appointed a district manager for thirteen stores, later expanded to sixteen, at a salary of $14,000 a
year. But after Meshulam Riklis stepped in to weld the disparate
chains into one massive retail network, the first team he brought
in shook up the executive staff and Ben was one of several district managers who were uprooted. He found himself in charge
of a relatively small New England district, almost but not quite
banished to oblivion.

In the next year, he demonstrated an unusual resiliency. He turned his district into the one which showed the best recovery rate in a one-year period. While his was one of the smallest of the company's districts, Ben was given the highest bonus of any district manager that year. Shortly afterward, he was brought back to New York and was appointed manager of a major district in the metropolitan area.

One day in 1964, he received a phone call from a Sam Neaman in Rapid–American's office and an invitation to lunch in Manhattan. "Ben," Neaman said, "I have been told that you are one of the most astute district managers we have in the variety stores. Now, as you know, I'm sure, things are not going well and I have spent some time in the field trying some new things, not that I am a retailing *maven*. But I would like to tell you of some plans I have, some projects I want to start . . ."

When Neaman had finshed, Litwak reached over and shook his hand warmly. "It all sounds great to me, Sam. But how can you do anything? Nelson's still running the show."

Neaman smiled knowingly. "Yes, of course. But you may be talking to his successor—and soon," he said. "I'm glad you like my plans, Ben. I will need people like you. Remember that the men who put the numbers on the bottom line will get the recognition—the rewards and the climb up on the totem pole."

They shook hands once more. "I like that kind of talk," Litwak said, grinning. "I've always liked it. I happen to have a lot of ambition myself."

Neaman delivered on his promises. Within a year after his accession to the variety-division's presidency, Ben was appointed to two successive regional posts, regional sales manager and regional merchandise manager. A year later, he was named one of the company's five regional managers. He had climbed the third rung.

In the new job, Litwak repeated his New England turn-around. Although the region he now headed had never been the first in the company in its profit margin, it was reorganized under his supervision and quickly became the best performer. He repeated that feat for a second year. And then Neaman asked Ben if they could meet at an opening in Westchester County of a new store in Litwak's division.

"I had a virus the day before," recalled Ben, "and when Mr.

Neaman called me I got my doctor to give me another shot and I went up to meet him. But, instead of touring the new store with me, looking into all the nooks like he always did, we sat down and had coffee. I remember the day like it was just yesterday. Thursday, August 7, 1968. All of a sudden, it dawned on me through my temperature and the beating in my head that he was telling me about his problems with Klein's. He said he'd given up trying to find a president on the outside; he was gonna handle it himself by wearing yet another hat, and he wanted me to switch over to that company."

"What was your reaction?"

"I was surprised. I knew they were having some problems there. I said to Mr. Neaman, 'Look, when you're getting the calling, you go.' But I'll tell you this—I didn't say a hell of a lot because I was feeling so lousy, but I wasn't so aye, aye about it."

"What position did he offer?"

"Senior vice-president of operations—the top spot under him."

"That's quite a job, isn't it?"

"Ah!"

"And you've been at Klein's ever since, struggling with its problems. What are they, anyway?"

"In '68, we were a company that was not organized internally from any standpoint—systems, procedures, people. We had a range of things wrong that would choke a horse, from whores to pimps to thieves to lazy people to dishonesty. But we've done a lot to correct all those things. Today, if you ask me, this company is as well systematized and organized as any retailing business in America."

Although Litwak's role at Klein's later changed from operations chief to general merchandise manager, he was taking pains to keep his hand in both areas. They were equally important—the selling-housekeeping-logistics as much as the buying-merchandising-promotion—and he was confident that the chain was definitely on the upgrade. But why was it taking so long? After eight years since it had been acquired by McCrory, why were profits still so elusive?

"I think when you reorganize a company," he replied, "and you have the problem of cleaning it up at all levels—merchandise, people, plant—you have to suffer. Didn't it take Gimbels' stores in New York eight or nine years to come out of their slump? You know, you're not dealing with small stores, these are 250,000, 300,000 square-footers—"

"Can it be done eventually?"

"Absolutely."

A tour of some of the Klein's stores tended to back up Litwak's claims of major improvements. The stores, particularly those in the suburbs, were clean, bright, inviting. Receiving-room operations appeared to be efficient and well-controlled. Stockrooms were clean and orderly. In the newest stores, communications and security were controlled by master closed-circuit television and radio in the store's front. But, in the older stores, the sales personnel seemed fewer than on previous visits and more than a few of these seemed to be indifferent to customers. The other problem, although nothing more than just an observation, was that the Klein's stores under Neaman–Litwak, appeared to be shifting from their traditional role as New York's bargain centers into general apparel stores with typical discount-store merchandise and prices. The flavor of the stores, in other words, had changed. Asked if the push for profits and especially the systematizing were robbing the stores of their homey individuality and their pull on the shopper, Ben Litwak shrugged. "We've modernized," he said. "Retailing is a changing game, isn't it?"

Since the post of Klein's presidency was still open, did he think that the job might naturally come to him? "Hasn't this president thing been part of your life," the interviewer said, "from the day you answered that first ad?"

"Sure, it was part of my life—from the minute that first store manager told me that if I worked hard and had common sense—"

"And?"

"I don't think so," he said. "Not since the change."

"What change?"

"You see, when I was with the variety stores, I thought I was a genius. But since I'm here, judging by the bottom line, I'm not quite the genius I thought I'd be. That's the change. Maybe I'm just an ordinary guy, after all."

"Maybe this is a tougher job?"

"Well, I appreciate that. I could be the president if I set my heart on it and I wanted it. But I've got different ambitions now. I want to go corporate. I think it's a bigger challenge. A company with over $1 billion in sales needs a general merchandise chief. Federated has it. Sears and JCPenney have it. Allied has it. So why not McCrory?"

He studied me as though convinced that I might not ever understand. "It's this way," he persisted. "I'm a little old to become the president—they've got to get a younger man with the experience—but general merchandising is more exciting anyway. I don't think being president is necessarily the most important job. I'm an ordinary guy, yet look at what I've learned, what I've accomplished. Why shouldn't I make use on a bigger scale of what I already know? Merchandising is where the action is. The president loses, other than having the prestige of having his title, and I've gotten beyond the stage of titles. I never thought I would get even this far, but look, I'm in the middle of the action. You know what I call the trick in selling merchandise? Fashionalize it! Fashionalize, that's the thing you gotta do. Me, I like to touch merchandise. I like to feel the merchandise. . . ."

Someone of Depth

McCrory's chairman, now doubling and tripling as the Klein's stores' chairman and president, was often accompanied by a thick-haired, serious young man who wore such eye-catching clothes as a red-and-white checked suit or a pale-green, double-knit sports jacket and maroon pants. When they walked together, Neaman usually strode a half-pace ahead. If they met a third person, the young man was promptly ignored. And when the young man spoke first, he checked himself with an intake of his prominent chin and studied Neaman's smooth face to see if the chairman wanted the priority before he seized it himself. At other times, the younger man blurted an expletive or a rash conclusion of his own, his stocky body quickly stiffening as to prepare for Neaman's correction.

At only thirty-two, Steve Jackel already held one of the department-store chain's highest posts. He was vice-president and general store manager, which made him a super-store manager, a mentor and supervisor of many older men. Despite his youth and brash tendency, however, he was widely respected for his knowledge of the business and for his occasional snappish remarks to Neaman. But he was otherwise obsequious enough and certainly respectful. He "believed" in Neaman, he freely admitted, and he hoped that Neaman "believed" in him.

He was one of several Neaman alter-egos, each one apparently filling a different but vital purpose. If Stanley Kunsberg, for example, was McCrory's front to the outside world and to the parent company, Rapid, he was to all intents and purposes the outside Neaman. The same with Norman Mallor, the go-between with the financial world; with Charley Gass, "Mr. Internal Audit," as the inspector-general; with Marvin Shenfeld, the computer *maven*, as the contact with the robotlike, steely eyed IBM men; and with Ben Litwak, Klein's chief merchandiser, who, if he were a bit slow and ponderous, nonetheless had the full confidence of the buyers and the manufacturers and spoke Neaman's language to all of them.

But Steve Jackel considered himself more of an alter-ego than the others. The reason was, he explained, that he was Neaman's teacher of store operations, a pivotal job in which he functioned as Neaman's fingers to Neaman's head, so to speak. Yet, conversely, Steve was often being taught himself. At a strategic point in his career, a slight misunderstanding, a misreading of Neaman's sometimes cryptic instructions impelled Steve as a store manager to issue instructions to another store manager to "straighten up and fly right" and thereby to come in with his entire staff on a Sunday to tidy-up a shabby store. Neaman had laughed about it, had kidded Steve about his peremptory command, but had begun to see him in an entirely new light. Inside of eighteen months, he promoted Steve into a new suitable post and shortly afterward gave him a vice-presidency.

Since Neaman, in those early 1970s, loved two things most—tinkering with the computer and visiting stores—he spent much of his time with Marvin Shenfeld and even more of his time with Steve Jackel. When the chairman found that some piece of the continuing puzzle of the ungainly Klein stores especially eluded him, it seemed natural to him to take to the road, to visit one of those stores and try to stare down the problem. Inevitably, as general store manager, Steve Jackel was with him, staring just as hard.

To many who knew him, the surprising thing about Steve was that despite his youth he actually had more retailing experience than many of the older men. Steve had been a "soda-jerk." It was retailing of the most basic sort, but it was not to be shrugged off. There is more give-and-take at the soda fountain, more pure merchandising and concentration on the initial and cumulative markup in dispensing malteds, celery tonic, banana splits, and chocolate egg-creams than one often finds in more dignified types of stores. This was the nature of Steve's early experience. He had spent many twelve- and fourteen-hour days and nights working in his parents' candy store in Coney Island.

The older of two sons, Steve completed high school in Brooklyn and at night attended Brooklyn College. In-between time he worked in the tiny store with which his father, an unemployed furrier, managed to eke out an income for his family. Steve started in the store at seven in the morning, left it to go to school, and returned to it until 1:30 the next morning. From friends, he learned to play the saxophone and clarinet, and he tooted and tweeted in a youthful band which played locally and in the Catskills. But the demands of the store, operating on a 17½ hour basis, took precedence so that he gave up his music.

In 1959, three momentous things happened which changed the life of the nineteen-year-old youth. One was that he married a Queens girl whom he had met through a fellow musician. Another was that he served briefly in the United States Army, and for the first time since puberty, he was free of the candy store for a prolonged period. And the third was that after applying to the main S. Klein's store in Manhattan, he was hired as a stockboy.

While Klein's had no formal training program, Steve was brought in at a slightly higher salary as a stockboy on the assumption that he could also function as an executive trainee. He moved stock from the backroom to the sales floor, learned how to handle the cash register, and performed other storekeeping duties. After nine months, he was transferred to Klein's buying office in the same building, was made a clerical, and soon became an assistant buyer. Not long after, he was appointed buyer and department manager of a leased drug department in a Klein's branch store.

In some ways, it was like running his own candy store again except that being responsible for patent medicines and health-and-beauty aids and working with a pharmacist substituted for dispensing malteds and chocolate egg-creams. Within a year, he took the volume from about $5,000 to $20,000 a week and had the concessionaire company hot after him to leave Klein's and join its executive ranks.

Steve's friends advised him to accept. It was unusual recognition after such a short time. And, they reasoned, Klein's would probably take him back if things didn't go well. After all, it already had an investment in him and needed "young hotshots like you." He took the new job, and in little more than a year gave the leasing company the first $1-million-a-year drug department it had ever had in any Klein's store. Three months later, he was named one of the firm's national supervisors and was earning $135 a week more than he had in Klein's.

Yet, despite his new job and his success, he was still physically working in Klein's. One day while in the Newark store, the store director became impressed with the young man's energy, the brisk way he spoke, and how he demonstrated what he wanted to the drug-department manager. The following day, the store director offered Steve a job as manager of several soft-goods departments at a substantially higher salary than the concessionaire paid him. Steve accepted and precipitated a battle between lessor and lessee companies in which their mutual contract was almost broken.

Smiling wryly, Steve Jackel recalled the situation. "By that time, I guess, I had become the leased operator's key man, and they didn't want to see me go back to Klein's. But the Klein's management said they wanted me back, and I had originally worked for them, and I was still really their man. It was a whole to-do which flattered me, but in the final analysis what it really did was raise my salary even more. Had I remained at Klein's for those eighteen months, I probably would have been making $10 a week more than I had. But the incident had far-reaching proportions. A couple of people who were responsible for allowing me to leave Klein's were on the spot because management couldn't understand why I was worth so much more money when I came back than when I left and so those people were let go."

Within the next eight months, Steve was again promoted to merchandise manager of the entire Newark store. Almost immediately, when an opening developed for the store director's post, second to that of store manager, Steve was selected over a man twenty years older but on an "acting" basis. It was in a period when Meshulam Riklis began making overtures to acquire Klein's and shortly afterward added the eleven-store chain to McCrory.

Sam Neaman did not wait long before calling a meeting of all the Klein's managers, giving Steve his first face-to-face meeting with the highly regarded chairman. With surprise, he heard Neaman set a pattern with the managers of the new company that had fallen under his wing by asking each to furnish a list of all the things they were responsible for. "Just put it on a sheet of paper, gentlemen," Neaman requested, "and sent it in to me." As it turned out, everyone, including Steve Jackel turned in a comprehensive list of his responsibilities, such as developing people, watching the cost of overhead, seeing that the lights were turned on and off, and so on. But no one gave any indication that he was also responsible for making money, for producing a profit. Neaman, of course, later used it as a frequent object lesson in attitudes and priorities.

Much of that first meeting was devoted by Neaman to a narration of his concepts of management and of retailing. His ability to reduce them to human terms and to explain them from the standpoint of individual responsibility electrified the audience. "His ideas were completely new to me," Steve said later. "I found them very exciting and very interesting. We all did." That may have been, but the twenty-six-year-old manager was evidently more stirred than anyone else. He decided on his own to apply Neaman's sales-per-square foot productivity to the Newark store, returning that same night to start it. On Sundays, at night and in his spare time, Steve put together a book-length volume, recommending that the store be cut from seven to five floors, measuring out the space from existing to optimum dimensions, and listing the improved results to come from it. He mailed the volume to the chairman.

Neaman phoned and asked Steve to come to New York to see him. "Your figures check out," Neaman said. "That's good for a man who's got no financial experience. Look, do you think you can take a little time off and look at the store on the Jersey Shore? It's a big headache to me."

"Sure. You want me to check in with the manager?"

"I will call him myself."

Steve spent several hours wandering unhappily through the big shopping center store, from whose third floor one could see a dazzling sweep of the sunlit Jersey shoreline. It was only a few years old, but it was unkempt and displayed few of the signs of top professional handling. The more he looked, the more upset it made him. It seemed to him that the manager had succumbed to the relaxed vacation environment that was one of the big lures of the area. Finally, he stalked into the manager's office. "F'cryinoutloud, Harry, this store is a goddamn disaster! I want you and your staff in here this Sunday—clean it up and re-arrange the fixtures so it looks like an honest-to-goodness retail store! This looks like one big craphouse!"

With that, Steve stormed out. But as he did, he heard the manager's shocked words trail after him. "Who the hell asked you to come in here and tell me what to do? You the boss all of a sudden?" As he drove away, it began to dawn on Steve why the manager had responded that way. Neaman had never called to say that Steve was coming.

When he came to see Neaman the next morning, he found him sitting at his desk, while Kunsberg, the president of McCrory, was standing at the window. Both their faces were round and red, as though they had just enjoyed a big laugh. "I kind of got the feeling, Mr. Neaman," Steve began, "that you made a *shmuck* out of me—"

Neaman shook his head, smiling hugely and glancing at Kunsberg. "No," he said, "that wasn't my intention at all. I wanted to see if you had in yourself the capacity to get angry and to push your weight around. So you have—and you did. Good. Let them come in on Sunday in Jersey Shore and do some work. It won't hurt them. But for you we have a new assignment. We want you to be in charge of several of our stores. We are going to replace you in Newark."

Enthused by his promotion and a sizeable salary increase, Steve soon found, however, that Neaman had more plans for him. In addition to supervising the activities of a number of the Klein's stores and coaching managers on how to improve their productivity, Steve was also asked to double as manager of the main store in Manhattan. But Neaman, Steve found further, had a plan-within-a-plan. He and Steve would use the New York store as a testing ground for new operational techniques and devices, new fixtures, and new ways of presenting merchandise. If successful, these efforts would then be applied to other Klein's stores and be incorporated into the blueprint for new ones.

And so, for the next five years from 1967 through 1972, Steve Jackel became involved in a frenetic regimen in which he worked seven days a week and most nights, in a complexity of roles. His new title was vice-president and general store director, but he also ran a school for new managers in New Jersey, escorted Neaman from one store to another, and functioned as his alter-ego in changing managerial attitudes and improving store decor. He was so swept up with the challenges and the quasi-intellectual, quasi-professional, quasi-logistical problems with which Neaman presented him that Steve became a combination of working and thinking machine. And despite all the time it took away from his wife and three young daughters, he had never felt as involved, consumed, or as fulfilled by anything that had happened to him before.

"Do you feel that you may be giving too much of your life to the job?" Steve was asked.

"Maybe," he said, "but it's become a way of life. My family has become adjusted to it; my wife, especially, has become acclimated to it. To me, right now, I know nothing else. I leave the house in the morning, and I never get home before ten or eleven at night. And on Sundays, I'm either in one of our stores or I'm on the phone for several hours or I'm working. I would say that at the beginning of that routine I did it because I saw Mr. Neaman do it, and I wanted to associate myself with him. I sort of did it for that reason. Today I do it because that's just the way I am."

"Which way is that?"

"Well, to make up my mind that I want to be successful and to understand that to achieve this kind of success you must really work at it. Sam himself told me. He said that I had crossed over the bridge."

"What does that mean?"

"I took it as a great compliment. You see, what he meant was that I had finally stopped working this way just to try and impress him, which at the beginning was probably all that it was. Now I'm doing it because I really enjoy working this way and it's become my way of life, and I guess that's what he meant by my having crossed over the bridge. I had made up my mind that I wanted to be successful and not to try to get there by saying the right thing and just trying to do it the easy way. Too many guys try and get there, but they aren't prepared to do what has to be done in order to be successful. . . ."

"How?"

"By being superficial and by trying to give the impression that something is done and that they have the depth and they are eligible and are really capable when they are not. . . . I think I have achieved what I need. I think I've become . . . someone of depth. 'Depth' meaning that I am being turned into being very good at what I do. I have Mr. Neaman to thank for that. And no matter where I am at whatever level I have to be I've learned to be good at it and not to accept or expect anything less from myself. And then, when you can consider yourself to be good at something, then you don't have to be ashamed again."

When he talks that way, rather tortured and yet happily honest with himself and the world, Steve Jackel tends to bend over his desk, his torso almost parallel with it. It is as if it strains him not to be able to demonstrate at that moment that behind those sweeping words lies a deep pool of self-discipline, infinite work, and total involvement. An outsider witnessing this and knowing Steve's particular background must think back to the long, lonely hours at the Coney Island candy store and wonder how much they are a spur or a shadow. The thought soon turned into a question.

"Do you think you succeeded in your career because of all the hours behind the soda fountain, Steve, or because you're running away from them?"

The torso slowly straightened up and the smile under the

rather prominent, jutting nose was rueful. "You reporters always have that knife ready, don't you?" Steve said. But his smile was friendly enough. One always had to be a professional to do a job right, it implied. "Maybe there is something to that," he conceded. "Lemme see if I can put a handle on it—"

As he spoke, it occurred to me that Sam Neaman sat in his office only forty or fifty feet away, deeply immersed in pulling the strings, imposing his personality and activating his credo on all his executives. He might not think well of what I suspected might be coming out of the introspective gropings of perhaps his most promising young executive. The relevance of that ubiquitous term of the period—counterproductive—hung in the air, but it didn't seem to occur to Steve Jackel.

"All right, did all the hours in the candy store help or hurt?" said Steve. "They helped to this extent—having to put everything I had into the effort of that time. At the beginning, when the money is not there, when the future isn't bright, when the sense of accomplishment doesn't matter because there isn't any, you still have to work like hell. And it continued that way even afterward. Most people don't want to work at something that doesn't produce for them; because, why do it? All right, to me at the beginning it had become a way of life. Then you got to remember that when I came to work at Klein's and found out that you don't have to work on Sunday, when I decided that I should work on Sunday, it wasn't so bad. Once in a while, I would skip it so that it was like a vacation, which is something I never had as a young guy. So at the beginning here I sort of walked from the candy store into something where working, working, working didn't bother me. So I didn't fall by the wayside like the rest of the guys that found that in a store you had to work six days a week and two nights. Not only did I work at Klein's, but I even had a part-time job. My father died and I had to help out in the candy store because my mother was all alone there. I used to leave here at six at night and go to Coney Island on the train and work until one and two in the morning and then come home. I saw my wife only on Sundays until my mother was able to sell the candy store. . . .

"Look, I think the candy store helped in two ways. It helped me to get used to working long hours and not be upset by it. It helped me because you're dealing with people all the time. And it's a personal kind of business so the relationship with a customer really comes home. In a large corporation people have a tendency to forget who the customer is, and he gets lost in the shuffle. But in a neighborhood candy store, everyone who comes in to spend, even the guy who just buys a newspaper, is important. The other way it all helped was that I worked so hard for so little. I think that feeling is still something inside me.

"Of course, there's that other side. I'll admit it. I never want to go back to that candy store again—not actually, of course, but figuratively. I have that awful desire to amount to something so that I don't have to watch my parents and myself be subjected to anybody that comes in to be an All-American spender for ten cents or fifteen cents and needle you in the bargain. This did more for me—never wanting to be subjected to that again, never wanting my children to have to see me the way I had to see my parents take that—it did a lot for me. I'm so inundated with the feeling of never again being faced with that torment again that I guess I just fought my whole life to become somebody and not just a kid standing behind a counter in a sweaty T-shirt that people naturally took advantage of."

The telephone rang. It was Neaman wanting to see him. Steve returned in about ten minutes, a slightly different person, no longer introspective, alert, about to be on the move again. "I have another coupla minutes," he said, sitting on the edge of his desk. "Then I have to scoot out to the stores. So shoot."

The mood was broken, yet there was a little left to say. "This conviction that you have become 'someone of depth,'" he was asked, "is that mostly Neaman's doing or yours?"

He didn't set out to become that way, he replied. But the fact that he was working with Neaman and wanted to continue to had forced him to become "very, very good at what I was doing and to gear myself to work at it constantly."

Steve added, "I thought I was a great store manager when I was twenty-five or twenty-six. I thought I was the greatest store manager in the United States. And I wasn't even a good store manager. He made me see that; that's what Neaman gives you. But you don't have to take it. It's a question of make or break or quit. I decided to become the guy I could be, and I now am.

You see, Neaman, if you want to become an executive of substance with him, if you're capable of it, will force you in spite
of yourself to become capable of doing as much as is humanly
possible. I mean, he doesn't let you off the hook. He keeps
pushing me until I'm begging to learn what I am supposed to be
doing. And I won't fold. Look, I don't have a goddamn thing
to complain about."

But it was obvious that he frequently showed the strain of
the pressure that he was under from Neaman. Perhaps because
he spent so much time with the chairman that he could be familiar or because it was not in his tough nature to fully idolize
anyone, he sometimes spoke in a sarcastic manner, even at meetings. Neaman didn't seem to mind much. He knew that Steve
Jackel had, to put it in his own words, "crossed over the bridge."

Efforts to jog Jackel into describing any of Neaman's "faults"
proved largely fruitless. Outwardly, Steve remained loyal, respectful, greatly devoted to his superior. He did not, for example, outwardly respond other than in the norm when Neaman suggested, as a morale-building move, that the Klein's
executives establish a Man-of-the-Year Award to the individual
who had contributed most to the organization each year. And
then when the executive committee reported that the consensus
had opted for Neaman himself, the chairman graciously agreed
to become the first awardee. An immense bronze plaque to that
effect was hung in his outer office. Steve Jackel did not complain.

Nor did Steve permit himself any known comment when
Klein's garden and nursery-products concessionaire proposed
that, as part of the dedication ceremony for the commemora-
tion of the long-standing relationship between the Netherlands
and the United States, a new tulip be named after Klein's chairman. In due course, the "Samuel Neaman Tulip" was introduced to the American public in the Klein's Garden Shops and
through the auspices of the Netherlands Embassy.

Steve was one of a big contingent of McCrory executives who
sat at a second dais a few feet from the main one when a prominent social-trade association presented the Retailer-of-the-Year
Award to Sam Neaman in the Advertising Club on Park Avenue. The citation for that year stated that Neaman had made

"significant contributions to the advancement of chain variety-store retailing in the United States." A press release in advance of the luncheon also said that Neaman would make a "news-worthy announcement during his acceptance speech." But this never materialized. Asked afterward how he felt about Neaman's award, Steve replied, if somewhat grimly: "He deserves it—and a lot more. Nobody in the country has done the job he did."

Several items relevant to the award luncheon are worthy of note. One was the summation for the press of Neaman's accomplishments:

Under his leadership, McCrory, a downward-trending company, was shaken out of its doldrums and infused with new vigor and vitality. Accepting the challenges of new ideas and concepts that flowed from the top, staff specialists and technicians developed and implemented a new breed of systems, controls, and highly efficient distribution technology. The turnabout in the company's financial condition was soon apparent and it became increasingly healthy as the newly developed systems took hold.

In 1963, the return-on-investment for the variety-store division was 2 percent. Two years later, following Mr. Neaman's advent, it rose sharply to 11.6 percent and is now averaging a return of 15 percent plus. . . . What makes his approach to achieving straight-forward corporate goals different, and thus worth recording, is his strong belief that the key to profitability and growth is not only modern management but also the active development of the company's human resources, its people.

One other notable item was Neaman's opening remarks in his acceptance speech. "I wonder how much business we wrote today," he said. "That is the most important part of this luncheon. Well, I hope we wrote enough business to justify ten percent of the exaggerated compliments paid to me. I don't deserve it, yet you know that I love compliments. But motivation is more important than compliments. I think it all started when Eve turned to Adam and said, 'I've got nothing to put on.' He said,

'Why don't you go shopping?' She said, 'What about some money?' He looked and found he had no pockets, so he said, 'Charge it.' Then the first retailer showed up. . . ."

The Dachau Memory

Neaman was always on the prowl for people in the organization who could be motivated to assume greater responsibility no matter what the cost. This was not so easy as it might appear, either for them or for him.

It was easy enough, of course, to offer a better job with more money and have people accept it as though they were deserving. Neaman knew this was hardly enough. For what he wanted to do, he needed the unusually motivated who could be made to rise to a job by being intellectually and professionally challenged, though flailed, perhaps, by the whiplash of his mind and by his dissatisfaction with the mediocre achievement. This compelled him to search for those seeking to compensate for a past failure, a past wrong, a past loss of opportunity. Such persons, he accurately sensed, had the visceral need to succeed and also the moral fiber, the unbending backbone, to take his lash. They had the reason.

Charles Witz was never quite sure if Neaman knew he had spent a year in Dachau after four years in a Nazi-policed ghetto in Lithuania. He always wore his sleeves down so that the concentration camp number did not show. A lanky, balding man with a heavy, Slavic accent, Witz attracted the chairman's attention because of his obvious European background and his persistence at his job as one of Klein's assistant controllers, despite the promotion of others over him. He never complained about this unfair treatment over two years, though his heavy-featured face was dark and parched much of that time.

But then it seemed that he was all but forgotten one day, discovered the next. In 1967, Sam Neaman walked into his office, sat down, sighed, and said, "Tell me a thing, Charles. If I appointed you the controller of Klein's, what would you do?"

"Do you mean how would I conduct myself?"

"Right. What would you do to improve, streamline, and run a beautiful type operation?"

Witz stared past Neaman at the intent, stolid figure of his boss, the controller, sitting in a bigger office not twenty-five feet away. What could he say? Was he being tempted to be disloyal? Or was this one of those rare moments which everyone dreads yet eagerly looks forward to when a display of courage and initiative could drastically change his life? Neaman waited patiently, his lip pouting a bit as Witz pondered. Finally, with a gutteral Russian accent, Witz began to speak. He went on for more than twenty minutes, not worrying about the words but about the meaning, ignoring the figure in the other office and concentrating on Neaman's face. At last, he finished with, "All this I promise to do in four months. Not more but not less."

"Four months?" Neaman asked, skeptically.

"Yes."

Neaman got up. "All right, Charles. Then you are the controller. The present controller is being promoted to treasurer. *Mazel tov.*"

The surprising thing to Witz was that the chairman had obviously been watching him, studying his behavior and performance, while Witz had convinced himself that he was being overlooked because he was a holdover from the previous management. Meshulam Riklis had bought Klein's for his usual bargain price from another company, which had been clearly headed for the rocks. When Klein's became part of McCrory, Neaman wanted all the accounting office procedures changed and new computer operations brought in. The shift displaced many people. Charles Witz, who had worked his way up from junior accountant to assistant controller in six years, was retained, but others were moved over him.

He had had one brief, prior meeting with Neaman. Some months after his firm's acquisition by McCrory, Witz had met Neaman emerging from the controller's office. "This, I believe, is Charles Witz? I am right?" asked Neaman.

"Yes. How are you, Mr. Neaman?"

"Charles," Neaman said, placing an arm around his shoulder, "you know a lot about the Klein's stores. I think you could be

very valuable in cutting expenses around here. When you finish
cleaning up the unfinished business from the old system, I will
have special projects for you to handle."

"Thank you," said Witz, hoarsely. "Thank you very much."

Neaman smiled, waved away Witz's gratitude and walked
on. The special projects never materialized. But more than a
year later, Neaman dropped into the assistant controller's office
and summarily promoted him.

From then on, Witz, who had always worked hard, nonetheless began a work regimen that might have ultimately killed
a man who had not already survived five years under the Nazis.
He put in as many as ninety hours a week, eating in and sometimes late at night napping at his desk only to start and work
some more. However, like Steve Jackel and most of the other
executives, Witz gradually learned to steel himself against
Neaman's insatiable demands for more details, for answers that
seemed to elude him and for the stretching of human and technical assets to and even above their capacity.

Early on in their new relationship, Neaman suggested a pact
with Witz. Only a few weeks after becoming controller, Witz
was summoned by Neaman. As the chairman ate his meager
lunch in the conference room, he told him, "I am pleased with
you, Charles. I sense that you have the capacity to grow, to develop beyond yourself. So let me suggest an arrangement with
you. You are a mature, sophisticated person who has seen many
things, including the mistakes of all the previous regimes, so let
us agree that I will never mention or criticize or even praise you
for your accomplishments. Instead, I will mention or criticize
only what you have not yet accomplished. All right? This will
be a constant challenge to you. You will never get off my hook,
Charles, but you will become a man who outdoes others. Can
you stand such a knife always sticking in your *tuchas* and your
brain?"

Witz regarded the chairman who, instead of waiting for his
answer, plunged into his Ry-Krisp and cottage cheese as if it
were haute cuisine. It was an astonishing request. Yet from Neaman's standpoint it was an obvious recognition of him and his
capabilities. It was also patently an experiment on Neaman's
part, and Witz couldn't help but wonder how much of that

was related to his already proven capacity to endure pain. Could he handle it? He honestly didn't know, but he knew one thing. If he refused, Neaman's estimation of him would wither. He had to try.

"I think that this could make a better man of me," Witz replied, rather weakly.

Neaman looked up with a happy smile. "Good," he said, still chewing. "That is already half the battle. We will meet here every morning at eight."

It was to be a test of endurance. But, difficult as it might be, it could not be a test of survival. He had already undergone that and nothing could be worse.

Witz's father had died when he was only two years old. Thus, starting in 1924 in the Lithuanian city of Kovno, which was renamed Kaunas after the German occupation, he grew up with a mother who also had to be a father. Everyone in the small family worked, Charles starting at thirteen while attending *cheder* and public school. But his mother, who worked alternately as a seamstress and cook's helper, insisted that he receive as much education as he could. After gymnasium, the high school, he took night courses at a higher school (equivalent to college) and learned bookkeeping and accounting.

It was not overly difficult for the scrawny, intense young man to get a job in a merchant bank as a junior accountant. But when the Russians overran Lithuania in 1940, incorporating it into the Union of Soviet Socialist Republics, the bank came under Russian control and Charles lost his post. He soon found another one, however, as an accountant in a Russian–Lithuanian food company. In June 1941, the Germans invaded Lithuania. For four years, Charles lived in the horror and uncertainty of a Jewish ghetto policed as a concentration camp by the Nazis, while many around him died of hunger and maltreatment. But even that, that nightmare of terror and scrounging for crusts, was better than what came after. In 1944, he and the pitiful survivors of that ghetto were herded into railroad freight cars and transported to the notorious Dachau camp in Germany.

Luckily, Witz's mother had died only a few weeks before the family was shipped to Germany. His only sister had also died earlier of illness caused by malnutrition. Only he, his brother, and his brother's family were left to make the trip to Dachau. In the year of horror that followed, his brother's wife and their two children died in the camp. On May 2, 1945, when the Americans liberated Dachau, only Charles and his older brother survived of the entire family.

The Allies and the German government under occupation attempted to provide some measure of relief for the liberated internees. Food tickets given to them were more liberal than those the Germans obtained. Houses formerly occupied by government officials and Nazis were made available. Charles was offered such a house but he refused it, preferred to board with a German family in Munich. He worked for a Jewish-language newspaper as its accountant and occasional interpreter. In that role, he translated a number of articles of Walter Lippmann, the American political columnist, into Jewish for the enlightenment of the small number of Jews left in Western Europe.

In 1949, he was one of the first Lithuanians living in West Germany to be repatriated by the Russian authorities. It was a sorry group that was being returned to Lithuania, firmly believing the widespread rumors that they would be immediately mobilized into the Russian army. Charles managed late one night to break across the German border. Keeping out of the way of the Russians, he made his way to freedom and decided to emigrate either to the new state of Israel or to the United States. He chose America. His brother had settled several years ago in New York, had remarried, and had begun to raise a new family. Charles also had cousins in Hartford. He received his papers and by the late fall of 1949 reached Connecticut.

He had already learned superficially to read and speak English, and he now brushed up on the language in night school in Hartford. A friend of a cousin, a minor executive at the Klein's stores, mentioned that the chain was building two monstrous-sized branches and would need some new people in its accounting department. Within a few months of having come to the United States, Charles had a job as a clerk in Klein's accounting operations.

The next decade had good years for the skinny immigrant. Through his relatives, he met and married an American girl and became the father of two children. He rose successively at Klein's to senior clerk, junior accountant, senior accountant, and then to assistant controller. He bought a house in Brooklyn and by 1960 was supervising fifty accountants and clerks.

But often in those years, he could not rid himself of occasional nightmares. The terror of his experience in the ghetto compound and later in the concentration camp haunted him in the morning's darkest hours. And strangely, in that decade's later years after he had stopped waking up in a cold sweat, he had other nightmares while wide awake. It was a premonition that it could all happen again in his new country. His fears were fed by books like *Gentlemen's Agreement*, newspaper stories about restricted-clientele resorts and hotels, and the demagoguery of Senator Joseph McCarthy. While the fears receded in later years, they never fully left him.

The next seven years, unlike the previous ten, were largely frustrating. After Klein's founder sold the business to a large, diversified company, the new owners brought in another controller. Two years later, he left and was replaced by another. A new senior assistant was then named over Charles Witz, who felt himself submerged by layer and layer of incompetents. And then, for the first two years under McCrory, the pattern was repeated.

Countless times in 1966 and 1967, Witz asked himself if his background weren't working against him. Did "they" think that five years of entrapment in a life-and-death situation had robbed him of his natural attributes of imagination, vision, or flexibility? Or did they think that his experiences had made him lose his courage? Or was it just the simple fact that he was considered a foreigner, with a thick, Slavic accent and a telltale I.D. number burned on his wrist? After prolonged brooding, he began, at least in his own mind, to behave as if it were so. Rings appeared under his eyes. And he found it difficult to meet the gazes of others, including his own workers, with a confident gaze of his own. Why in God's name weren't hard work, devotion, and good intentions enough?

That was why, on that amazing morning when Sam Neaman walked in on him, he was so unprepared for the promotion that was being handed to him. It spelled the end of his nightmares, the real ones, and almost but not quite the wide-awake ones, too.

As he reviews his life, there is a rueful tone which creeps into his voice. "You know—as I look back upon it—in my fifty years the hardest thing to do was survive," he says. "I had more of that pressure than probably anybody else around here or in most other places. When I was in the ghetto and in Dachau, later when my management overlooked me for seven years and—" he adds weakly, "even now."

He says, "Each time, I survived somehow. And now I think maybe I will also survive. You learn something every time. Or maybe it is just that you hope you learn."

Can you really equate human and professional survival? Witz's answer is to smile and lower his eyes. "I do not mean to equate them," he says, "or even to compare them, except that each of those three important periods in my life was like a great mountain which I had to climb," he says. "You climb up, you fall, you pray, and then you are up on the other side. You have a new life. And then you see a new mountain and you start again."

As he spoke, something else became clear to him. It was not just that those three "mountains" were plateaus that successively led to the next one, but that each was directly responsible for the other. Perhaps one could readily compare human and professional survival as if they were both oranges, but the simple fact was that each mountain appeared to him at the time to be as insurmountable as the next one. Did it matter, he wondered, that to climb one you had to pass through fire and brimstone while on the other you were inflicted with a consuming depression?

What emerged, too, as he thought more about it, was the cause-and-effect relationship of each. If surviving the beleaguered ghetto and Dachau when almost all the rest of his family perished gave him a cause, wasn't the prolonged frustration of being stepped-over for seven years all the greater because of the past injustice? One could only agree with this, sensitive and introspective as it was. There had to be "just a little something" to the theory, he insisted. And, he continued, having been recognized at long last by management, wasn't his taking Neaman's whip and not letting it beat him into insensitivity all the more vital because of the endless years of disappointment? Of course. It was hard to disagree with him.

But he sighed and observed that there were many compensations. "I am personally in debt to Mr. Neaman," he said. "He discovered me."

The chairman's encouragement, Witz went on, helped him personally and professionally and also benefited the company. "The suppliers today are getting paid automatically," he said proudly, "while in the past there were a lot of skipped invoices. They got lost, so the company couldn't pay and the vendors had to come back and claim later on. I am also very proud of our tight controls, especially the profit or loss by square-foot statements, which few companies have. It was only by his generosity that we in our department were able to get the priority for this program."

There was on a personal basis, he said, more to it than mere pride in accomplishment. "Mr. Neaman has been instrumental in inspiring me to regain the confidence I lost all the years when I was on the sidelines watching people come in over me," Witz said. "There were maybe six to twelve controller-type people available at the time to handle the controller job but he decided to give me the opportunity. Afterward, he inspired me to go through with everything that I told him I would do. Many times, he said, 'I didn't put the brains into your head.' But even so, he opened up my brains and he gave me the chance to use them."

After pausing for a drink of water, Charles Witz added, "He has also been instrumental in provoking me. In my opinion, he is the most ironic man I have ever worked with. Maybe that is not the right word. But, you know that we have an arrangement that he will never praise me. So he is never satisfied with half-jobs that are mediocre-accomplished. For example, on store operating statements, he would challenge me on certain expenses and items and question so many different things that would make us do a further review, to start a more detailed and professional analysis so we can satisfy the gentleman."

"Don't you find all that prodding a burden?"

"If you have an understanding why the demands are placed upon you," Witz said, "then you take it, because you know that they will make you a better person. This man took me after I was passed over, without my having fancy titles in schooling, and gave me a chance. Don't forget—the time I should have been in college I spent imprisoned in a ghetto and in the concentration camp. In place of it, I had to work very hard to learn my trade, to learn how to motivate people, and to learn how to accomplish what I have done without the proper schooling. I should complain if Sam Neaman demands from me things that make me a better person?"

"I see what you mean."

"Do you? My strongest asset, I have learned, has to be my dealing with people. I would say that probably the lesson that I learned very young in my life—to be on my own and to witness the destruction of many human beings—has put different values in my life. That has been a great help to me in dealing with people. One of the things that you learn by going through a concentration camp is that you have to be sensible. You have to enjoy life, because you have witnessed thousands of people around you who share the same faith lose everything they have gathered—including their lives. That kind of experience motivates you to enjoy every day and not to put it off for the future. And that's why I feel I can take whatever Sam Neaman wants to give me, because it is sensible to achieve the most that is in you. It has already made me an all-around better man, and I feel like I am a different person. And it's not just that I always have to say 'yes' to him. I disagree with him many times. I think it has also given me a maturity. Do you know what I did recently?"

"What's that?"

"After seventeen years, I stopped smoking cigarettes last week. I told myself that if I can be a better person in one thing, I can be like that in another thing. So I stopped smoking—from forty cigarettes a day to none."

"What made you stop all of a sudden?"

"Just an article in *Reader's Digest*. Since I have demonstrated will power in other things, I thought why not stop smoking already? So I did."

He sat at his desk, nervously stroking his thighs as though he might really be missing a cigarette, but he was apparently still thinking about his relationship with Neaman.

Looking up, Witz said, "You know what the chairman told me a few weeks after he made me controller? 'Charles, I'm a happy man that you didn't walk out on us in those years that you were pushed aside and so many people were put on top of you.' But what I didn't tell him was that I used to be so unhappy those days, and yet I didn't want to leave the company even though I was getting other offers. I went home many times and cried. That was funny, you see, because after Dachau I thought I would never cry again."

The Dissident

But some couldn't stand the gaff. And some didn't want to. It was not, however, because Sam Neaman ran everyone through the same wringer. He chose only the most motivated, those who didn't mind overcompensating for past inequities to meet his greatest demands. For others, he scaled down his criteria. But these, it was generally conceded, were greater than the maximum criteria of most other companies. So he was actually tough on everyone.

He tried several presidents at S. Klein and went through them. He imported specialist executives and went through them. Accustomed to other management milieus, other styles, most of these found it difficult to work with Neaman from the moment they arrived. So they came with hope, worked with frustration, and left with bitterness.

One of the more revealing cases was that of Hi Leder, fortyish but youthful, fat, brilliant, possessed of a striking comic flair and a gift for mimicry. A skilled advertising man who had worked as sales promotion manager and as advertising manager for two of New York's top promotional specialty-store chains, Hi Leder was one of the city's best-liked store executives. He hadn't a nasty bone in his fat, soft body, everyone decided. But his brain and tongue could rip through affectation, hypocrisy, doubletalk and make the writhing subject wish for those moments that he was miles away.

He went to work for Klein's in 1966 and was fired in 1969.

On a hot summer Sunday, Hi Leder weighs hard on the straining webs of a lounge chair, smoking a cigar with his left hand and swigging beer from a can with his right. He wears only a pair of Bermuda shorts, and his heavy torso is smeared with perspiration. It is two years since he left Neaman's employ, and he is now well-situated with another local retailer. He burps with heavy satisfaction, drains the can, and heaves it with a wink toward a neighbor's lawn. The pollution problems of Long Island are of no concern to him.

"You've put on weight, Hi, since I saw you a few years ago."

"Thanks. You should have seen me when I worked for Sammy. I was the fattest skeleton you ever saw. I've been trying to get back to myself ever since."

"How do you look back on those years?"

Reaching over for another can in a tureen of ice cubes, Hi replies, "I had a three-year contract with them. I stayed there for the full length of it. For me, it was a financially wise, career-foolish move. I would have done better for myself if I'd signed up with some Georgia chain-gang."

"What was the real problem?"

"Neaman, who else?"

In retrospect, two incidents revealed the chairman in ways that Hi Leder couldn't forget. Chameleon-like as the changing moods and behavior of Sam Neaman were, those two incidents were like a bizarre frame to the shifting picture that could never change.

In one of his numerous attempts to jar Klein's oversize stores into a better profit stance, Neaman called a merchandising meeting of some 200 people in the chain to explain new developments. The group of top, middle, and junior executives was greeted by Duffy Lewis, a grizzled but soft-spoken merchandiser who served for something less than eighteen months as

Klein's president. At that point, he still held that title. Lewis had a teacher's way about him, although his simple diction and passive behavior were hardly that of a leader. Sitting in the front row, Hi Leder glanced around the large group which filled the Klein's cafeteria in the New York store and wondered why Neaman had decided not to attend. He sensed a strangely expectant attitude, a hesitation—especially among the younger men, the buyers, their assistants, and the younger financial and operations people. It was clear to Hi, who had been around, just what it was. It's hard to accept concepts in a meeting called for the purpose of engineering change without the chief engineer in attendance, too.

Up on the platform Duffy Lewis stood before a slide projection of a typical floor plan and pointed to salient details. His voice appeared to waver, and he looked back and around at them all as if he had lost his direction. But he tried to cover up. Staring out at the audience, he said, "I got this feeling that most of you aren't giving me the benefit of your full attention. I—"

At that moment, a ripple of awareness moved across the audience, its lagging attention seemed to reignite itself and almost every head in the room moved wheatlike in the breeze to the side door. Neaman had come in. He walked on his tiptoes, his head lowered. Obviously, he didn't want to disturb Duffy Lewis's presentation.

As Neaman sought a seat in the back, Hi Leder thought, "Verily the dramatic entrance. I bet it was instinctive, too. He doesn't even have to practice. Nothing he does, not even picking his nose, is practiced. The guy is a consummate actor, a real Boris Thomashefsky." Behind him, he heard Neaman protesting in a whisper, "No, no, please, I will find my own seat," and then, a moment later, his full voice telling Duffy Lewis, "I'm sorry I interrupted. Please to continue."

Duffy resumed, his voice feigning strength and authority but lacking conviction. Hi thought that Lewis had been heartened by the arrival of the chairman but the after-reaction was one of dismay, of the pupil—even the senior pupil—cowed by the attention of the mentor. He stopped for a long, long pause. Then Neaman stirred in the rear, held up his hand, and asked, "Duffy, please. Can I take it from here?"

As Neaman walked briskly ("Pranced, was more like it," said Hi Leder), Duffy Lewis sat down in the audience and was no longer heard from. Neaman smiled fondly down at Duffy and took up the commentary. ("It was the summary dismissal—in other words, sit down and stop the bullshit—in front of everyone," as Leder put it.)

Neaman spoke for two hours. People squirmed. He ignored it. It went past the noon hour. That, too, was ignored. Case history followed general concept. Rhetorical and hypothetical questions flowed from the platform. Then Neaman had two buyers come up and debate positioning of merchandise. It was a demonstration lecture in combination with a philosophical treatise on retailing by the country's best-known nonretailer.

"He had the damned thing organized down to every detail, even a claque. A couple of hacks got up toward the end and asked, in effect, 'Do you mean that after Monday comes Tuesday, then Wednesday?' Hi recalled, "and then Neaman reassured them. 'Yes, my friends, Tuesday does come after Wednesday and you can depend on that every week.' That was the effect of it."

Then as the meeting appeared poised for conclusion, a young assistant buyer arose and asked, his voice hoarse with the wonder of new knowledge, "Do you mean, Mr. Neaman, that if you follow those rules, it will come out right every time. In other words, sir, is it A, B, C, and then D?"

Neaman glared at him. His face, according to Hi Leder, turned into a mask. He wiggled a finger at the boy. "No, no! Oh, no! Are you trying to get me to give you the exact answer? No, it is not A, B, C, or D. It is A, B, C, and then E, L, X, but better still whatever answer is indicated by facts, plans, execution, supervision! Those are the keys to successful management—not a bunch of alphabet soup!"

"Sir, I'm sorry—"

Neaman ignored him, waved at the audience, and walked off the platform.

Then, the Man-of-the-Year Dinner.

To his surprise, Hi Leder found himself running it along with three others in a four-man committee. The others spent a good part of their time outside the office so that Hi, who didn't, had to handle a lot of the arrangements. This brought him into further contact with Neaman, the first awardee. Undismayed by that fact, the chairman insisted on approving all the details—the decision to use a hotel ballroom instead of the company cafeteria, then the exact hotel, then the agenda, then the keynote speaker, then the content of the speech, then the selection of the honor guards who would usher the awardee to the dais, then the precise seating of all the executives on the three daises . . .

By the time the night arrived, a balmy Saturday evening in April 1968, Hi Leder's head felt as though it were permanently spinning. He had never suspected that a man who was receiving an award could involve himself so totally in its preparations. But everything ran true to plan, including the presentation speech given by an old-time Klein's executive who knew everyone in the chain so well that Neaman figured that the presentation by him would have the grass-roots flavor, the connotation of unanimity to make it all seem authentic.

"The only trouble with him," Hi recalled, "was that he was a toothless old gaffer well into an advanced stage of senility. Nobody in the organization was loved more or respected less. We figured that Neaman had an ulterior motive in tapping him. You see, he was a sort of buyer without portfolio. After he was replaced by a younger, more capable guy, Neaman kept him around the buying offices as a sort of symbol that the new management was humane, paternalistic. So his choice of him for the presentation was a sort of act of mercy—the sort of thing that only a real, honest-to-goodness Man-of-the-Year could be expected to do."

Hi pointed out that he couldn't, of course, write a speech, or for that matter, even make one, since he lacked an adequate bridge in his mouth. So a plan was drawn up. First, a speech would be drafted and sent up to Neaman. After several drafts, it would, hopefully, be approved. And then the old-timer would be fitted with a new mouthful of teeth.

"He got through with the speech but not without breaking down at least twice. He was genuinely maudlin, more or less thanking Neaman for being born so that he could come to Klein's and whip guys like himself. I tell you, it was cloying, nauseating. . . ."

The dinner's highlight, of course, was the presentation of the award itself. It was, according to Hi, "like getting the kid the biggest toy in the world." What was it? An eight-foot, electronic map of the United States, with every store in the McCrory empire marked by a tiny light. Each division had its own differently colored lights. "I could easily imagine Neaman," said Hi, "sitting up all night in the dark playing with the lights."

Accepting the award, Sam Neaman made an interesting comment. "I look forward to the day, gentlemen," he said, "when there is not a square inch left on this map which does not have a light on it. There is no reason why our concept of guided autonomy, of average people with average talents working together, cannot be applied anywhere at all in this wonderful country. Can anyone in this room think of such a reason?"

No one could. Neaman beamed.

There was no question in anyone's mind, even the subject himself, that Hi Leder was a dissident by nature. Circumstances made him even more so. In an environment geared to group achievement, he was an individual, not average as a person or in his talent. But it is likely that he would have been a sore-thumb anywhere. In this one, though Hi believed strongly in a hard-work ethic, Neaman quickly became aware of him as a potential threat to genuine group effort. Perhaps it was because Hi—fat; ebullient; happy in his raunchy, creative style—was frequently overheard protesting he would damn well not be submerged in a "fucking, socialistic, workmen's-circle atmosphere."

He married a Manhattan-born girl (who appreciated his sense of humor although not always his jokes), sired two children, and finally reached his goal as a retail advertising manager at the Klein's chain. One of Neaman's several unsuccessful presidents was the prime mover in hiring Hi Leder, having known and admired his work in an earlier connection. Less than a year after joining Klein's, Hi was appointed a vice-president by Neaman on the urging of his sponsor, who shortly afterward was fired.

"From the minute Neaman kicked my rabbi out," Hi said as he sipped beer on his front porch, "I knew I was in trouble.

Maybe if I had kept my big mouth closed, I might still have gotten on the good side of Neaman. But, I confess that I never learned how to do that."

His early impressions of Neaman were good ones. He saw the chairman at first as a very unassuming person, a man of the people, a sort of Nikita Khrushchev but "Jewish folksy." Neaman used to "walk around, looking into every office like a friendly, fat rabbit, like he really had nothing much to do but didn't want to butt into anybody's business. How wrong I was."

Increasingly, he found Neaman involving himself in sales promotion and advertising, which were Leder's provinces. He was the same in regard to Klein's merchandising, credit, operations, and control and accounting. These were not Hi's provinces actually, but he was occasionally involved in some of them. Everywhere he went, it seemed there was the chairman with a routine reminiscent of the Duffy Lewis meeting: silent observation, then abrupt takeover, then domination, and then a prolonged lecture.

In the sales-promotion and advertising meetings, Hi related, "before I knew it, he took over, rambling at first after which he treated us to an avalanche, so maybe I could pick something out. But it was all guidelines and pep talk, nothing I could sink my teeth into. He just didn't want to be a partner to a decision. I believe a boss should have balls, otherwise he's not a boss. But he insisted that all he had to do was set you down at a crossroads, tell you what was in each direction, and then turn his back on you and walk away."

Maybe that was the right method to clear the cobwebs out of a person's mind, Hi conceded. But it often tended to create havoc among people who thought they knew their business and suddenly found the big boss questioning all their concepts. "One of the things Sammy always said at those meetings," Hi observed, "was, 'I am not a retailer.' Well, I have to agree and I did it many times. I told him, 'You're right, Sam. You're certainly not a retailer.'

"About the third time I told him, his head snapped back and his face turned into that mask. His eyes snapped shut like iron gates. I knew he would never forgive me. That's what I mean by not learning to keep my big mouth shut."

But Hi, already on a disaster course, did not run away from it. He had something to prove, to declare. "I guess if you pin me down, it was myself, my own goddamn, feisty individuality," he said, "and I was not about to sell that out to anybody, even to a guy that so many people swore by like Sam Neaman."

From then on, the Neaman–Leder relationship worsened. There was scarcely a media schedule, a radio commercial, or a printed ad that the chairman seemed to like. At the later meetings, he would put Hi through a defensive exposition of "tell me, please, who is our customer?" and the fat, harassed advertising man would try patiently to explain that it was the blue-collar worker, the housewife of uncertain income, and the medium affluents who liked to think they could save money. Neaman, in turn, would listen patiently, and when Hi's breath ran out, comment, "Please forgive me, but I still do not know who is our customer. Work on it some more."

And when Neaman would leave, Hi related, "I would tell myself—'I'm no psychiatrist or psychologist. I wouldn't know a schizo if he talked to me simultaneously in a soprano and baritone. But this guy has got to be a paranoid. He's certainly a megalo close to the edge, if not already over it.' Sometimes, at larger meetings when I wasn't on the griddle, I used to lean back and look at him and realize that he was just a self-protective, nondestructive bastard. It wasn't necessary to find a silver bullet or a wooden stake to put in his heart—I mean he wasn't a vampire. And then I wasn't sure."

As a confirmed dissident and sometime iconoclast, it was easy for Hi to feel critical and even intolerant about Neaman. He would have preferred to like Neaman, but instead he grew to hate him. The chairman, in Hi's view, did things that seriously conflicted with his "kibbutz" philosophy. He displayed favoritism. He indulged in prejudice. And he had an autocratic attitude that turned him off on any dissenter, even though he often publicly professed that "I don't like yes-men."

Hi watched uncomfortably and resentfully as Neaman seemed to surround himself in the Klein's offices with a coterie of young men whose lives he dominated. For months, he brought them into two- and three-hour lunches while he ate his spare meal and put them through a think-tank session. Sundays, like Saturdays a full-time day for Neaman, became for a while a meeting day for the group. He created "new-fangled" titles for the group of six young men—merchandise movement director, budget control manager, inventory-flow administrator, and so on —using them to devise new methods and systems that the older executives with the standard titles were too dogmatic and ingrained to think of. He reassured the young men that they were being trained to succeed their older superiors.

But he once jokingly criticized Neaman to Klein's personnel director, with whom he occasionally ate lunch and exchanged confidences. "Christ, Hi, straighten yourself out," the personnel man said, "you're grabbing at straws. Sam considers you a malcontent and a guy who's careless on budgets and disorganized. If you give him any more reason, he's going to dump you."

Hi shrugged in reply. "Maybe. But I don't think he'll do it until my contract runs out in about eighteen months. I'm the first ad manager and sales-promotion man that Klein's had in years who's done a real professional job, and Neaman knows it. And what's more, Klein's is his big problem. He needs all the help he can get. There are enough guys around Riklis at Rapid–American who are damned happy that Neaman has got a tombstone like Klein's."

"Come on, Hi," the personnel man told him. "Neaman has got so much going for him that he's bound to survive. He's done a fantastic job—probably one of the most dramatic turnarounds in American business today. Sure, there are guys near Riklis that hate Sam, but that's natural. They're all fighting for Riklis's favor so one guy pushes, the other guy pulls."

"Oh, shit," Hi replied, "I'll admit there's a good side to Neaman. He's not a retailer, and so he doesn't enter into a project with any preconceived notions except his own. He's perpetually dumb. The four keys of his are good, I guess, but look, when everyone's a cog, the machine just keeps rolling without any change in direction even when you need it. There has to be a leader—or leaders. Any business is only as good as its capacity to keep up with change."

The personnel man had a feeling for people, which was why Hi liked and respected him. But he shook his head at Hi as if it were impossible to get through to him. "I don't know, Hi, you just don't seem to understand that Sam has accomplished a miracle by going against tradition. I would think, being the kind of individualistic pain-in-the-ass you are, that you would appreciate that. He doesn't accept the logic or tradition of rules that have always been around, the little-by-little things, or the stupid inane things. He questions them. He makes people reexamine their pet ideas and habits, and he makes them think clearly."

"Yeah," Hi said. "I'll buy that. He's got what they call 'the *yiddishe kopp*.' But I also happen to think he's one of the world's great hypocrites."

Hi Leder was wrong about one thing. A week before his contract ran out, the personnel man came into his office and handed him a note from Neaman informing him that his contract wasn't being renewed. Neaman wasn't waiting, in other words. He wanted him out a week early. But what hurt even more, Neaman wanted him out that very day. That morning, in fact.

"Okay, if that's what he wants, I'll clean out my desk and go," Hi said. "I'll drop in on you later and say good-bye."

"No," said the personnel man. "You can't. I've got to stay with you while you clean up and usher you out of the building. Neaman's orders."

'That sonofabitch!" Hi exploded. "What's he afraid of? I'll steal some paper clips?"

"Whatever, Hi. That's the order."

"And that goes for you, too," Hi said, bitterly. "You could have talked him out of that, you bastard. What do you think everyone around here will say when they see you escort me out?"

"I can't help that."

"Friends like you I need like another asshole."

Men Found

As he prepared in late 1972–early 1973 to grapple with the biggest merger yet—the absorption of the 740 J.J. Newberry stores into McCrory's 800-odd variety stores—Neaman had the satisfaction of knowing that he had prepared well for it. He might be having his troubles with the Klein's situation: its top executives; its super-sized, unwieldy stores; its unprofitable product mix. But, when it came to McCrory's biggest division, the variety stores (which produced three times the volume and seventy-five times the profit of Klein's), he had solved all of its problems, particularly its human ones. And, after all, the human problems were the most important. This, he was fully convinced, augured well for his overcoming all his other problems.

A man sensitive to his ethnic differences and difficulties, it never failed to amaze Neaman when he realized how smoothly and effectively he had achieved his miracle in the variety-store division, which was known as one of the most "Gentile" chains in its field. Perhaps it was because for decades all of its top and middle management had come from the predominantly Wasp areas of the Atlantic states—south Jersey, western Pennsylvania, New York State, upper Connecticut, central Maryland. But that was all beside the point, since it had gradually dawned on him, despite his deep ethnic awareness, that there is a core in people that overcomes, reaches beyond religious, national, and racial differences. The core was stamped "need."

If people really needed one another, if peace-of-mind, happiness, and fulfillment (not to mention survival—not actually survival perhaps but balance, calm, even sanity) depend on their maintaining a constructive or productive relationship, then ethnic differences are just so much fringe matter.

So it seemed to him, even though at times he would have a twinge of self-doubt as he paraded the labyrinthine halls and warehouse aisles of the York distribution center, followed by a team of the division's executives.

He had not only found his men in the important McCrory variety division, but he also had such an excellent relationship with them that it frequently made him swallow with happiness, gratitude, and self-appreciation. He had come at a surprisingly strategic time in their lives, as they had come into his. Their relationship, with an obligation on him that sometimes hung heavily, was the foundation of his continuing achievements.

Whatever his problems were with the seemingly intractable Klein's department stores, despite what appeared to be a growing sniping from Isidore Becker and others at Rapid–American, and despite his failure with unproductive types such as Hi

Leder and others whom he didn't discharge but whose contracts he failed to renew, his relationships with the top men and everyone else at the McCrory variety division sustained him. They also helped to produce the profits that were the mainstay for the corporation. (And, more importantly, those relationships with those men were synergistic.) From Neaman's standpoint, they were men found. But from their own standpoint, they were men who had found themselves.

Bearer-of-the-Pennant

The best of Neaman's relationships—not an easy choice to make—was the one that bloomed with Frank Patchen. It became a standard for the entire organization, an example of a golden, productive relationship on a one-to-one basis.

It impressed many. This was because Patchen, a thoughtful, respected retailer whose quiet blood and low-key manner represented the old guard at its most smug and satisfied, adjusted to the Neaman style and credo as though he had been waiting for them all his life. Yet that was a superficial aspect. Not many knew the details of the most difficult years of Patchen's life, especially those when he had been struggling to find his way and when he had been seriously ill.

An indication that much lay behind the surface of the relationship was what happened to Patchen at the end of a six-month convalescence after nearly fatal surgery. Instead of relegating him to a shelf as expected, Neaman gave Patchen an interim post as research director, and a few months later, elevated him over the heads of several tiers of superiors to the post of president of McCrory's variety chain. Thus, in his early fifties, pale-faced, weakened and probably anemic, Frank Patchen found himself raised to the pinnacle of a career that he had assumed was already over.

The new responsibility also proved a therapy, perhaps because the challenge stimulated him as though it were adrenalin. He seemed to thrive on it, his eyes brightening, his slack jaws showing muscle, and his slowed step turning springlike. But his pallidness never quite left him.

On close examination, one of the oddest things about their relationship was that it bridged normally insurmountable extremes of national and racial backgrounds. There were 6,000 miles of distance and ages of difference between Neaman's upbringing in Galilee and Patchen's on the Atlantic coast of the United States.

Patchen was born in 1913 to a family which was devotedly Protestant, convinced that its meager circumstances were its lot, and painfully moralistic about its behavior. During the Depression, the father, John Patchen, lost his job as an electrical engineer but refused to accept relief. He got odd jobs, all menial considering his background. Although a poor salesman, he tried to sell the then new "Monitor Top" refrigerators produced by General Electric and failed. Then, living with his family near the summer resort colonies in Connecticut, he bought bread at wholesale and sold it at retail from a battered Ford to the resorts and the families living in cottages by the lake. He hired a small trailer and hauled 100-pound bags of peat moss and topsoil which he sold to nearby residents.

As a boy, Frank was sickly and contracted scarlet fever twice. He loved to read, but he had to wear glasses and was often reminded by his parents that glasses were expensive and he should be careful not to break them. Recalling it, he said many years later, "When you say this to a young child, you structure his living habits to some extent. The way this affected me was that I took more interest in school than I might have, and I developed a passion for the library. I remember taking out two or three books a week for many weeks. When other children were out playing, I would be inside reading. My parents had emphasized to me the fact that my glasses might break if I were playing. And if I broke my glasses, they would have to get another pair, and they really didn't have enough money for it. The rest of my life I was a great reader."

In the first fifteen years of his life, the family moved to five different towns and cities. Three principal memories linger from those years. Living in a small town near Wilmington, Delaware, young Patchen and his mother would sit on the porch in the summer evenings and sing two-part harmony with the neighbors. He also remembers the mixture of a sinking feeling in his stomach and a surge of pride when his father would appear at their rented home with yet another temporary means of support —an ice-cream truck, quantities of bread in the old Ford, and even once, sitting in back of a truck as part of a crew erecting cyclone fences. And then there were the difficulties with several teachers who kept telling his parents that "he can be a fine student if he would only put his mind to it," but failing to explain adequately to them all that there were some subjects he loved but others he hated.

After the age of ten, he grew up in New Jersey, Connecticut, and Rhode Island. A quiet, well-mannered boy, his reserved behavior reflecting a rigid family atmosphere. He managed to get into Brown University in Providence by obtaining a grant-in-aid, assisted by some cash from his grandfather. Anxious to please his mother, who wanted him to become a doctor, he pursued a pre-med curriculum for three years with little success. He was finally summoned by the dean. Frank admitted that for three years he had pursued subjects he hated, particularly chemistry and biology, only to please his mother's ambition. The dean drew out of him that what he especially liked were English and literature and suggested that he switch to majoring in education in his senior year. He finally told his mother what he had been advised to do, and after swallowing her disappointment, she agreed. He took six courses, two over the normal amount, received all A's and B's and made the Dean's List on graduation.

Qualified to teach at the high school level in 1935, he found himself in a quandary to find a job in the heart of the Depression. He could have a teaching job for $25 a week, but first he needed a year's experience and he could have that without pay. A bank offered a job, but it paid only $10 a week. He could hardly help his family or support himself on that bare stipend. But a florist who needed an assistant carefully studied the serious twenty-one-year-old young man and gave him a job for $15.

He worked there only briefly. An application he had made in his senior year resulted in an offer three months after graduation to become a trainee at the McCrory variety chain. Frank became a stockman in a Bristol, Connecticut, store at $18 a week, a sum he later described as "princely at that time." The town was 120 miles from home, and he was lonely away from the family. But the constant fare of working nights occupied him. That first year, he had one night off in four months, thinking nothing much about it. Retailing, after all, he had been carefully instructed, was a service business.

The next five years were filled with sundry adventures and assignments, all seemingly leading to nowhere. He tried to cast off a growing feeling that he was drifting. Coming from a disciplined but narrowly confined background, he could only react to late nights, lonely railroad flats, and repetitive assignments by withdrawing into himself and hoping that somehow it would all help him in the long run.

First there was the odd manager he worked for in Bristol. He was a "decent man but he talked more than he worked." Before leaving for supper, he would line up chores for Frank. By 7:30, when Frank would return from his own meal, the manager would be back, taking up the trainee's time and attention to describe in colorful terms his own career in retailing until 10 P.M. or so. "Oh, you haven't got your work done, have you?" he would then ask. "Well, then, I'll see you in the morning." And Frank would work until midnight and later. A fourteen-hour day was not unusual.

Then, months later when he lined up a job as a manager-trainee at a clock company, he spent his last long days at the McCrory store unhappily, realizing that he had become an important fixture in the store. Everyone would come to him with, "Hey, Frank, where is this? Where is that? Do we carry an awl? A set of chisels? Can you find it for me?" It was just before Christmas, the biggest season, and it would be chaos without him. He decided to stay on but never told the manager why.

Then, a year later, he was promoted to another store where he became a "combination man." This involved stock work and the opportunity to assist on the sales floor. Three months later, he was transferred to a Massachusetts store in the same role. There, he met Molly Hope, one of those people one unexpectedly meets and who helps to shape a life. She was about forty years old, a twenty-year veteran saleswoman in that one store and just about the homeliest woman he had ever met. Almost forty years later, when she was almost eighty, they still corresponded, and he vividly remembered the warmth of her personality and her lovely plainness. He remembered the way she studied him—a callow, serious young man who had a good education banging around in his head but who had made little use of it and who knew little about his work except that he had to work hard. She taught him everything with the proprietary fondness of a spinster aunt—why things are displayed as they are, why space is allocated as it is, how things are changed Friday night to prepare for Saturday, the big day, and so on. In a matter of months, the tall, angular woman with the pock-marked face, large nose, and marvellous smile imparted to him much of the wisdom she had accumulated in twenty years.

Summoned by the district manager to become a stockman again in yet another store—a large, new one—Frank willingly moved again. Each transfer took him further from home, and the wrench never left him. Although he would still be a rung or two under an assistant manager, he was given an assignment similar to the two assistants in the store. One such chore was to lay out a typical counter. He spent several long nights in his hotel room, plotting space from a stock book on several sheets of paper strung together to approximate the dimensions of his counter. This was his own method. Next morning in the store, he assembled the counter in a couple of hours, a fraction of the time it took the assistant managers. The day before the opening, the regional manager, McCrory's top field executive in the area, came to the store and was amazed to learn that the young stockman was working on his eighth counter while the assistants together had only done four.

Unusually impressed, the regional manager asked Frank to take on still another new store and to repeat the stunt. But the manager in the next store didn't get the proper message. He merely understood that the young man had been assigned to him, and he put Frank to checking freight. It was no happy undertaking for the young stockman, who thought he had done so well in his previous assignment. A week later, the regional head appeared and was stunned to find his man being wasted. He set things straight in a hurry.

Then, finally in 1940, after eight stores, Frank became an assistant manager. His ability not to surrender his zeal and to retain his loyalty through one mundane assignment after another made an impact on his superiors. The following year he became a store manager.

Asked much later why he hadn't lost interest, especially when the young are usually so impatient to advance, he replied, "Why should I? Each time they moved me, I got paid another dollar a week. Besides, I met my wife-to-be in the Westfield, Massachusetts, store when I was an assistant manager and she was a salesgirl. I call that progress."

After only nine months as a manager, he was inducted into the United States Army and served in Europe. He became a staff sergeant in charge of regimental transportation. But, during the Battle of the Bulge, he was captured by the Germans and was a prisoner-of-war for six months. By the time he was liberated by the British army, he had lost fifty-nine pounds and weighed only ninety-six pounds. He spent several months convalescing in a British hospital, returned to the States, and trained recruits in Texas until his discharge in 1946.

At that point of his life, Frank Patchen recalls with a trace of wryness, "I had changed, perhaps for the first time in my life. Somehow, after the struggle of finding myself in McCrory, becoming manager, getting married, becoming a father, serving in the army, and being captured, I had become a man-of-the-world. One never really changes I suppose, but when I returned to McCrory for a refresher course, and in January 1947 when they gave me a store in Dedham, Massachusetts, I felt as though I were capable of any challenge. I was armed by having weathered so much, you see. . . ."

But companies being what they are, things didn't really change, he adds. In 1949, after managing a second store, he was promoted to district manager and then, in the inbred manner of variety-chain appointments, he was moved from line to staff and was made buyer of notions—thread, shoelaces, sewing equipment, and the like. It was a boring, unchallenging job, and so he went back to school at night. Eventually, in 1956, he received a master's degree in the science of retailing from New York University. During those seven years, he held various buyerships, including drugs and footwear. Summoned one morning by the head merchandise manager, he was told, "We don't want you to buy footwear anymore. We don't think you're doing a very good job. We want somebody else to do it. Come in on Monday, and we'll have a new job for you."

"Is it to be a handout?" he asked.

"No."

"All right, I'll take it."

He became notions buyer again and began to think seriously of leaving the company. "Perhaps it wasn't a serious consideration," he says, trying to recall his true feelings, "but I was getting that old feeling that I wasn't going anywhere again. The company was going through its various administrations, trying many things which were mostly not working out, and I and many others were the butt of it."

And then suddenly he was promoted to associate merchandise manager and then quickly again to supervising buyer. It was difficult to know where he stood. "Where does anyone stand," he asks, "when the firm you work for is floundering?"

It was about that time that he was told that a representative of the parent company wanted to see him. He came into a cubicle next to the office of the variety-chain president and found a stolid, bald man sitting at the desk with no nameplate before him. "I'm Neaman," the man said. "You're Frank Patchen? Come in, come in. Let's talk a little."

Neaman, then still trying to function unofficially to correct top management mistakes and misjudgments without upsetting the division president, had gotten hold of a letter that Frank Patchen had written as a supervising buyer to all the store managers. Waving Frank to a chair, Neaman said, "You are offering all 1,100 stores the opportunity to buy a quantity of Kleenex and Kotex?"

"Yes, sir."

"But not all the stores are the same size?"

"No."

"Do you think the store manager of the smallest stores will use the same judgment in ordering this merchandise as the big ones? Do you think there is a possibility that the small store manager will order things he doesn't need and overstock himself?"

"Yes," Frank said. "I think there is a possibility of that."

"So would you then consider sending a follow-up letter to the smallest stores withdrawing the offer?"

Frank regarded Neaman thoughtfully, thinking that he liked the man's directness and pragmatism. He wasn't quite sure of the notch in the line of authority that Neaman occupied, but he recognized logic when he heard it. "Looking at it from that point of view," he observed, slowly, "I would not make this offer to 250 small stores."

Neaman beamed. "I appreciate your flexible thinking, Mr. Patchen," he told him. "I hope that you and I will see more of each other."

As he left, Frank remained thoughtful. It was his first experience with the concept that everything bought should not be exposed to all managers. Central buying with total distribution had been a McCrory tradition for many years. From then on, in an instinct combining both an awareness of impending change of authority and his recognition of common sense, Frank structured all his buying on the basis of the size, nature, and the performance record of the bottom quartile of the McCrory stores. With gratification, he saw the method beginning to work as the markdown and return rates of goods he handled inched downward.

Six months after his meeting with Neaman, Frank was gratified to learn that the short man with the guttural voice and the pouting lip had been appointed acting division president. Somehow, he thought, it seemed right, and he felt hope stirring in him that many things which had appeared aimless and frustrating in his more than a dozen years with the company would change. Within weeks, Neaman was creating new titles, and Frank Patchen was tagged with one. He was called "head merchandiser," a job category distinct from "head merchandise manager" and "merchandise controller." The lines among them were blurred. Patchen did not fully understand where his authority and those of the others began or ended, but he had faith in Neaman's thinking process. But even before this was clarified, Neaman had still another new assignment for him.

"I want you to go down and stay at the York, Pennsylvania, distribution center," he told Frank, "and see why they are having all kinds of problems in the warehouse. There are trucks full of goods that they can't get unloaded because they are not allotting the right space for everything."

"You ought to get a warehouse man to go down there."

"You're my warehouse man."

"So after ten years, I'm a stockman again?"

Neaman laughed. "You're in training."

"For what, Mr. Neaman?"

"Who knows?"

Patchen put his house in Connecticut on the market and moved to a motel near York. He needed a house in the area for his wife and two children. While he didn't ask for Neaman's help, the chairman assigned a man in the York center to help find some likely homes so that Frank could concentrate on his assignment. But he found that Neaman did not tell the chief of the McCrory warehouse that he was being replaced. Only that an emissary of his was making "some studies." The chairman told Frank that "this fellow is doing his best, but he is failing and I need time to find something else for him to do. I want you to make that time. You know by now that I do not like to fire anybody, especially one who tries."

Instructed to get the job done without stirring up resentment, Frank managed to do so, mostly by talking to other executives and making suggestions, much in the Neaman manner, at least in its superficial aspects. What he couldn't accomplish, he did by sending detailed letters to Neaman who pushed the right buttons in New York. Yet, he found himself characteristically putting in long hours and much effort. Months after he arrived, he made a decision that later proved to be strategic. Obedient and loyal to Neaman, he had his own mind, too. "Mr. Neaman," he said, "I think I have done just about all that is necessary to get things straightened out. In a month from now, you will find that the inventory levels have come down according to our plan, the space allotments here will be proper, and incoming truck shipments will be handled properly."

"Yes" Neaman commented cryptically. "I'm glad to hear you think so. I have gotten complaints that things are not going as smoothly as you say."

"I'll stand on it, Mr. Neaman. In fact, I have a month's vacation starting tomorrow."

About ninety seconds of silence crackled over the phone line. "All right, Frank," Neaman said in a monotone. "Go on your vacation. But please leave your destination with my secretary."

At the end of the third week in Florida, Patchen received a one-word telegram from Neaman. "Congratulations." With trembling hands, he folded the paper and slowly crammed it into a pocket. He knew he had scored in a major way with Neaman.

When he returned to York, he did not feel well. The company nurse took his temperature. It was almost 103 degrees. He drove back to Connecticut where he still lived and entered a local hospital. His illness was diagnosed as a virus infection and in a few days he was out again. But ten days later, he was back in the hospital again with a much more serious infection. It was diagnosed as lymphatic disease.

The doctors were troubled by the presence of lymphocytes in his blood and speculated that he might have a fatal form of lymphatic cancer. He was quickly operated on for the removal of his spleen, which was many times the normal size. But the doctors learned that he didn't have cancer and could be cured. He stayed in the hospital for another two months. Neaman sent him flowers, books, and a letter informing him that he had a new assignment waiting for him. He was to be McCrory's research director.

Those long months in the hospital and later at home were a period in Patchen's life in which he could meditate on all that had happened to him, especially on the great influence the company's chairman had had on him. He didn't really believe that Neaman was holding an "honest-to-goodness" job for him. It was not in the mold of big companies to do such things. Though he had advanced in the McCrory concern, it had been a fitful thing, and it was only after Neaman's appearance that he had really moved up. Now, he was convinced that there was an even chance that the research job was simply a way of gracefully putting him on a shelf.

Lolling about his home, reading, relaxing, Frank decided that there was no way to find out if Neaman was serious until he returned. The dynamic chairman was a hard one to figure, capable of unexpected acts. Patchen recalled two of them as he convalesced. One night in 1965 at about 8:30, Frank had put his hat and coat on and passed Neaman's office on his way out. The chairman had been seated at his desk, studying some computer print-outs and looked up at him with a smile. "Why are you leaving so early?" he asked.

"Well, it's the only way I know of, Mr. Neaman, to see my wife and children for a little while. Sometimes, I forget I have them."

"Yes, my friend. That sounds like a good idea."

A week later, when Frank arrived at his office early in the morning, he had found something new on his desk. It was a large, elaborately framed photo of his wife and children. Attached to it was a note. "Maybe this will help you remember while you work. Sam Neaman."

The other incident occurred some months later when they were working together in Neaman's office one evening. After a prolonged discussion, Neaman leaned back in his chair with a sigh. Fixing Patchen with a curious gaze, he asked, "Frank, what do you want for your future?"

"I think I would like to be president of the company when you move up."

"You would?"

"Yes, sir."

When Frank returned to York, he found a folder-full of assignments from the chairman, waiting for him to perform as a research director. But Neaman did not accept Patchen's findings easily. He questioned them in the light of the methods he used, and Frank would either defend them or restudy his techniques and findings. Yet, it was obvious to him, as it must have been to Neaman, that they worked particularly well together, probably because they attacked problems in a similar way. If Neaman thought that Patchen had benefited from absorbing his work-ethic and philosophy, he never said so. But Frank knew he had changed and that he bore the Neaman imprint.

In June 1967, Frank's phone rang. It was Neaman. Without a greeting or other preliminary, Neaman asked, "Are you well enough, Frank, to be president?"

"Yes."

"Good. Because I have already announced it in New York."

Patchen found that being the division's president, supervising

1,500 people in the variety chain's home office in York and some 20,000 in the field, wasn't really so much different from being research director under Neaman, except that he now had the authority to hire and fire. He still involved himself in both short- and long-term projects. His role was a thinking one of grappling with problems presented and solutions sought through a Neaman-approved thought process. And he still spent hours on the phone with the chairman on questions posed in New York. At times, he was convinced that Neaman was a sort of Talmudist, presenting an accepted thesis only to strip it to its fibers and rend it of its meaning, and then returning reinvigorated but loyal to its precepts.

So, in a major way, he himself became a Neaman minus the final authority, minus the burden of taking a major stand that could prove a backlash. It wasn't an easy role, as he surmised others around him assumed it was. There was no point in talking or dealing with Neaman unless one was the complete master of what he was doing, because Neaman never let anyone get off the hook. And so he taught himself and he taught others to school themselves in a manner that Neaman respected. He bore the chairman's pennant. And it suited him well.

"Do you sometimes feel that working under such a tight relationship might be robbing you of your initiative?" After almost five years as division president, Patchen doesn't blink under the thrust of the question.

Austere but methodical, he slowly shakes his head. "No, not at all," he replies. "This is a team effort aimed at bringing out the best in people, from the president down to a truckman. I'm acclimated to it because I was trained as a teacher, and that's really my main role today. In our business, there are so many more questions than answers that groups of people making decisions together represent a forum for discussion not unlike a classroom. One man is simply not capable of seeing all the different points of view and making the right decision by himself."

"Doesn't that gum up the decision-making process?"

"Possibly. But it's more important to make the right one, because if you don't examine your practices of the past, you are, to paraphrase Santayana, doomed to repeat the mistakes of the past. Let me give you an example. Mr. Neaman has taught all of us that most retailers are bad businessmen and that their judgments quite often make for bad business. Let's take a major expense item—remodeling of stores. They decide to remodel for any of one or more reasons but least of all for what it will do for sales. Most retail chains spend money on stores that could not possibly be amortized—recovered—within the existing terms of the lease. Improvements that would take more than five years to be paid off are often being made in stores where the lease is less than five years. Is there a bottom-line relationship to the remodeling? There should be, but most of the time it is overlooked."

"But don't you sometimes have to spend money other than what would be sales productive?"

"Of course, but that's a different kind of decision. It should be made from the total realization that you're not going to get a recovery but are doing it for other reasons. My point is that in the past we made no attempt to separate the two, and most other retailers are still not doing it."

"A personal note, Mr. Patchen. Looking back on your career of about thirty years with McCrory, with only the last eight under Neaman, do you feel fulfilled, totally self-productive? Do you feel at this juncture, at the age of sixty with your present situation, that it was all worth it?"

Frank smiles, more than a bit self-consciously. "I do," he says. "I feel that everything I have ever done prepared me for the role I perform today. Some people may tell you that I'm just a carbon-copy of Mr. Neaman. But no matter. I subscribe to all he does, and I am not dismayed by anyone who casts aspersions at me. Absolutely not."

His smile becomes fixed, a symbol of patience and understanding over the interviewer's groping questions. In the quiet of a Saturday morning on the town's outskirts, with a warm May sunlight filtering in through the half-drawn blinds of his office, Patchen is a study in relaxed awareness. The medium-sized gray-haired man—with his gray slacks, knitted blue shirt, and canvas shoes—may truly be Neaman's average man. The only atypical notes are offered by the austerity of his thin, pale face and the precise way he pronounces the "s" and the "t." There is in him clearly the superiority consciousness and the thoughtful pause of the pedagogue. His smile widens under the scrutiny.

"I can sense your doubt, or at least your skepticism," he observes. "That's your earmark, perhaps. But mine is to teach our people to think without emotion and to work together toward a common goal. I know that people call me a follower, not a leader, and they say I'm a puppet on a string. Mr. Neaman and I are a team—a team within a team. And the same teamwork permeates the innards of our organization. I enjoy my work, and in the process I'm happy to carry Mr. Neaman's pennant. Nonetheless, I am convinced that I am still myself, Frank Patchen."

Alter-Ego

Like rain pattering on an upturned metal drum, self-accusations and doubts pecked away at Harold Hughes. In those early months in New York when it seemed as if Sam Neaman didn't quite know what to do with him, Hughes used to try to avoid meeting the others in the hallway, in the men's room, even in the cafeteria. But he could scarcely avoid himself or the nagging questions of who he was, what he was, and where he was going. Insecurity added to disappointment sapped his emotions.

He could only conclude that he was a charity case. Having been demoted from district manager to store manager by Nelson, Hughes was acutely aware from the beginning that Neaman's impulsive offer in a Long Island shopping center for him to be his administrative assistant was an act of kindness to someone in distress. How could he then feel pride in his new job? The short space between the two extremes of the situation gave him no room for adjustment.

One day, for example, he is the manager of Store No. 127 on Long Island, an unhappy, disappointed man suffering the trauma of demotion. The next day, by a stroke of happenstance, he is the administrative assistant of the new president, Sam Neaman.

For many weeks, he searched Neaman's brown eyes for signs of condescension, of disgust, of reproach toward him. But the chairman behaved with dispatch and realism. "Please look into this matter," or, "Harold, I have to question Steve Jackel's report —double-check me, please," or "Inform the management board we will meet tonight—no absentees, please." Polite and matter-of-fact, Neaman's manner could not have been better therapy. Hughes learned that the best way to get rid of a bad mood was to throw himself into work. Neaman gave him no alternative, involving him in multiple projects at the same time. Neither did he leave his moody assistant with any opportunity to slough off, rejecting what he accurately appraised as less than the best that Hughes had in him. However, since he observed that Neaman treated everyone else the same way, Hughes had no feeling of discrimination.

Nonetheless, the pin-pricks of doubt persisted. Finally, in late 1964, or roughly six months after he had been given a small office next to Neaman's large one, his doubts began to dissolve and soon vanished.

The main reason was unexpected. It was not that Hughes, never really to change from the sagging, worried figure he had become years ago, peered into Neaman's soul and finally discovered no revulsion there against him. Nor was it that he found that something had changed in relation to the charitable nature of the opportunity handed to him. Instead, as he studied Neaman, it was the chairman's own role in their relationship that quite suddenly turned everything around. Neaman needed him. It was that simple. At least Harold Hughes became convinced of it. Obviously on the way up to even greater things, Neaman, as chief executive of the variety-store division, had his own insecurities and needed someone—admittedly, someone inoffensive and hardly likely to use any visible weakness against him—to help him over his occasional fumbles and more basic inadequacies. Not that Neaman ever said anything like that. But, as he increasingly used Hughes' ear and common sense to pretest a planned speech or new method, the assistant noticed with a pounding heart that the chairman would pause and carefully observe Hughes. After a while, Neaman would ask, impatiently, "Well, Harold, talk to me. Let me hear your opinion, please." The question at hand was often language. Although he spoke English well, Neaman would occasionally slip into the sing-song expressions or hardly translatable idioms of Yiddish in attempting to express a difficult point. Or it was a question of logic, as, for example, the progression of criteria he should observe in making demands on a particular individual. Somehow assuming that Hughes knew everyone in McCrory because of his twenty years (minus five in the War), Neaman relied on his assistant's opinions of people. Or the issue was the matter of the timing of a new method or system. Hughes didn't smile much, at least in those days when he was recovering from a deep feeling of personal inadequacy, and this appealed to Neaman. He liked a taciturn imperturbable, first-night audience—a screen through which he could strain both oral and psychological presentations before unloosing them on their intended objects.

And so, in less than a year Hughes became comfortable with, if not valuable to, Sam Neaman. Frank Patchen's relationship with Neaman was the obvious one of the number-two in the division bearing the pennant for the number-one. Patchen carried the Neaman style and philosophy to the staff and did it well. But Harold Hughes' relationship to the chairman was more personally essential to Neaman. If Patchen proved to be the equal of Neaman in a discusson of logic and technique but rarely contradicted him, Hughes did not have to be the equal of the chairman nor did he have to contradict him. He became Neaman's second self, a man trusted beyond the relationship of friend or co-worker. Yet, Hughes, being and knowing what he was, never quite lost his intense awareness of the chairman's demanding nature. He developed into a believer, a thoroughly self-effacing individual whose pulse could race with alarm if he felt he were not living up to his superior's need of him.

It was interesting to an observer visiting Hughes in his office in the York, Pennsylvania, division headquarters that, besides the big frame picture of Sam Neaman with the credo, there was another object on the wall above his head. It was one of those large, framed mottos in Old English type. It read:

> "There's No Limit to What
> a Man Can Do as Long as
> He Doesn't Mind Who
> Takes the Credit."

Hughes, there is good reason to believe, wasn't very much different in temperament at five or fifteen years old from what he was at almost sixty. Born in Cuba in 1914 to an American couple, he was a quiet, introverted child who seemed to have difficulty playing with the Cuban children. He had an early facility for language, but something in him quailed at their boisterous, expressive behavior. When he was eight, his father, a mechanical engineer who had worked for a Cuban construction firm, obtained a post in New Jersey and the Hugheses moved to a small house in Perth Amboy. Yet, while he grew up in the same community from his public school through his high school years, he remained shy and hesitant when it came to involving himself with other young people. Recalling it many years later, he observed with a twisted smile, "In Orientes, I was an American. But in Perth Amboy, I was a kind of Cubano."

Taking their example from their father, he and an older brother decided to become engineers. His brother managed to get his engineering degree. But Harold, in his high school senior year, took college geometry and found it incomprehensible. In 1936, he graduated from the University of Missouri with a bachelor's degree in journalism, having majored in advertising. His attempt to find a career in advertising in that Depression year was fruitless. Someone suggested that he get into it through the backdoor by working in the advertising department of a retail store. He was offered a trainee's assignment by the McCrory chain at $18 a week, went through a program of successive advancement, and 3½ years later became a store manager in Great Bank, Massachusetts.

Inducted into the army in 1941, he obtained a commission as a second lieutenant on the basis of his R.O.T.C. training in college. In the infantry, he was assigned as a training officer stateside and remained there. Discharged as a major, he returned to McCrory, and on the strength of his military occupation, was made training director. Five years later, he was promoted to district manager in Long Island. After two years of what he candidly admitted later was "only moderate success" as a district manager, he indirectly became a victim of Neaman's early success.

Fired by the nonretailer's achievements in Indianapolis, Meshulam Riklis gave the word that an entire district set up a game plan to establish an "Indianapolis" model within a 30-mile radius of New York. It was decided, however, that the presence of a career variety-store man as district manager would inhibit the brain-storming effort. Would he, Harold Hughes, accept a transfer to either the Pennsylvania or the Arizona districts, either of which would be available to him? He was reluctant to move his family, his wife, and two children, and kept delaying his answer. Finally, disgusted with him, Nelson, then McCrory president, demoted him to the managership of tiny Store No. 127.

The purely coincidental nature of his meeting Sam Neaman outside one of the Long Island stores, both being attracted by the temporary opening of the store's restaurant on a Sunday, was one of those fateful events that sometimes penetrate the lives of small men but more often those who live on a more dramatic scale. Many times afterward, Harold Hughes recoiled when he remembered the sad, forlorn spectacle he had presented to Neaman when he had first refused to enter the store with him. What sort of excuse was "Since I was demoted, I haven't been myself"? What worse introduction could anyone have arranged to a man destined to control his future? The trouble with being down, Hughes told himself, is that "you start thinking of yourself as a down, not an up, guy and you act that way."

Those early months with Neaman were unpredictable if thoroughly insecure. The first week, Neaman told him, "Harold, let us arrange this between us. I will teach you management, and you will keep me from getting into trouble with the retail. Then, when we both get our feet on the ground, we will think of a new arrangement."

Once he rid himself of his doubt and cynicism about their relationship, Hughes began to thrive under the benevolent lash and persistent demands of Neaman. Whether or not there was a certain element of masochism in the administrative assistant's changed attitude was not very relevant, Hughes insisted to himself, because he felt himself charged with more internal excitement, with more of an intellectual and professional challenge, than he had felt in all his thirty years with the company. "Mr. Neaman . . . has a way of making my life, as a working life, a very, very interesting experience," he explained later.

Hughes found that working with Neaman was stimulating

because he would never know what project or activity would be undertaken the next day. But, over the months and years, he found that it didn't matter, that the irritation of being cast into a totally different project before others were completed was offset by the growing closeness between them. "I started seeing," he said, "that we were becoming very much alike. Mr. Neaman called me his 'alter-ego.' But, sometimes, I thought it was sort of the other way around. He was me, with more get-up and dynamism, and of course, a much better brain. Today, I can generally anticipate what he is going to want or how he is going to approach something. You see, before he decided to take over the running of the Klein's stores, I used to sit next door to him. He would call me in whenever he had a meeting with someone so I could listen in and later help him analyze it. The exception was when there was something confidential, or sometimes when it was very confidential he would talk in Israeli, or Hebrew I guess it was, so I wouldn't understand. But, mostly, when the fellow would leave, Mr. Neaman would discuss with me the conversation and what we thought the man was thinking and what Mr. Neaman's reaction was, and we had a lot of good interchanges. So, maybe because we had hundreds, probably thousands of those conversations, I got to thinking like him. And after working with him for so long, I developed many of his characteristics."

More human than most people—at least this was what Hughes considered himself because of "my weaknesses and my failures"—he was pleased and chastened to find how "human a person" Sam Neaman was. Perhaps because the chairman allowed him more time than he did anyone else, certainly even more than his own wife, Cecelia Neaman, Hughes saw things that others could not.

He noticed, for example, that whenever Neaman sat too long he became restless, or if he were preparing to make a prolonged dissertation, he would get up and walk back and forth. His pacing became furious, like a frustrated tiger, even though he would only cover a small area. It was also very noticeable when he was in a situation where creative thinking was required. He would get up before a group in his office and pace around his desk, speaking to them face front or with his back turned. At such times, he did not appear to care about their reactions.

During those meetings, ideas would pop from him not singly but in clusters. He would start with a logical premise and then build on it, rarely growing illogical. Knowing his boss, Hughes always carried a notebook, and early on in their relationship he took a crash night course in Pittman shorthand so that he would miss nothing. Neaman's habit the next morning would be to ask Hughes if he would repeat for him all the chairman had suggested at yesterday's meeting. He would obviously enjoy hearing it repeated. If that were really a secretary's job, Harold didn't mind. He knew Neaman relied upon him. And when someone relied on you, especially someone like Neaman, wasn't that enough?

Demanding as he was, Neaman was often critical of people. But he had developed his own method of criticism, which he considered most effective. He had found that when he roasted someone directly, the man usually appeared to tune him out in the immediate interest of building up a response. So Neaman decided to bring in two people, the man to be criticized and another man who was to be the pseudotransgressor. For this role, Hughes himself was most often utilized. The ploy was used with various degrees of subtlety. "You are not thinking clearly, Harold," Neaman would say, glaring at Hughes and occasionally at the real culprit. Or, "Lately, your reports are sloppy." Or, "If you didn't like sitting on your backside so much, Harold, you would get out in the field and see what's happening on the battle line." The technique was that Harold would not reply but that sooner or later the real culprit, either voluntarily or beginning to sense what was really going on, would say, "Sam, Harold isn't the only guy who's guilty. I'm a culprit, too, I guess. It's so easy to get into bad habits. I've got to shake that one off." Of course, it didn't always work. But the percentage was surprisingly good.

As things improved in the division, Neaman put together a management committee, appointing some of its members as vice-presidents. To give Harold Hughes some degree of stature, he shifted him from administrative assistant to executive assistant,

and true to his promise, came up with a "new arrangement.'
Giving birth to new ideas and new projects in clusters, Neaman
turned them over to Hughes, who would develop them to a
point where his superior felt they were sufficiently advanced to
turn over to an operating executive. He also gave Harold the responsibility of integrating outsiders into the company. It wasn't
an easy assignment, especially if they came in from some form
of the retail business other than variety-store retailing.

The variety business, it appeared, was different in many ways.
Neaman often said that variety-store people were the "Barry
Goldwaters of the retail industry." He explained that they, like
the senior Republican senator from Arizona, were very conservative, adapted very slowly because they hated change, and
tended to mistrust outsiders. Neaman himself had some difficulties because of it, or at least, he found many of his people slow
to change. From the first, he worked hard, traveling all day
Saturdays in his chauffeur-driven Cadillac from store to store
and spending all day Sundays on his private communications
system in his Manhattan apartment talking to his executives all
over the country. To watch Neaman—only Harold Hughes was
permitted to do so—at his complex set of electronic equipment
(the Citizen's Band system that fed directly into Frank Patchen's
office and home also had terminals plugged into the York, Pennsylvania, switchboard, into the five dispersed regional offices, and
into selected district offices) was to see a zealot dedicated to constant communications. Neaman was convinced that an ongoing
dialogue would ultimately sweep aside confusion and prejudice
and that irritants caused by it were not important because variety-
store people were generally intractable, anyway.

Because, as Hughes pointed out, his predecessors were "very
formal," Neaman would eschew their standard uniforms of gray
or blue suits with a printed tie and white shirt and visit the
stores Saturdays in a sport shirt or a sports jacket. He would
tell the manager, "Call me Sam," and address him on a first-
name basis. Privately, he studied their names and faces from a
book with photographs carefully prepared and kept current by
his executive assistant so that he knew many of the store managers.

Neaman remained very sensitive about his Jewishness, particularly because not only McCrory but all large variety-chains were almost totally Gentile in content. Asked about this, Hughes agreed, adding, "Mr. Neaman is very sensitive, but then he is sensitive to anyone who may be prejudiced toward minorities. Frankly, he doesn't generally like the Wasp-type person. He has the impression that because they're the majority they look down on everyone else." But, Hughes emphasized, there had never been any religious or ethnic problems between them, though Hughes was an Irish Catholic. "One day, I told Mr. Neaman that there was nothing much different between an Irish-man and a Jew except that we believed in a different God," Hughes said. "But our philosophy otherwise was very much alike." The chairman smiled and told him, "I'll tell you what, Harold, I'll take care of you on earth if you will take care of me in heaven."

When he came into McCrory in the odd position of being a Jewish president of thousands of Gentiles or so, Neaman also decided it must be time to increase the proportion of other mi-norities as well. Not long afterward, he called in the division personnel manager and "tested the water," so to speak, as Hughes sat by. The response on blacks was negligible. When the man left, Neaman told his assistant. "He'll still be our personnel man, but, Harold, that man has to come up to the times. He doesn't know that the day is here when all minorities have to be accepted. He doesn't know it, but he's prejudiced. I want you to work on him." Shortly afterward, Neaman named a black man to a new role as civil affairs specialist, a move that sent ripples throughout the organization. Catholics, Jews, Negroes, who would be next?

Studying Neaman constantly, Hughes became more and more impressed with the man's personnel policies. He never dis-charged anyone, even if given substantial reason, unless the provocation left him no room to maneuver. Difficult people were transferred to assignments that would make them more productive or would convince them that there really was no place for them in the organization. But there was one excep-tion, according to Hughes. "One thing he will never accept from anyone," the executive assistant said, "is when they tell him the reason they did not blow the whistle on someone stealing or perpetrating some sort of disaster on the company was because they were afraid of the consequences. One case that stands out especially in my mind was a vice-president whom Mr. Neaman called on the carpet because he was instrumental in passing on a decision by the previous management in which they pissed away $5 million for not very valid reasons. This vice-president said he knew it was wrong but decided he had to go along because he had no other alternative. He would have been fired. Mr. Neaman said that he had had an alternative—and an obligation to Mr. Meshulam Riklis (the head of the parent company), to the stockholders, and to the other employes. So Mr. Neaman promptly fired him."

As he intensified his search for suitable people, Neaman once told Hughes, "Look, you know we don't have enough talent around here, so see what you can do to bring new people into the company." The assistant contacted employment agencies and began interviewing applicants from discount houses and traditional department stores. But, as he put it later, "What they really wanted was to jack up their salaries $10,000 to $20,000, even $30,000 a year to come with us. Or they wanted a five-year contract. The others who came to us were the job-jumpers, or the losers, or the nonproducers." Some were hired, but the vast majority were turned away. In the main, Neaman soon realized that the decision was a simple one. Make-do. He told Hughes, "Well, we have a lot of round pegs and square pegs around here, so let us rebuild our organization chart and take a lot of round pegs and put them into square holes and then put the squares into round holes and see what we get." The results proved quite successful, although there were more than a few failures. But Neaman's technique with the failures was to keep reassigning them. When an important job, even on a minor level, could not be filled adequately, he divided the responsibilities into two or three parts, assigning men to each until one surfaced as the most productive one, whereupon he was given the title.

All this moving around helped to bolster morale because it meant that everyone had a chance, somehow, to make good, even though the criteria for performance were stiff and growing stiffer. Asked if this technique weren't reducing everyone to a state in which they thought the company would take care of them regardless of their failures, Hughes denied it. "Just the reverse as it worked out," he said. "The proof of the principle is that Mr. Neaman built his company that way. Some of our people are new, but most have always been here. It works on the effectiveness of a lot of normal people, of a management of equals, and it is not a lot of bullshit. It's a lot more dependable than taking chances on bringing in many outsiders on their own terms or hiring a few geniuses. Mr. Neaman has always felt that geniuses are great in art and in certain situations, but when it comes to business, they're risky. And I must tell you that I agree with him."

In 1965, Neaman created a management board for the division. In 1966, he also created an executive committee, a super-management board which met twice a year and included executives from the home office and the field. In 1967, when he moved the home office of the variety division to the York, Pennsylvania, distribution center, he appointed Harold Hughes administrative vice-president of the division and Frank Patchen its president. With the troublesome Klein's stores refusing to show the same degree of malleability as the variety stores, Neaman had no qualms about taking the titles of chairman and chief executive officer of both divisions, operating Klein's with his right hand and McCrory variety with his left.

For the first time, Hughes was physically separated from him, but that was only a one-dimensional change in a relationship that had come to assume many dimensions. They continued to be on the phone with each other constantly, and there were many visits to one another either in New York or in York.

Over the years, it became evident that Hughes had changed. Visitors and reporters who met him in the early days of his assignment with Neaman were unimpressed with him, tending to ridicule him for being Neaman's new "male secretary." His own drooping, obsequious manner helped to support that appraisal, and it took no gifted observer to conclude that Hughes wasn't getting over his demotion after so many years. But, a year or two later, he appeared absorbed by his work yet self-contained and more confident. He put on a little weight, and occasionally, as one greeted him, he would break into a warm smile. His open admiration for Sam Neaman might have been embarrassing to a stranger once, but it appeared to become more submerged the longer he worked with the chairman. It had become deeper and wider, if less open.

In his office in York in the mid-1970s, Hughes was a man at ease and at home. "For almost two years," he observed with that easy, new smile flashing, "I sat in New York almost as though at the feet of Socrates. I became a disciple, although only a shadow of the original. But he allowed me to start my life over again. Let's forget emotions, which always get in the way of things anyway, but let's talk about age. In your mid-fifties, you tend to get a bit stale, but now I have a very broad existence. From 1936 till 1964, I was strictly a variety-store manager or district manager. But since then, I have moved a whole company down here, I have become involved in engineering and construction, and I have become a personnel man. I have created and have under me an entire audio and video studio which produces tapes and films for training. I have created an entire security division, and I even do occasional research projects for the Klein's chain. You see—I'm not alone. If you look around here and in many of the offices in New York, you'll find numerous examples that this theory of the effectiveness of the multitude does work. I reiterate to you that it is not a lot of bullshit."

The telephone rang and his secretary broke in to say, "New York's calling." He shrugged happily, and displaying the new smile, took the call. He even winked at the departing visitor, as if to say, "Guess who?"

The Achiever

Not all who rose to the heights in the country's fourth-largest variety-store chain were either retreads or pseudolosers doomed to anonymity until tapped by Neaman's magic wand. Some were powerful performers who could have had bigger jobs in competing companies but remained loyal and motivated under shifting mangements at McCrory. They had reserves of energy and personal depth which the table of organization had yet failed to tap, and perhaps never would have.

Ed Luedtke was one of these. Burly and muscular despite his average height, he had a big, square, ruddy face and several unusual habits, all testifying to a decisive, deliberate temperament.

Before rendering what he considered an important or striking point, he would flash his eyes or blink them several times and stare hard across his desk. If about to make a decision, he would flick the fingernail of his thumb with a rasping sound against his index finger or forefinger. And, sitting in his office only twice removed from that of Frank Patchen, the division's president, he was one of the few executives who wore a short-sleeved shirt and no jacket, despite the low temperature of the constantly humming air-conditioner which was deliberately set at that level to accommodate the nearby computer and EDP system.

When he was asked, "Aren't you cold?" Ed grinned and answered by loosening his collar.

He was unquestionably the most outwardly dominant of the executives in the McCrory variety division. He had little subtlety about him, but few appeared to find it lacking in view of the excellent rapport he was able to create with everyone around him. He was bluff, genial, loud, and totally open in his reactions to people. He was particularly successful with the stores' rank-and-file and with the store managers. His greetings and comments were so direct and pragmatic that their reactions were natural and friendly. Those who thought he was patronizing them saw in a brief glance the friendly sparkle and the sheer absence of guile and felt guilty about doubting him. So their immediate reaction was warm, even though he was a stranger, and it grew warmer every time they saw him.

His superiors recognized him for what he was but failed to sense what he could be. They seemed to miss the basic element of his makeup. He was an achiever who came from a family of achievers. On both sides, but especially on his mother's, there was a determination to reach as high as one could in a society where all seemed possible. They were the sort of Lutherans who looked upon their church's creed that they must work to ameliorate social conditions by including themselves, too, in that goal.

They also believed that people should in their essence sweep aside the materialistic trappings, which are only selfish, and seek to attain a role in which they could perform the greatest service to others.

Intertwined in this was their deep satisfaction with the country's democratic ideals. Ed's maternal grandfather had come to the United States at the turn of the century, seeking a better life removed from the military and class society that kept small-town life in many parts of Germany bare and wanting. He had instilled his ideals in his children. Ed's mother married a man, who, though he never reached beyond a career as a postal clerk in Kingston, New York, nonetheless believed in the self-purity of work and the obligation of people to seek constant self-improvement. The marriage was a happy, productive one, yielding four sons and two daughters.

The first in the family to reach a high level of attainment was Ed's uncle, an older brother of his mother, who received an appointment to West Point, became an All-American tackle, and had a brilliant military career. Before his death in 1926, he had satisfied his ambition of becoming a general and was buried with three stars on his tombstone. As Ed put it later, "He sort of started off the family. Mother always used him as the example of what the rest of us could aspire to."

An aunt, his mother's younger sister, became a soprano for the Metropolitan Opera, specializing in the exacting roles composed by Richard Wagner and Richard Strauss. She, too, was held out as an example to the children. "We had," said Ed, "some pretty tough examples to follow, and everyone tried hard. Mama was the pusher and my father backed her up 100 percent."

The sons had to excel in school or sports, preferably both, and spurred by the growing family tradition did quite well. All went to college. The daughters were not pushed as hard but were good students, gracious, and intelligent, although their education ceased when they graduated from high school. Both married soon afterward.

Ed, the third of the sons, was a high school athlete and received a scholarship to play basketball at Rider College in Trenton, New Jersey, where he became a four-letter man. At twenty, in 1944, he served for a year in the navy before returning to finish his last year at Rider. He became interested in Sears, Roebuck and Company, using that company's new rural store concept as the subject of his thesis at college. He felt at home in a store. As a member of the Luedtke family, he had worked in a local JCPenney store. The manager liked the Luedtkes; Ed's mother, sister, cousin, and one of his brothers had been employed there as Christmas or weekend extras. In high school, Ed sold dungarees and work clothes there on Saturdays. While at JCPenney and later in talking to the Sears' manager, who had helped him on his thesis, Ed learned that few college graduates were going into retailing. Most of the store managers had amassed long years of service but had only high school educations. The realization spurred him to apply to the McCrory stores after graduation. McCrory was growing at a faster rate than either Sears or Penney, but as a chain it was still much smaller than either. He reasoned that his advancement there might be greater than at the larger chains.

He became a management trainee in a store in Plainfield, New Jersey, where he trimmed windows, received freight, and occasionally waited on customers. But Ed was disappointed when he learned that the store manager, who realized that the youth would soon be transferred, refused to allow him to become involved in merchandising or buying. Ed immediately saw it as a deterrent to both his learning process and his advancement.

After six months and after having discussed it with his mother, who thoroughly supported his decision, Ed waited until the district manager came to make his biweekly visit to the Plainfield store and cornered him. "I can't learn anything more in this store," Ed complained. "The manager won't let me. If I don't get a transfer, I'm going over to Sears or Penney."

"Well, we don't want that, do we?" the district manager observed, with a smile. "Not after a six-month investment in you. You say you want to learn? Fine. I'll send you to Bill Wasserman, the roughest, toughest manager we've got—and the best we've got. You'll either make it with him or he'll get rid of you."

Bill Wasserman was a broth of a little man, perhaps a *kasha* was more like it. Tiny, squat, with juglike ears and a thin-lipped mouth that frequently spat both commands and insults, Wasserman operated one of McCrory's biggest variety stores. Located in a major western Pennsylvania city, the store was also one of the chain's most profitable even though it was next door to the area's largest department store. His aggressiveness and pugnaciousness had grown in the twenty years since he had come to the store and had carved its success out of the hide of the giant emporium next door. He had never been transferred, was already the oldest manager in point of resident service, and would remain there until he retired. He knew that the company could not afford to transfer him.

Ed came in one morning with his suitcase and introduced himself to Wasserman, who regarded him sourly. "Big and square, ain't you?" the diminutive manager asked. "Okay, I can use a good Dutchman around here. I guess I deserve a third assistant after all these years." He told Ed to find himself a room in a nearby boarding house but to leave his suitcase there and immediately return ready for work. "We'll be here late tonight," Bill said, searching his face for any objections. "We work late in this store every night, even when we close up, except Sundays when we're shut. I hope that fits in with your plans."

Work they did. Ed, born into a family with a strong work ethic, never put in as many hours in a day as he did in the next three months. But no one came in earlier or left later than Wasserman. Somewhere along the line, he had taken time out from his duties to find himself a wife and have a son, but as far as his co-workers were concerned, his family was nonvisible. In his first two years at the store, the tiny, bustling manager had no home other than the second-floor storeroom, where he kept a tiny cot, eating breakfast by himself at the sandwich counter before the store opened and the rest of his meals there after it opened. He still did the same, except that he now slept at home.

Wasserman believed that an important part of his obligations was to teach his assistants. A few weeks after Ed arrived, Bill saw that the new man was to be his best student. It was a constant on-the-job training. Wherever he was in the store, he would yell in his raucous voice for one or all the assistants when he found something he wanted to tell or teach them. If they were at the other end of the floor, or even on another level, they were supposed to respond quickly. Customers were treated to frantic yelps most of the day, and the spectacle of a yelling manager and scurrying assistants became one of the odd traits of the McCrory store. Once he came there, Ed was the one who hurried the most to the calls. The manager was pleased. "I like that damn Dutchman," he told everyone, even the other chagrined assistants.

Bill had some odd habits, his new protégé found. He was stingy in one way, lavish in others. He didn't raise the assistants' salaries but paid them liberally for overtime. He deliberately worked them harder than other managers did their assistants, but when it came to Christmas, he managed by pressure and even threats to the district manager to ensure that they received larger bonuses than assistants in other stores. Though he was one-dimensional on the job, insisting on complete attention to the store's needs and that there be no malingering or personal matters on anyone's mind, he was solicitous after hours on everyone's personal problems. He helped one assistant to make arrangements for his wife on the impending birth of their first child and spent hours in the hospital, sitting with the young man and filling him with coffee until he became a father. When Ed was attracted to a young, blond salesgirl in the store, Bill suddenly became a matchmaker, although he took pains to relate to each the failures of the other, and he hovered over the two of them to make sure that they would carry on their budding romance only outside of the store. When they were married in 1950 in a local Lutheran church, he was the only one who didn't even give them a token gift there. Then, he showed them a handsome, large apartment he found for them with a bedroom suite, which was to be his and his wife's gift to them.

His greatest influence on Ed was that he taught him many things about the business. Recognizing the young man's motivation, Bill revealed with startling insights many standard operating principles that he had learned in over twenty years in the store and in ten previous years at another retail chain. For example: That while one must stock as many as 200 different items in a department, it was only vital that prime attention be paid to the stock depth in the twenty or thirty items on which eighty percent of the sales were rung up. That there were three things that must be done to keep customers loyal: make sure that there is an adequate amount of inventory available on items advertised; take pains to ensure that size assortments were adequate because almost as many shoppers turned into walkouts because they couldn't find their sizes as those who couldn't find any merchandise to buy; and keep the store neat and clean at all times and especially watch the housekeeping of counters and racks, the floors, and the customer's washrooms. That despite the fact that the McCrory variety stores bought their goods centrally—that is, through buyers stationed in New York and in York—the local store manager had to remain highly vocal and selective in taking only what he was certain he could sell. Otherwise, he would be held accountable for goods he didn't want.

During his vacations, Ed decided to apply some of Wasserman's ideas to earn some extra income. With his wife, he rented space during the summer at the Allentown Fair where he sold hot dogs broiled on roller grills. The first year, he cleared $200 in eight days. The second year, Ed recalled Bill's conviction that customers often needed time to consider a purchase; and he decided it was worthwhile having two small counters, one at each end of an aisle, instead of one large one at its head. Ed rented another grill. His wife manned a smaller one at one of the first aisles, while Ed stationed his grill almost at the end of the last aisle. Together, they netted about $385 in the eight days.

After three years as Bill's assistant, Ed was recommended by the peppery little manager to take over a troubled store in Philadelphia. As he and his wife stood on the Reading Railroad station with Wasserman awaiting the train to Philadelphia, Ed stared down at the tight, working face and mouth of the veteran manager. Bill seemed to be impatient, evidently wanting to get back to the store. "Glad to get rid of me, Mr. Wasserman?" Ed asked. Bill shrugged. "What the hell, nothing ever stays the same," he said. "I'll miss you, Dutchman." Then he turned to Ed's wife. "You, too, Mrs. Dutchman."

Looking back years later, after the company had changed hands again and Sam Neaman had come into the picture, Ed realized that Bill Wasserman was one of the few really motivated executives in McCrory whom Neaman never recognized by elevating him to a higher post. It wasn't that the chairman didn't know of Bill's performance or of the tight, clean ship he ran. He seemed to visit Bill's store once every couple of months. But Bill remained the store's manager until he retired in 1970 at sixty-five. Ed concluded that Wasserman was probably one of the few people who in Neaman's view had realized his full potential, both for the company and himself.

From 1953 to 1960, Ed was a troubleshooting store manager. Wherever a store seemed moribund in the Atlantic states, management decided to give it one more breath of life by turning it over to Ed Luedtke for a year or less. His record was excellent. He turned around the Philadelphia, Chester, and Penns Grove stores before he was assigned in 1958 to the toughest assignment of all. This was an old, once highly successful store in downtown Washington on the fringe of the core area. Theft was high. Volume had fallen, and profits had turned into deficits. McCrory was about to close it until the regional manager said, "Let's give Ed a crack at it. He's got the touch."

It was his first store in an area rapidly turning black, as the ghetto inched closer and closer to the downtown shopping area. Yet, when he arrived, he was surprised that while blacks represented more than sixty percent of the customers, the percentage of black salespeople was less than twenty percent. Too many black shoppers were crossing the street to shop at Woolworth's, which had a higher percentage of black employes, and to the older department stores nearby, which seemed to be holding their own more than McCrory's despite the erosion in the area.

After three days, he summoned the personnel manager of his store, a white woman about forty years old, and told her he personally wanted to see all the applications for salespeople. When she asked why, he explained that he wanted to hire more black salespeople to bring up the store's ratio.

"The staff won't like it," Pearl Stone, the personnel manager said. "There have been a few incidents already, Mr. Luedtke. I seriously advise you not to do this right now."

He regarded her steadily and realized that she, and probably all the others there, weren't aware on what a skimpy lifeline the store hung. But there was no point in scaring her by telling her the truth at that point. "I know how you feel," he said, "but times are changing, and we've got to change with them. I want you to spend a few minutes today studying how our white salespeople treat our black customers and how the customers behave here. Then, you'll see why I'm doing this."

Within a week, he hired two black girls as salesclerks. Mrs. Stone walked around the store with a frozen face, grimly listening to the complaints she had anticipated. Some of the staff talked about confronting Ed.

A few days later, Mrs. Stone came in with a fur piece over an attractive suit, explaining to those who asked that her husband was taking her out to dinner directly after work. But at 5:30, when her husband arrived, she found the fur stole was gone from her locker. The Stones went directly to Ed's office. Her eyes blazing, the personnel manager accused him, "You see what I meant? Invite them in—and they steal you blind! It must be one of those two new girls."

After a while, he calmed the couple down, even suggesting that they have a night "out on the town at my expense." The husband refused. Ed finally got rid of them after promising to conduct a thorough search himself. When the store closed, he obtained a master key and opened over 100 lockers without finding the fur piece. He checked all the offices, the stockrooms, and the employes' washrooms. Finally, after several hours, in one of the toilets in the women's washroom, he found the sodden fur stole, stuffed down inside one of the water tanks. It was obvious to Ed what had happened. One of the unhappy white employes had taken the woman's stole, hoping to create an incident in which one of the two new black employes would be blamed. It was not a very neatly planned scheme, Ed thought, since the stole would have been discovered eventually anyway.

He took the stole home, dried it, and tried to smooth down the fur. The next morning, he returned it to Mrs. Stone and told her he had found it in the stockroom. "Evidently," he said, smiling at his lie, "somebody mistook it for a piece that should be in the inventory."

"But we don't sell furs," she said.

He shrugged. "I know. Look, Mrs. Stone, have it dry-cleaned and give me the bill." She seemed unconvinced but was happy to have it back. She never gave him the bill, however.

While there were no further incidents, there was a lingering problem of importance. The shoe department was one of the store's biggest, but it was losing money quickly. It didn't take him long to discern the problem. The white salespeople worked in the department only reluctantly. They disliked waiting on the black trade. Black families would come in with three or four children who needed shoes. But the white clerks complained that the children had dirty feet, that it was an unpleasant task, and so customers sat around in the shoe department vainly waiting for attention.

Certain that he could sell all the shoes in his stock if he could only get the right salespeople, he searched through the applications and had Mrs. Stone call in a young black woman who had had sales experience. When she came into his office, he studied her and noted that, like many of her kind, she had a hurt, surly look as though she didn't expect anything good to happen during the interview. He studied her application carefully as she sat before him. She stirred restlessly. Looking up, he asked, "Miss Fletcher, why did you leave your last job?"

"I couldn't make it with the department manager. She was a bigot."

"She didn't give you a bad reference," said Ed. "We called her. She said you had a lot of energy but you had a chip on your shoulder."

"I guess that's so. But so would you if you had so much trouble getting a job and then got yourself hired by a bigot. I've been walking the streets now for almost a month looking. What're you gonna tell me now? We'll call you?"

Ed smiled. "Don't try to second-guess me, miss. I can't even do that myself. Do you like to sell? Have you ever sold shoes?"

"The answer to the first is yes. No to the second."

"I've got a shoe department that's just waiting for the right saleslady."

"Try me."

Ed put her on. The woman was a whirlwind. He found out later that she was on her own with a young child, her husband having walked out on her. Within three months, she increased her initial weekly sales from about $500 to over $1,700 a week. She was brisk and yet understanding with the black families. She was also an example to the white salespeople in the department who found that they, too, had to hustle to avoid looking bad by comparison. At the end of the three months, the pace of the department had changed drastically. Ed ordered the entire stockroom of shoes be moved forward onto the sales floor so that the customers could be better serviced and the salesclerks could save time without incessantly running back and forth.

Ed remained manager of that store for 4½ years, during which it not only returned to profits but became one of the most profitable in the district and region. His bonus rose from $400 that first year to $8,000 in the fourth year. Since his bonus was based both on profit as well as rate of increase, his almost turned out to be so prohibitively high that someone in New York decided everyone but Ed would be better off if he were put back on the troubleshooting assignment. He was just too good.

In 1963, he became district manager in charge of the eastern Pennsylvania area. This made him Wasserman's boss. After congratulating him with "Goddamn, Dutchman, you did it— like I knew you would," he told Ed. "Boy, am I sorry I taught you all I know. Now how in the hell can I fool you?"

The next year, because he hadn't hesitated to register some unhappiness with unwise instructions from New York, Ed was given a smaller district. He smouldered under the tacit demotion, but it didn't make him shrug off his responsibilities in the new district. He now had a portion of Philadelphia and several of the city's near and farther suburbs. It was another challenge, but his future looked uncertain.

In 1965, when Neaman began traveling as division president, he came to see Ed. "I wish to see the stores and the managers," Neaman said. "Will you please show me around?"

The district manager was amazed at how quickly and accurately Neaman perceived the real nature of the stores and the men who ran them. "He knew within an hour or two which guy was trying to cover up and which wasn't," Ed recalled later. "He had a fine sensitivity to bullshit. When we got back to my office two days later, he sat there giving me a rundown on every store and every manager, and you know what, he hit them right down to a tee."

Neaman also told Ed something else. He had studied his record and had decided that Ed was ready for a series of new assignments—regional sales promotion manager, regional sales manager, and then regional manager. That would take him about five years, or into 1970, at which time, Neaman told him, "I think you will be ready for the ultimate assignment for you. In the meantime, you will have a chance to soak in responsibilities at a higher level."

"Mr. Neaman," said Ed, grinning as his heart pounded away, "What did I do right?"

Neaman arose, looking impatiently at his watch. His chauffeur and his car waited outside. He had another district to visit that day. "I'll tell you what you did right, Mr. Luedtke. You did a good job. No matter what, you gave every assignment all you got in you. And that makes you lucky, Mr. Luedtke. You'll never have the problem most of the people have of trying to impress the boss. You don't worry about the boss because you're concentrating so hard on your job. You got what my people call *mazel*. It's some kind of good luck."

True to his word, Neaman elevated Ed to the jobs he had promised. And then, in 1970, he promoted him to vice-president and general store manager, the third highest post in the division. Ed was still only forty-six. He had, in a way, reached his generalship. With three stars at that. He wished Mama had lived another five years.

Company Country

June in York, Pennsylvania, is like June in a thousand towns along the Atlantic seaboard. Maybe it is the sparkle in the warm sun that makes one smile tolerantly at the shabby taverns, monotonous gas stations, and tawdry diners along the countryside. But frequent billboards promoting new homes, Roto-rooter, and garden and utility services, as well as confident chamber-of-commerce trend-data, testify to the municipality's economic progress. Even in a growing recession, York, Pennsylvania, seems to be thriving. But perhaps it is only the summer's hope and breathlessness, the abrupt, sensuous change from storms that batter the coastline, eroding the flatlands. One feels a new season in the heart as in the weather.

Even the industrial parks that fan out from the highways, a testimonial to the success of the innumerable efforts by the counties to "balance agriculture with industry," do not seem as grim in the new summer's sun as they will a month later in the baking heat or much later in the snow and hail.

Massive acreage has been carved from the farmlands and the unproductive brush to create this neatly laid-out industrial area. Separated by two- and four-lane highways, it has been squared off in approximately equal blocks. Truck-trailer access has been provided by narrow bisecting streets and a sprawling parking area. Everything has been provided to lure outside business to the B.A.W.I. programs—low taxes, tax holidays, inexpensive footage, cheap utilities, less costly labor—and many have moved to the Yorks of the country.

Number 2955 East Market Street is the McCrory Building. The 760,000-square-foot, beige-painted facility is four stories high, about 200 feet wide, and perhaps 600 feet long. Its frontage and about 100 feet of the rear is constructed of beige brick, but the remaining 500 feet of the rear is of corrugated aluminum. The same paint, however, has been used on the metal as on the brick, so that from a distance of about 150 feet the structure gives a unified appearance.

About 3,000, or roughly fifteen percent, of all the variety-chain's employes work within the building, representing the staff of the chain's home offices and distribution center. The forty or so top executives have large but not sumptuous offices. The 250 others—buyers, assistants, and managers of smaller departments—have cubicles, about eight-feet square. There are three conference rooms, a large second-floor cafeteria, and a sizeable recreation room. About eighty-five percent of the immense structure consists of a central warehouse, holding a constant but moving inventory that is worth about $50 million at wholesale cost.

At the rear end of the distribution center are five large truck bays at which trailers are loaded or unloaded twenty-four hours a day. This merchandise center is the conduit for three other warehouses in New York, Nebraska, and eastern Pennsylvania, as well as three relay points in-between. After all, there are about 1,100 stores to be serviced from Bangor to Miami and from Wildwood to San Diego.

In the office area, a sharply cooled, antiseptically clean, and virtually silent room of about 2,500 feet is devoted to the computer. This is about five times the size of the computer room the center had when it first opened in 1967. Since then, the size of the computer, its scope, and its surrounding area have been successively enlarged. Gradually, the McCrory variety chain became known as the most computerized in the industry.

In the individual offices, one notices with a touch of shared identity the displays of individuality that are scattered among the manuals and the samples of merchandise. A dress buyer, for example, has her graduation hat taped to her diploma from the Fashion Institute of Technology hanging on the wall. Amid toasters, blenders, and styler-driers, a housewares buyer has deposited a football painted white so that it cannot be missed. An assistant merchandise controller has nailed above his desk last year's auto plate, announcing that he is a York, Pennsylvania, volunteer fireman.

In the top executives' offices, however, there is no such personal indulgence. The uniform exception is a photo of the occupant's family unobtrusively stationed on a corner of the desk. But on all the walls hung at the approximate same height and position over the executive's head is the framed Neaman photo and the credo. Each is signed with a flourish by the chairman. The smile in the photo is identically fixed in every room.

Decor and furniture in all the top executive offices are simple and contemporary. Pastels predominate and among them pale blue, peach, and beige are the norm. Files are spare and tightly modular. There are extremely few loose papers or folders on any of the desks.

Control, including the low hum and the cold throb of electricity, is evident along the halls. The offices and distribution center on any given day are visited by guests from other companies, schools, and even government agencies. All are eager to observe the highly reputed efficiency of the York, Pennsylvania, operations.

If the division's table-of-organization is T-shaped—with the executive committee and the management board forming the arms and the executive, operations, and services units forming a heavy trunk—the manner and dispersion of the 300 executives' homes resemble more closely a series of semicircles. The nearest semicircle consists of buyers' and department managers' apartments and ranch houses a mile or two away. A few miles beyond them are the split levels and raised ranches where senior buyers, merchandise managers, and operations and service managers live. Several miles further, the heavy Tudors and the white colonials of the major department heads and officers.

None is more than twelve to fifteen minutes driving-time from the office. As one of the boons of living and working in a small town, the short commuting time was one of the pleasant surprises that the relocated New Yorkers discovered when the home offices moved to York, Pennsylvania. That, along with the more subdued, relaxed atmosphere of the town of 4,000, helped to offset the disappointments and difficult adjustments they experienced in the move. But, because the men were always absorbed and deeply challenged by the rapidly evolving changes in the company, they were able to submerge the trauma of the move.

Like thousands of families being moved around the country and even overseas by American businesses, their wives and children had perhaps more prosaic but deeper challenges. Living in a changed milieu and adjusting to new types of people, to new regional mores, to new schools, and to values both subtly and harshly different, the families had the greater adjustment to make. But make it virtually everyone did. The overriding consideration was the man's job and, of course, the livelihood it provided.

On this June weekend, the families were as relaxed and as informal as many in the suburbs of the large cities.

The first of the four visited were John and Mary King. King was the home-office division vice-president who heard in 1963 about Neaman's startling field research among the Southern stores and joined him in his travels. Later, when Neaman took over first as division president, then as chairman, and then as president of the total corporation, King was promoted to senior vice-president and head of buying. Four years later, in 1970, he was named executive vice-president.

Now, ten years after he had first met Neaman, he and his wife, Mary, a childless couple, lived in one of the town's finest homes. It was a California-style ranch, ripe with birchwood walls and open beams and novel by having a series of semicircular roofs or cupolas. In the center of each was a square window which permitted light to filter through. The house to a first-time observer was startlingly different, modernistic, and ostentatious. But if its style, more than somewhat Moorish but certainly striking, was warmer and more dimensional than its residents appeared, the comparison was not necessarily in their disfavor. Obviously, one thought, glancing around at the heavy contemporary Western furniture, there was more to the King family than appeared at first glance. John was frail-looking, about sixty-five years old, thin-faced, blue-eyed, spare but not tall. He was genial and somewhat nervous but comfortable in his red-checked sports jacket and gray slacks. His white turtleneck shirt provided the right touch for a leisurely Saturday afternoon. Mary, about five years younger, was an attractive blond, the occasional gray tufts not detracting much from a still pervading youthfulness. Her pink sari showed a mature but good figure. Both spoke easily in a Southwestern drawl. And, somehow, one immediately guessed that they had dressed up for the visitor. But one also guessed that the large, ice-filled tumblers of scotch they promptly provided were not "dressed-up." They were standard.

The Kings discussed the company, their lives with it, and themselves easily. It was not hard, however, to sense a reluctance to delve beneath the facade of a couple well-integrated into the life of McCrory. Try as much as one could to avoid it, it was difficult not to feel the evocation of Neaman sitting in on the conversation and censoring it. Probably, though, it was no more than John King's close and loyal relationship with his superior that caused him to curb his mind and tongue.

Mary King often glanced at her husband before she spoke. They had been married almost forty years and all of it while he was employed by the same company. Had his being in the retail business proved onerous in their married life? She shook her head. "Well, it's a demanding profession," she said, "but then I think that everything is, isn't it? If a man is to be successful, he has to be truly interested, and his wife must go along."

"Was there ever a period in your marriage when you thought your husband was overdoing it?"

A glance at him. A smile is exchanged. "Yes, yes. That's in the early days." Fights? "Uh huh. But not many. You had to get accustomed to his long hours and later his many trips out of town."

"Do you think Mr. King could have had a more rewarding or interesting career in another field?"

"No. Not him. I think that this is his life's work."

"But, it's been a long time, hasn't it? Is there something else you would have preferred him to be?"

"No, I really don't think so. That's something that a man has to decide for himself—what he wants to be—and no one, wife or anybody else, can tell him, can they?"

They met in 1932, when he was about twenty-two and she was a few years younger. He was the manager of a McCrory store, one of the original chain, in a small eastern Texas town. He had never gone beyond high school and, coming from a poor family, had been fortunate in getting a job as a clerk in the hometown store. Two years later, he became store manager. Mary, who came from Phoenix, was teaching public school in the Texas town and met him on a blind date in October. They were married the following March.

But she was soon compelled to surrender her job. During the Depression, according to the local law, married teachers had to give up their posts to single ones. Things looked bleak for the Kings the following year when, like many other smaller retail chains, McCrory was forced into receivership until it could become solvent again. John remained with the company at a reduced salary. But, in 1937 when McCrory had recovered and was beginning again to build new stores, he was appointed manager of the San Antonio store. A year later, he became district manager. After army service in the Post Exchange system, from which he emerged as a major in 1945, he returned to the company in a higher post, regional manager. In 1949, he was transferred to New York as a store operations executive, a job he held until he became a vice-president in 1956.

Mary had managed to obtain several teaching jobs over the years. Saddened by her childlessness, she decided to provide the nicest home surroundings possible for John and also to take up a number of hobbies. She developed a modest talent in painting oils and, encouraged by her husband, took instruction from several prominent local painters and teachers. But, as she admitted to her visitor in York, Pennsylvania, she never fooled herself that she possessed "any real sort of talent." She also learned to become an adept sewer, advancing into macramé. And with John away so much, she became a fastidious homemaker and decorator. She also decided to keep herself young-looking through careful eating and exercise.

When her husband started coming home first with dismay and then with praise for the "new president they brought in, this Jewish man Neaman," Mary wondered if some new phase might not be opening up for John. She was not troubled that it could be a bad phase. Surely, anyone who worked as hard as John—who did not mind being on the road half the week, who still looked gratefully on his job after all those years and really thought of little else beside his work and his wife—would only be recognized by a new management for what he was. And later when John was promoted by his new superior to a senior vice-presidency, she knew she had been right. And then, four years later, when her slight, self-effacing husband became the division's executive vice-president, she was very proud.

All this was brought out in the conversation in their home—some by words, some by gestures, some by the glances between them. Asked how her husband had changed over the years in an environment as difficult as the merchandising business, Mary replied, with a warm smile at John. "I thought he was a very nice fellow the night we had that blind date. Forty years later, I still feel the same way."

But didn't *his* experience under the new company regime change him as it had many of the other executives? It was now John King's turn to talk. He shrugged. "Not that I can tell," he said. "I'll say one thing. Mr. Neaman demands a lot. You either give him a lot or you don't survive. But I have always given my work everything, anyhow, so I had no particular problem."

Would he identify the main thrust of the Neaman-styled management? "Motivation." Was it motivation—or pressure? "I would say the two relate closely. It would be hard to find any difference." A matter of style? "No, approach." Have you, he was asked, ever had any differences with Neaman on approach? The shrug again. "No differences, but I might have thought his approach at one time or another might have been drastic." Did you raise any objection? Once more, the shrug. "He would sometimes ask me if I thought he was too rough. Once or twice, I said yes. Mostly, I told him no." Can Neaman take criticism? "He is the kind of person that when you talk to him, you should have your information well-documented. And if you can document your point with facts and figures, he'll take criticism. Otherwise, he will climb all over you."

Did he, the interviewer pursued, ever climb over you? "Never gave him the chance. I fortified myself with facts. I had the knowledge. I should have—after all this time."

Mary showed the way to the garden. She wanted to demonstrate something she was proud of. And well she might be. It was one of those jewellike, miniature Japanese gardens—full of tiny trees, sprays of red and pink leaves, the smell of jasmine, and the rustling of precise, little waterfalls. After observing this scene with verbal appreciation, John, who had come along, interjected, "Mr. Neaman's done something no one else has done in the forty years I've been with McCrory. He did not claim to be a retailer, but he brought management to this company and he's building more of it. That's been the big failing of all the variety-store companies, from Woolworth and Kresge on down. They did not bring the people in or bring them along to become top management. He's got a wonderful concept, you see. He puts together the people that have some knowledge of different areas, but all together they have the knowledge of everything. That's why in just the few years he's been running things we've come from the bottom of the heap to the top. He's given everyone a new lease on life."

"He's a wonderful person," Mary put in. "Very intelligent. I also happen to like him as an individual."

Back in the living room, John was asked, "Will you answer one more question?" He nodded brightly.

"When Sam Neaman was running around down in the Southwest driving all your managers crazy, why did you decide to fly down and join him? Were you sent or was it your own idea?"

"Both," said John. "You see, Mr. Nelson, who was president at the time, asked me to run down to see what was going on, but it was only after I informed him about what was happening. Some of the district managers had called me, you see. I hoped he would send me, but I could hardly ask to be sent, could I? But I immediately knew that I liked Mr. Neaman. I liked his direct approach, the realization that if you've got a problem, the only way to solve it is break it down to its parts and attack each one. That means work—and I've always believed in that. You see, because of my lack of education—I never went past high-school—I have had to outwork everybody else. That's why, when Mr. Neaman came on the scene, I think he recognized me."

Outside on the lawn, the unusual house was striking. Mary admitted that she had fallen in love with it from the first moment. Since it had stirred her "artistic core" she had twisted John's arm to buy it, even if it "cost us an arm and a foot."

"Well," said John King, putting an arm around his wife's waist, "I am very partial to it, too. Don't you like it? It's just a lil ole twelve-room house."

About two miles away, as our car worked its way back toward the distribution center and to the area of somewhat less affluent homes, we stopped at the McClellans' house. It was a small colonial, modest structure about thirty years old. Paul and Mildred McClellan were a tall, friendly couple of about sixty. Paul was McCrory's vice-president and national merchandise director, a calm, genial, rather heavy-set man with glasses. Mildred was a tall, attractive, vivacious woman with a big, grayish bouffant. She wore a handsome, long white dress. Evidently, they, too, had dressed up.

After the introductions Paul said, "I'm going to let Milly do all the talking. She's got a lot to tell you. I'll just sit in the living room and watch the TV. I'll be back when she's finished."

We went into the small dining room and sat at an oval table. Mildred McClellans' large brown eyes sparkled and her breast heaved with repressed eagerness. "Paul is so right," she said. "I do have a lot to say, but I hope I won't bore you. You see, I believe that religion and business life are closely intertwined. May I tell you?"

What ensued was a marathon monologue, only occasionally interrupted by questions, much of which went as follows:

"I can't believe all of the good things that have happened to me through the years, ever since I met my husband and he went to work for the company.

"I met him when I was a college girl working in the Abilene, Texas, store where Paul was the assistant manager. Then, after we married, he became a store manager in Arizona, then Oklahoma, and then back in Texas, where our one and only, our precious daughter—our beautiful daughter—was born. Then Paul went into the army. He came out two years later and was appointed a district manager. In 1956, he was sent to the New York office to become a buyer, and we bought a house in Garden City, Long Island.

"By then, our daughter was of college age. In 1962, we sold our house and moved to Manhattan and I loved every single, solitary minute of that. All through the years, my husband has been so good to me. Chain-store men have always had long hours, so he was very good to me to let me fill my time. I was always actively involved with church and club work, but my main work was with young people, youth.

"When we lived in Arizona, he trusted me. We had been married in July 1936, and he let me take our automobile and drive about 3,500 miles on a trip. I went as a delegate from the local YWCA in Arizona to the Rocky Mountain regional Y conference. Then when I returned, I was made a YWCA board member for the young people. Things like that have happened to me through the years. Wherever Paul has taken me because of the company, I've always found a place and he has allowed it. And that's why I say that the company has been good to me, because it's been good to Paul and he's been good to me in turn.

"When we moved to Manhattan, we lived on East 56th Street, and it was just as exciting as I had expected it to be. Our daughter came home for the summers and worked on Wall Street. Paul walked with her every morning. It was safe for her to walk home at night. In those days, it was. In New York, it was no different for me. I was very fortunate, as I have always been, to meet the right person. I continued to be actively involved in my church. My background is Southern Baptist, so I was raised that way and I attended Hardin-Simmons University, which is Baptist, where I was an A-plus student in Bible and history. I am not a graduate, just an alumna. But I was always church-oriented. Started teaching Sunday school class when I was seventeen. . . .

"The company, through my husband's salary and bonuses has made it possible for me to have my own car. I've always had my own car, and he has always been willing to furnish the gasoline for all my needs. . . . If the Depression hadn't come along and hit us very, very hard in west Texas, I might have gone on to graduate as a drama or speech major. But in Clinton, Oklahoma, I was in a singing group and I had the comic lead which my husband, Paul, allowed me to do by going out at night. I was also singing before Kiwanis groups, their benefits, in plays, that kind of thing. We were very good bridge players, and we were just all-around good people, may I say that? I don't think that makes us very dull, because we have always been faithful to each other.

"And I don't think he's ever had any cause to be jealous of me. And I don't think—well, maybe a few times; I wouldn't be a woman if I didn't, if I weren't jealous of him. But maybe he would say the same thing about me. But we've never had any problem as far as that kind of thing is concerned which, I'm sure, you would find in some families.

"I'm one of those stupid people. I'm so happy, I guess, and my time is so filled. There were times that I got angry and frustrated. But as it turned out, it was as though there was someone watching over us.

"Like when we had been in Arizona a year and a half and another store had been mentioned to us but instead we were sent to Oklahoma and I don't know to this day why. But the way it came out, it couldn't have been better. And that has turned out to be my faith. And then again I was personally very angry when we had to move from San Antonio to Memphis. It wasn't Paul's fault, of course, and I don't think I've ever upset him so much. I just didn't want to leave San Antonio. I loved it.

I gave Paul a hard time; I was horrible. But three weeks after we moved to Memphis, I was called on by a lovely person who was the aunt of one of my neighbors in San Antonio. She knew all the right people in East Memphis. By the time I had lived there three months, it was as though I had never lived any place else.

"I'd like to say something about Paul. I have always thought his progress was slow, because he was always a fantastic merchant, a fantastic person. I don't think he had yet come into his own, and I'm not sure he ever will. But Mr. Neaman made him a vice-president in the fall of 1968. In fact, I may say that everything has happened since Mr. Neaman. But that takes some explaining, doesn't it?

"But first I would like to tell you that I've always believed in one thing: I believe in tithing. And, as I've grown older, I've come to believe in the tithing of time as well as money. I guess both of these things come from the fact that I am convinced that God says love Him best and give Him the best and you don't have to worry about anything else. My greatest fortune came when I married my husband. I always gave of myself to clubs, Campfire Girls. When I grew older, before I had a child, I was with somebody else's child—I was teaching Sunday School; I was an officer in a women's club. It was all a kind of quiet life in a little west Texas town. But the real excitement in my life started when I married Paul. We couldn't have had that kind of life if he hadn't had the salary.

"What I am building up to tell you is that when we moved from New York to Dallas, I was angry again. As I said, I loved living in New York. From there, shortly after Mr. Neaman came into authority, Paul was ordered to go with a group to Indianapolis for some experimental work. He was then to be reassigned to Dallas. Just about then, I was in the Harvard Club in New York at a dinner, and my husband was sitting there with Mr. Neaman who was explaining to him the reason for that change. I had recently spent the entire summer in Texas with my daughter, and I didn't care a thing about going back. But, by October, there I was back in Dallas, a big city I didn't know much of since I had always lived in the small towns.

Paul was traveling from Monday to Friday so I enrolled in the Dallas Theater Center, but somehow I wasn't much interested in that. One Sunday morning, when Paul was at a meeting, I walked down to a park near a beautiful church, the Park City Baptist Church. I walked across the street just outside the church and stood looking up at it and then, as always happens to me, I met someone. Two women came out. One of them was a woman that you could call Mrs. Dallas—she was that important—and she saw my interest and started talking to me. Well, she took me in hand and we walked along and we found out all about each other. It turned out we had some mutual friends. She invited me on the spot to join the Symphony Auxiliary, the City Opera, and all of that. In the meantime, a class was being dismantled in the adult department of this church, and this woman happened to be the superintendent of the adult department. When she heard that I had been a Sunday School teacher once, she asked me to become temporary teacher in this adult class.

"Now, this is what I want to point out to you—if Mr. Neaman hadn't sent my husband to Dallas, none of this would have happened to me. You understand, there is such a connection here that I can't separate it at all. I had never taught an adult class of women, and our daughter is a psychology major and I have all the graduate-school books. I said I would take the class just one Sunday but that's all. I surrounded myself with these books, because one time in the years long ago I had had the same thing happen to me. I had taken a class of adults when I was very young and knew that I shouldn't. I was talked into it. And I was fired—because I didn't know how to teach. They just went ahead and said, 'We can't stand her another Sunday. Get rid of her and get us somebody else.'

"So here were all my books spread out on the table—the maps, everything to do with the Bible. I studied seventy hours that week. When my husband came home Friday night, he rang the bell. He looked strangely at me. I had transported myself. Or somebody did. I was with the Children of Israel, building the Tabernacle. And I actually felt that I had lived with them. Paul looked strange to me. He didn't have a beard, a turban, a shepherd's cane, and I was the Children of Israel. . . . I stayed with the class, they liked me, and I kept studying. It was one of the most rapturous times of my life. I kept teaching the class until we were transferred to Florida, and the same kind of things started to happen to me again because of Mr. Neaman. . . .

"As you may know, when Paul reached his fortieth anniversary with the company, Mr. Neaman and the top management honored us. They gave us two wonderful weeks at their expense in Switzerland. It was made at a presentation in the conference room at the home offices in York, Pennsylvania. There were quite a few present and they had cakes and liquor and cocktails. Paul was given the envelope and a clock, and I was given a beautiful corsage and a basket of fruits and other lovely things. And while we were in Europe, my heart was so full that I wrote a letter of appreciation and a poem dedicated to Mr. Neaman. Paul thought it would be all right and I did it. Would you—may I show you the poem?"

The poem read:

Tribute to Samuel Neaman

Day was long; filled with woe.
  Night was too soon ending.
Man was aimless; no place to grow.
  His spirit. His will. Bending.
Silent plea. Answered. Rapid fire pace!
  A genius, a gracious man, generous man,
Statesman of God's Chosen Race
  Arrived with prodigious plan!
Reviewed records! Examined stores!
  Interviewed personnel! Ascertained cause
Of diminishing returns! The whole score!
  Then onward and upward sans pause!
Rekindled exuberant vision in man;
  Removed from him doubts and fear.
The distinguished personage with the plan:
  Philanthropist, warrior, financier.

Now day is too short for to reap and to sow;
  And the dark of night is too long.
Man's aim restored; new places to grow.
  His spirit! His will! Unbent! Strong!

The next family visited presented a picture that has become a standard on the American landscape. Still closer in to the Mc-Crory distribution center, on a curving street with two identical rows of ten-year-old ranch houses, the Powers were relaxing on the patio behind their home. Earl Powers, a forty-two-year-old McCrory buyer supervisor, paddled around in a kidney-shaped pool and waved in greeting. Alternately watching him, working on her fingernails, and reading was his attractive, blond wife, Sheila, sitting under an umbrella table in a blue, floral muumuu. Their seventeen-year-old daughter, Dot, lay sun-bathing in a bikini at the edge of the pool, a tiny transistor radio blaring away. A shaggy-eared, foolish-looking dog completed the portrait.

The Powers, Brooklyn-born and New York-oriented, had hated moving to York, Pennsylvania. Sheila had been a professional model. Earl had graduated from New York University and had worked first in Macy's executive training squad and then as an assistant buyer. Macy's had just promoted him to department manager of shoes when Sheila met him at a party.

Their courtship had been quick, in the manner of many New Yorkers. In little more than fifteen months, they were married and living in a small Cape Cod in Syosset, Long Island. Sheila had given birth to their first and only child. She gave up her modeling jobs and they settled down to the life of a typical suburban family. After six years, Earl left Macy's for a job with more responsibility at McCrory. But, when in the fourteenth year of their marriage McCrory had asked the Powers to move to York, Pennsylvania, so that Earl could work at the new home offices, the request had presented a difficult turning point. They could, and often did, dine out and take in a show in Manhattan or go boating on the Sound, and yet they still enjoyed the homogenous life of a Long Island enclave.

"I was adamantly, vehemently opposed to the move," Earl

said, standing behind his wife, a big bath towel slung around his shoulders. "I told them at first I wouldn't go. Even when they said there was another promotion involved, I said it didn't cut any ice with me."

"Earl always goes on record with everything," his wife said.

But they had decided to discuss it calmly, the effect of the move on his career and their ultimate income. They realized that it was foolish to fight a company policy that called for relocating all its merchandising and buying executives either in the home office in a Pennsylvania town or in the field. Besides, Earl sensed that his Macy's background had to give him an edge in his career with the company. He was already a senior buyer and well regarded. They moved.

"Truth to tell," said Sheila, smiling, "we love it here now. But it took us quite a while. I was very lonesome. Dot had to make new friends, and it wasn't easy for her. Earl didn't like it much. But things change. We changed. The uprooted feeling left us after a while, and I can't imagine living in any other place now. Can you, Earl?"

He shook his head. "Nope. This is it. They came through with not just one promotion but two. I even get a decent bonus now. How can you fight it?" With a happy shrug, he went into the house to change.

Sheila's tone became confident. "For me," she said, "things definitely began to pick up two years ago just before Earl's birthday. You didn't ask me if I have an occupation. Well, I do. I'm the only McCrory wife who does. I'm a travel agent. I did it to start with as a part-time thing. The days got kind of long and boring. After all, I used to be a model. After a year or more of playing bridge and committee meetings, my days felt empty."

It began when Sheila decided that Earl's fortieth birthday was an event which required unusual recognition. Tall, cleancut, emotionally balanced, and a devoted husband, Earl had every attribute and more than he had had during their whirlwind courtship. She wanted to give him a gift that he would regard as a clear sign of, as she said, "My love and my respect for him." But buying it from her household money would have been impossible. So she looked for a job and found one with a local travel agency. "I truly only intended to work from January to the end of April when we were having the party for him," she said. "But it turned out that this opened up a whole new vista for me. I began working at it full time and I absolutely love it. Earl wasn't crazy about it, but he thinks it's a fine idea now. I'm a lucky woman."

Her tone was husky; her eyes sparkled. It was easy to see how the personable blond could be an asset in helping people decide where they ought to spend their vacations.

"You never said what you bought him for his birthday," she was reminded.

She laughed. "No, I didn't. I bought him a new little black box. It was the most expensive I could find."

"Little black box?"

"Yes. His attaché case. I've always said that if I ever had a rival for Earl's affections, it was that little black box. He always brought it home with work to do. But why should I complain? It's done everything for us. That's why on his birthday I decided to get him one made of elephant leather. It cost me $240."

So, with Earl Power's career, Sheila's job, and their daughter beginning to develop her own friends, they were happy in York, Pennsylvania. Sheila said she was particularly buoyed because last weekend she and Earl had celebrated their eighteenth wedding anniversary, and they had been treated to dinner. "The big boss," Sam Neaman, had decided that year to send every couple in the executive ranks a check for $50 so that they could mark their wedding anniversaries with a dinner on the company. Without great fanfare, the gesture was clearly an expression of appreciation for a great year for McCrory, for the work done by the executives and behind the scenes by their wives. "I think it's a very nice thing," Sheila said, simply.

Her husband emerged smoothly shaven in gleaming slacks and a powder-blue sport shirt. "I guess you can see now the secret of my success," he said with a grin. "The girl Sheila. Executive wife, mistress, and travel agent."

They were dining out that night with several McCrory couples. "We never used to spend much time socially with company people in New York," said Sheila before she went in to dress, "but we do now, of course. It took me a little while here to get used to meeting someone from the company every time we turned a corner. But it became natural to associate with them. After all, we *are* a sort of community within a community. In fact, we have even given up people that have left the company, and we have gone out of our way to welcome new couples that have been sent here. The wives get together separately. A lot of the husbands travel a good deal, and so the gals instead of mooning around meet for coffee and cocktails."

"Do you ever get tired of being locked into a company community?"

This time, it was Earl who answered, as Sheila nodded in agreement. "When we get tired of it, which is every once in a while, we just jump into the car and take a trip," he said. "We've been to Williamsburg to the restoration, we've gone to Philadelphia, and we've even driven back to New York lots of times. It's a nice place to visit, but I wouldn't want to live there. Especially since we can't anyway."

About three miles from the home office was a sprawling apartment house from whose top or fourth floor one could see the McCrory sign on East Market Street. The last couple to be visited that late afternoon lived on that floor. Both were company executives. But only one of them was at home. Marge Schiller—a forty-five-year-old buyer of foundations, bras, girdles, and aprons—relaxed in a lounging robe. Her husband, Robert, the division purchasing agent, was back in the distribution center doing some paperwork. His picture on the top of a new Zenith console color television set showed the strong, stolid face, intent eyes, and firm mouth of a confident man in his late forties.

The couple had been married only about two months. The Schillers had taken only one day off to be married. Upon their return they had waited a full week before mailing an announcement of their new relationship.

Marge was a plump, pleasant brunette with a matter-of-fact manner. She discussed matters crisply and listened as if she meant to remember. In twenty-eight years with the company, she had come all the way from a seventeen-year-old clerk-typist to the buyership of a major department. Along the way, as McCrory grew, developed new branches, merged, and merged again and again, she became manager of a clerical department of twenty-five in the buying division, then superintendent in that division, and then assistant buyer.

She was, in her way, typical of many woman buyers who develop dominant personalities in a world of men and bottom-line priority. They tend, as she did, to exude an aura of no-nonsense. The only major difference between them and Marge Schiller is that she fell in love and married after twenty-eight years of working. The others either marry much earlier or never do.

"I'm a Jersey City girl," she announced, smiling. "Robert is from New Hampshire. Both our families are practically all gone. I guess that was one of the things that brought us together. I knew him in New York when he was a store manager there and I was an assistant buyer, but we never dated. That didn't happen until we all moved down here." She paused, then added with a winsome turn of her lips, "I guess we were just two mature, lonely people who were attracted to each other."

While both now worked in the same building, she said, they saw each other only occasionally during the day. Robert left the apartment in the morning about 6:15, while she didn't leave for another hour and a half. Sometimes, either of them would pop a head into the other's office with "Hi, how goes it?" But they made it a practice to leave together every night at about 5:30.

"Of course, I miss New York," she admitted. "When I came here, I came under protest. I agreed that I'd come for six months. I was going to set up the department for them and then leave. Mr. Hughes, our administrative vice-president, said at that time, of course, I would get a job with another division in New York. But I wouldn't go back now. I miss New York for shopping, but I go there a minimum of once a month on buying trips for the company. I work much longer hours here, often into the night, which doesn't bother me because I don't have all that travel time. Robert and I have made many friends in York. It's a slower community—you're not running like you do in New York. I think both of us accomplish more here and at a better pace, and we're not knocking ourselves out all the time."

As a professional buyer, Marge was pleased with the changes under the new management. All the systems were being automated with a sophisticated IBM computer. There was a very extensive records department. Paperwork had been rendered more efficient and practical.

"Of course, even with all that," she admitted with a frown, "we buyers seem to have more paperwork to do, but it's for the best in the end and it has to be done. It was very sloppy before. So many things not accounted for."

But what was especially noteworthy, she stressed, was the new attentiveness and concern of suppliers. "I'm sure they realize that we have a very professional, more demanding management, and they are snapping up. Now, we make our vendors adhere to shipping dates, since it takes four weeks to get goods out to our farthest stores. You know, we could miss a whole season by a few weeks with late deliveries. So we have an expediting department now which polices our orders with vendors and sees that shipments are on time."

Did she plan to keep working? She smiled at the patently unnecessary question. "Oh, yes, I wouldn't know what to do," she replied. "Robert and I won't have any children. It's too late for us. So maybe the company will be our child or vice versa."

She gestured toward the large color TV console. "That's Mr. Neaman's wedding present to us," she said. "When he heard about us, he phoned Robert and then he phoned me. He said he was sorry he didn't know about it ahead of time; he would have liked to do something. So this was his wedding present after the fact."

"Why did you keep your marriage a secret?"

"Well, we didn't really mean to keep it a secret so much. We just didn't want to stir things up. You see, in our department there are normally two buyers, but the other one left a few months ago which complicated things. So I just wanted to do everything quietly and not take any time off and this is what we did. In fact, we had to delay getting married a week or two because I was so busy. That's the kind of business we're in."

The interviews were over. It was evening, although still light. My driver, a beefy young man with blond hair down to his jacket collar who had been assigned to me by Frank Patchen, the division president, asked if he was to drive directly back to the motel.

"Can you go by Market Street?"

"Yes, sir."

No. 2955, which came up between the buildings of a large, electronics company and a smaller, but more anonymous-looking research laboratory, still seemed to be busy at past seven on a Saturday evening. The front of the McCrory Building had many lights on in the individual offices. Buyers, department managers, assistants of all kinds, and maybe even some senior executives were obviously working. Was the IBM 360 making for more work or less? It was not a fair question—the EDP goal, after all, is more efficiency, not less work. More controls, hence fewer unpleasant surprises. But, judging by the lights in the building in the evening, not to mention statements by executives, the computer hadn't robbed the McCrory staff of its motivation or drastically lightened its work load.

As we pulled past, I pondered the questions. Others arose, too. Why had Sam Neaman allowed me to interview many of his top executives both in New York and York, Pennsylvania, when it was obvious that he was offended by criticism and mistrusted the press? Obviously, he hoped that by pre-selecting most of the interviewees he could channel the discussion and mold a positive appraisal. As I subsequently learned, he placed two calls to each interviewee, one before and one immediately after the interview. The first was to coach the man not to get involved in either criticism or controversy. The second was to ascertain just what questions had been asked and what the answers had been. But what he obviously couldn't control were the unauthorized interviews, of which there had already been a number and more were to come. He learned of some, although not all, through the spy system he had created. That espionage network was to be refined later under the pressures of subsequent developments.

"Johnny," I asked the driver as we pulled up to the motel, "what do you think of the big bosses—Patchen, King, Hughes, Luedtke and Paul McClellan?"

He turned in his seat with a grin. "Gee, I like 'em all," he said. "They all treat me great. Mr. King, the exec veep, he's an unusual guy. I mean he's so quiet, and yet he got to such a high job. Proves you don't have to have a big mouth, don't it? Mr. Patchen, he acts like a president or maybe a college professor. Always using big words. Sometimes I don't understand him. Sometimes, the other people make fun of him but I think they all respect him. He spends an awful lot of time talking to everybody. Mr. Hughes is a very nice guy—he always says hello to me like he really means it. He's got one of the toughest jobs in the place, but he never gets ruffled. But Mr. Luedtke, he's different. He's the tough guy. It's like on a football team—he's not the quarterback, he's the big halfback that everybody gives room to. Now, Mr. McClellan he—"

"What is your opinion of Mr. Neaman?"

He blinked. "Sorry, I don't know him. Is he up in New York? A lot of them come down here. . . ." The young driver suddenly looked worried. "Gee, I've got a lot of talking to do tomorrow. I have my six months' raise coming up and my boss told me he don't think I deserved a raise. I got kind of peeved at him and I told him a few things. I'd hate to lose this job."

Four DOES A COMPANY HAVE A SOUL?

13. The Happy Centipede

So those were the Neaman years.

In the late 1960s and early 1970s, the believers and many of the doubters wondered if a vital, new, hybrid institution wasn't being created. Combining human motivation and the operation of a business for profit seemed to make sense sociologically. People will break their backs if given an authentic opportunity. Implicit in it was the class struggle. Wasn't it, someone asked, Thorstein Veblen, that economic pundit with the demon's intellect, who exorcised and then impaled the question of why revolution doesn't simultaneously erupt everywhere between the proletariat and the capitalists? The answer, pronounced Veblen, was that the lower classes do not want to kill the upper classes because both groups really shared the same ambition, even if they wouldn't admit it. This desire once carried out leads to social stability.

Businesswise it made even more sense. Someone even recalled the old Mormon hymnal: "The world has need of willing men. Who can wear the worker's seal. Come, help the good work move along. Put your shoulder to the wheel." The country's work ethic, too, had been identified by no less a businessman than Henry Ford: "America is not a land of money but of wealth, not a land of rich people but of successful workers."

But then, scoffed a Neaman critic, Ford was about as consistent as he was prescient in asserting that Americans only would want cars painted black. "The average worker, I am sorry to say, wants a job in which he does not have to put forth much physical exercise—above all, he wants a job in which he does not have to think," Ford had also said.

And when in some confusion the believers and the doubters looked at the Neaman accomplishment, just what did they see? A moribund company of some 50,000 tired, sad-eyed people had convulsed and come alive under a new sort of pressure in the midst of which a challenge was dangled. Ordinary men could be extraordinary. Triumph waited only for the latent dynamism that existed in their numbers. It was the old principle that the sum was greater than its parts, particularly if all the parts moved in the same direction with equal energy and zeal. But should the parts not march or even crawl in unison, the total organism would collapse. However, its leadership provided the ultimate example, the constant spur. Neaman, ceaselessly. Whether he sat silently in the back of a room yet dominated all its activities. Or ate his Ry-Krisp and cottage cheese while he heatedly talked to others. Or hovered over the elaborate communications system in his den on Sundays and kept up a running multiple conversation with his executives on weekends. Or drew on a sport shirt on Saturdays and traveled from store to store to needle, kibitz, and coach managers. Or boasted about his lack of knowledge of everything but that one frail ingredient. He was the expert of nothing, yet the *maven* of something. The mechanism of people.

Everyone watched. Competitors scouted him. Academicians pricked the phenomenon. Their needles of doubt drew no blood. The press scoffed but sooner or later published glowing reports. Wall Street stared aghast at the fat, pouting anomaly. What was he after? He owned nothing, being neither wheeler-dealer nor empire-builder. He sought nothing—except power, of course—not the power of money or of bricks and mortar. He wanted to prove nothing—except maybe that he was better than Riklis. Through it all, Neaman beamed, intrigued by the bafflement that he created.

No subject was more on the tongues and minds of those at Woolworth, Kresge, W. T. Grant, McCrory—even Sears, Roebuck and JCPenney. To have engaged the curiosity of one's peers, not to mention their attention and consequent confusion, was a mark of recognition that Neaman savored. He was hardly alone in this in the McCrory organization. Everyone enjoyed the notoriety. For years considered one of the most backward of retail chains, the division was now one of the most distinctive and one of the most consistently profitable. Its techniques and systems were being copied. And its unusual management style was like a dash of fresh, cold water in the face of a sleepy, anemic industry.

The question that badly needed asking was being asked. Had a nonmerchant come up with the equation that had eluded all the professionals? Was it really that simple? To convince the ordinary, the normal, the average that their number, with all its variations of racial, genetic, and natural differences, could be more imaginative and productive than the extraordinary, the above-average, the talented, the naturally creative? How could that be? But it was. It was. Even the doubters, and there were many, could not deny it any more than they could deny that a new, vital company had been created from the ashes of the old.

In the division and in the company in general, the new pride was great. Neaman had created a new *esprit*, admittedly as much by injecting the constant awareness of himself and his demands as by igniting something dormant in people. But the result was an improved performance and more self-respect. Neaman's worst critics, such as Hi Leder (the obese, highly independent advertising manager) or Izzy Becker (Riklis's financial alter-ego) tended to reduce by 100 percent what Neaman had accomplished. Quasicritics, such as Steve Jackel (the Klein's general store director) subtracted about half. But, regardless of the mathematics of their cynicism, it could not realistically amount to 100 percent. Neaman was there. Neaman had done. Neaman had produced. Naturally, among the believers, who easily outnumbered the doubters, their admiration knew no bounds.

If among them there was an occasional tremor of foreboding, perhaps a sense of doom, it was shrugged off as a natural effect of euphoric change. Things were going so well, in other words, that they just could not continue that way. Many of the executives in the variety-store division, in the department-store group, even in Lerner's (the big chain of dress shops) were acclimated enough to the retail business to know that a bad season usually followed a good one and a good one a bad one. It was one reason why there was such a high incidence of ulcers, of hypertension, and of heart attacks in the business. But even when good seasons follow one another without interruption, the old sense of doom doesn't actually leave. In McCrory's case, the lingering conviction that destiny, the law of averages, or happenstance would catch up with the Neaman miracle was bolstered by the final way in which he had cut the strings with the parent company, Rapid–American. Support from it, everyone now knew, would come only as long as McCrory under Neaman continued to produce good earnings. It was, without question, a sword hanging over the head.

But Neaman himself had no foreboding. In his makeup, there was no allowance for a bad season following a good one. Such an eventuality, he clearly implied, was possible only by a letdown among people. He did not intend to let down or be let down. His enjoyment in the respect he received for his accomplishments, and for those of his staff, was so obvious that no one had the heart, or the courage, to predict that everything could not continue at that high level of success. He would not have listened.

Success was his, in a measure not often given to most men. It was direct and indirect. Direct because not only profits but promotion and respect came to him in excess. In spite of the carping and personal animosity of some in the parent company, in 1972 its board took the unusual step of setting aside almost $600,000 for Neaman to borrow at a low interest rate so that he could take advantage of an attractive stock option. And in the ensuing fiscal year, his salary and compensation were raised to about $375,000 a year, keeping it the highest salary in retailing. His success was also indirect in the sense that his name had become magic and drew spontaneous attention and support.

This yielded at least one dramatic moment. When he lent his name to a prominent Israeli university to establish a "Samuel Neaman Institute of Business Management" as a new graduate school, the sponsoring committee rented the ballroom of the New York Hilton Hotel for a pledge-raising dinner. Sitting proudly at the center of the dais with Cecelia on his right and a smiling Meshulam Riklis on his left, Neaman looked out at an audience of 1,500 that included many of his suppliers and trade acquaintances. One by one, men in the audience rose to announce with "pride," "humility," "with a full heart," "with deep gratification" sums from $10,000 to $100,000. The ground swell reached a penultimate height when Walter Straus, the head of the recently acquired J.J. Newberry chain and a Gentile at that, strode to the microphone and pledged $25,000 of his own money to the new institution. Considering that Straus had merged himself out of his job by agreeing to have his company taken over by McCrory, it was more than Neaman could manage to remain unmoved by Straus's spontaneous action. He bolted from his chair and embraced Straus at the rostrum to the accompaniment of thundering applause from the audience. Tears rolled down the cheeks of both men as cameras clicked and the waves of sound rolled over them.

But even that applause was only a small measure of what exploded in the large room when the grand total was announced. Only $3 million had been earmarked for the amount needed to establish the institute, yet three-quarters of it had been pledged in only half an hour. Weeks and months later, when the figure refused to rise, no one except one or two professional money-raisers was concerned. It was as if much of the nation's supplying industry had opened its heart in joy and spent itself in the process. One could understand such emotional exhaustion. Neaman never forgot the event or the spirit it had evoked.

Naturally, many of his executives pondered the reasons for his and their success. Inured to failure or a more hapless existence, they found it difficult to accept blithely their achievement. Each attributed it to a different reason. Ben Litwak attributed it to the fact that ordinary men naturally exult in an opportunity to be a capitalist. Norman Mallor saw it as the successful combination of controls and discipline. Charley Gass described it as a "simple win-or-lose proposition where guts pay off." Harold Hughes viewed it as a moral verity, "a management of equals." But Steve Jackel, who couldn't help scoffing at the success because he was convinced it couldn't last, was intrigued by the centipede concept.

One morning late in 1972, after having read up on the properties of that insect, Steve dropped into Charley Gass's office and confronted the short intense "Mr. Internal Auditor."

"You know what the hell all of us, including Neaman, are?" asked Steve. "We're a centipede."

"What?"

"You know—a centipede. What we kids used to call a 'thousand-legger.' "

"Why?"

"Because all of us are marching to Neaman's tune, like a hundred different bodies joined to that bastard. Each one of us is like the appendages on the centipede's body—we do every goddamn thing that the head does, the mind thinks, the psyche controls. We don't do a thing on our own—."

"C'mon get the hell out of here," Gass said testily. "I got a million things to do, with all these crooks around here and all the mistakes everybody makes."

Steve grinned. "There you go, that proves it. He's got you so keyed up to find an irregularity in every desk drawer that you can't even see what a slave you are. You're just another goddamn appendage."

Smarting from Steve's prodding, Gass entered Steve's office later that day with a triumphant look in his eye. "All right, you sonofabitch," he said, "I looked it up, too. Did you know how dangerous and ferocious a centipede is? Their bite is as dangerous as a scorpion's, and when they're attacked they're deadly as hell. They keep biting until they die. And when you realize that most of the species are blind, eyeless anyway, you gotta admire their guts."

The discussion drew several others and for a good ten minutes the debate raged. The observers and participants were divided about equally in their sentiments between Steve's and Gass's views. A junior executive was posted at an intersection of the hallway in case either Neaman or Stanley Kunsberg, the president, appeared in view. The debate more or less ended when Charley Gass, looking at his watch and wincing, conceded, "All right, you bastard, so we're a centipede. But you gotta admit we're a happy centipede."

"Charley," said Steve with disgust. "if you read up on it as much as you say, you'd realize something. There ain't any such thing. No centipede ever lived that was happy. How could it be—with 200 legs and only the head knows where they're all going?"

14.   The Plan

The fall 1972 acquisition of the J.J. Newberry Stores by Mc-Crory completed a full circle. It not only climaxed a series of takeovers begun a decade earlier but gave McCrory a scope that put it into the supergiant group which already included Woolworth and Kresge. It was one of those catapulting jumps. By absorbing the 740-store company—a huge, motley agglomeration of variety, department, discount, fabric, shoe, and dress stores—McCrory added half again to its annual sales. The loss of under $2 million from Newberry's operations could be written off against taxes due.

It was the latest—and the biggest—fish that Meshulam Riklis had tossed to Sam Neaman, who leaped to the new catch with gusto. Within a few months, he had restructured the new firm, integrated it into his own company, closed a slewful of untenable stores, sold off another group of them, and realized the gratification of operating a firm with annual sales of over $1 billion.

To Meshulam Riklis, the Newberry takeover was significant but in a totally different way. With a $1 billion subsidiary pushing out earnings of almost $3 million after giving effect to the Newberry loss and with inventory having a wholesale value of about $250 million, he had achieved the ideal money funnel for acquiring further properties. But, unbeknownst to Izzy Becker, whom he had made a vice-chairman of the parent company without tipping off Neaman, Riklis decided that the time was ripe for a move that was strategic and dramatic.

For most of the decade, Rapid–American had operated like an immense head with two massive bodies. One body was Glen Alden (the New England holding company for mines, real estate, and theaters) which he had gradually merged completely into Rapid. By doing so, Riklis had increased his company's share of Glen Alden's profits from 51 to 76 and finally to 100 percent. The other arm, McCrory, he had used for seven of those ten years as a conduit for cash and collateral. Now, with the important Newberry deal concluded, Riklis realized that he no longer wanted McCrory as merely a funnel. He wanted all of it. He sensed a recession coming in the later course of the 1970s and knew that 100 percent of McCrory's profits would be a better hedge than the current 65 percent. Equally important, Rapid, the original company and the parent one, by its very nature deserved the priority for growth. As a $3.5 billion empire, which it would be once it swallowed up McCrory's, its position would be unshakable.

Besides which, he realized, the timing was good. McCrory's stock, like most others in the down stock market, had fallen some 30 percent in value. So it would not take much to buy the remaining shares.

And the federal government would scarcely oppose such a merger. Rapid already had working and majority control. A full merger would not be any more anticompetitive than the present working control was. The government, he concluded, would have neither the case nor the inclination to fight it.

There would be only one problem—Neaman.

The night before he decided to leak his plan during a speech before the New York Society of Security Analysts, he told Izzy Becker. It was almost 8 P.M. and Izzy came in with his coat on, ready to go home. "You're not ready to leave yet, Rik? What's cooking?"

"We're going to bring McCrory 100 percent into Rapid."

Becker's brown eyes sparkled. He put his hat on the floor and sank into a chair. His bald pate suddenly seemed to be gleaming with a fine perspiration. "Wow!" he said. "The banks will love it. It will give us more muscle. And what a balance sheet. What about—?"

"Neaman?"

Becker nodded.

"We'll see."

At 2:20 the following afternoon, a reporter phoned Sam Neaman and asked him for a reaction.

"A reaction? To what, my friend?"

"Haven't you heard, Mr. Neaman? Mr. Riklis just told the security analysts society that he's going to make a tender offer for the rest of the McCrory shares. He wants to merge your company into Rapid–American."

Neaman sat silently for a few moments. The reporter heard his heavy breathing through the phone. Finally, Neaman said, "There is no reaction," and hung up. Within moments, his lower lip pouting and a tiny tic working under his left eye, he had his whole team in his office, questioning each one about whether he had known anything about the startling news. Kunsberg, Norman Mallor, Charley Gass, Ben Litwak, Steve Jackel, and Charles Witz. Then he placed calls to York, speaking briefly to Frank Patchen, Harold Hughes, John King, Ed Luedtke, and Paul McClellan. No one knew anything about it, but their reaction was uniformly shocked. Then, thoroughly angry, he cut off the inquiries that his questions had aroused and phoned a friendly informer at Rapid headquarters. He received confirmation from the man, who was one of a group who had been summoned by Izzy Becker and had been told the news at the same moment Riklis was informing the analysts at 15 William Street near Wall Street.

Realizing that the logistics of the action had been perfect, Neaman knew that there was only one thing he could do. He placed a call to Riklis's office and made an appointment that afternoon.

As the two faced each other an hour or so later, it would have been difficult for an outsider to know that there was a conflict between them. Both smiled, relaxing with one another. Riklis sat at his big mahogany desk, leaning back against the leather and sipping a large gin and tonic. His secretary had supplied Neaman with what was known to be his favorite. Tea with lemon in a thick glass. He drank slowly, staring at the tiny, dapper Riklis. "Our current quarter," said Neaman easily, "looks very good. The recession, I think, will bother the retail business last. The McCrory company even later. Of this, I am very confident."

Riklis's face softened. "I know," he said. "I have only just recently come to that conclusion myself. Much of that, Sammy, we owe to you."

"You are very kind, Rik. Too kind."

Riklis shrugged. "Only to those," he countered, "who deserve it."

"This *chochma*, this trick, this bombshell you gave me without warning this afternoon," Neaman said, "is this for the publicity? Or is this your considered decision?"

Riklis straightened up in his high-backed chair but his head still remained below its top. "I mean it, Sammy," he replied. "The publicity and the newspapers can all go to hell. It is time to bring in McCrory. As I did Glen Alden. I need the full return. I need the balance sheet. Let me put it another way. This is the payoff for all the troubles I have had with your company."

"All the troubles? You have had only *nachas* since I am there."

"All right, the *nachas*, too. But now is the time."

"And what will I do?"

"You'll come with it. You will be chairman and chief executive of the wholly-owned subsidiary."

"This is what I have earned?" demanded Neaman harshly. "To be submerged into a subsidiary of another company? To be subservient to a—to a *schwantz* like Izzy Becker? To take orders from a—a *klutz* like Leonard Lane? To bask in your reflected glory, Rik, when you will decide to send a little bit in my direction?"

Riklis did not answer. Neither of them smiled anymore. The telephone rang. It was ignored. "I think that maybe you shouldn't say yes or no right now," suggested Riklis. "Think it over for a week or two. Logic is on my side, isn't it? And there is a precedent for it, after all. Sammy, you should have known all along."

Neaman moved the glass of tea away from him. He got up. "There is nothing to think over," he said. "If you are serious about this plan, I give you my answer right now. I will resign."

Riklis emitted a deep sigh. "You mean it, too, don't you?"

he said. "I should know by now. Sam never does anything half-way."

Neaman acknowledged nothing. After several more moments in which they stared at each other, Riklis shrugged. "Well, we'll see. If you do resign, don't forget there are others who can take over. You've been training a lot of people over there. Maybe it wouldn't be so hard to scratch up a few successors."

Neaman nodded. "I see, Rik, that you don't understand. If I resign, you see, it is not just Neaman who resigns. Because if I go, I can assure you that my entire top team and the layers right underneath will resign, too. En masse. Over fifty of the top executives, the biggest jobs, will resign in sympathy with me. I will see to it. So the company will be—how shall I put it?—decimated of its senior management. I promise it."

He walked to the door, his back to Riklis. Opening the door, he turned to stare once more at the other man. Riklis had thrust back his chair but still sat in it. His face was red and he was breathing rapidly. "You mean it, too," he said, incredu-lously.

"I said I promise it." Neaman's lip pouted but his eyes were triumphant. "Can you imagine what this controversy will look like in the papers? The publicity in the *Times* and the *Wall Street Journal* alone will make the stocks of both companies drop five, maybe ten points. And the banks, the banks that Izzy Becker worries about so much, what will they think? Di-sasters come in small doses, right Rik? This will be a mouthful, maybe a stomachful. . . ."

Neaman paused a few moments more in the doorway, long enough to see Riklis begin to smile and to hear him say, "What's all the excitement, anyway? You know that I never force a merger on unfriendly partners. It would only be a mar-riage and a quick divorce. Who needs it? Let's not talk about it any more."

Within the next few days Neaman quickly pressed his tacti-cal advantage. He met with Riklis again under much more amicable circumstances and exacted an understanding that there would be no merger while he remained chief executive officer of McCrory. That meeting, however, resulted in an unusual communications gap. Neaman told a newspaperman that he had compelled Riklis to sign a codicil to his employment contract that precluded a merger between the two companies. Months later, when he was asked about this, Riklis vehemently denied it. He said that it would have had to be disclosed to the Securities and Exchange Commission because it was an action binding on two public companies and therefore affected stockholders. Still later, Neaman was reminded about his statement by the same reporter, but he denied ever having made it.

Yet, regardless of whether there had been a written agreement or not, Neaman's stiff resistance and threat had turned the trick. McCrory's last merger would not take place.

Most stunned by the turnabout, even more than Riklis, was Izzy Becker. When Riklis told him about it shortly after the meeting with Neaman, he thought that Becker would react by having a stroke. The heavy veins in his forehead and neck bulged with stress. He began to cough violently, and Riklis had to pound him on the back to quell the phlegm.

15. "I Hate Him, I Hate Him"

It was only a few weeks later that Becker realized a lifelong ambition. Those who thought they knew the lanky, intense, financial man well, who assumed that the heavy furrows on his big bald crown and piercing brown eyes often veiled under tired lids bespoke only the concentration on the balance sheet, couldn't have been more wrong. Although for almost fifteen years he had been under the shadow of Meshulam Riklis's ambition and personal drive, Becker harbored deep ambitions of his own. He had long thrived under his reputation as one of New York's most astute and creative corporate financial chiefs. But more recently he had felt dismayed by being tagged with a label as a specialist, although apparently incapable of running a large company. Even his appointment as the company's vice-chairman, though gratifying, had proved frustrating. He had been brought so near and yet was so far.

So, shortly after Riklis's confrontation with Neaman, the Rapid–American board met and devoted a portion of its regular monthly meeting to an action proposed by Riklis. With Riklis smiling and chattering happily at the head of the table, the directors summarily elected Becker president of Rapid–American. Riklis, who had held both titles, chairman and president, would continue as chairman and chief executive officer. After the unanimous vote of approval was tallied, naturally Riklis was the first one to leap from his seat and pound Izzy Becker on the back.

Afterward, Riklis explained to the press that it was all a matter of delegating his responsibilities, that Becker had earned it not only as vice-chairman and financial man but as concurrent chairman of a major Rapid subsidiary and that promotions are earned not dispensed. Neaman, who was on the board, had not been able to attend and he was apparently not missed.

But speculation on Becker's promotion did not overlook the possibility that the move was aimed as a deliberate counter-offensive, as a blow to the pride and aspirations of the stubborn Neaman. If he disliked anyone more than Riklis, it was Izzy Becker. He had said so often, not caring if it reached Becker's ears—and it did. Becker, on the other hand, had little use for Neaman's "mumbo-jumbo," as he called it. If Riklis had wanted to slap Neaman's ears hard, he couldn't have done it better, many reasoned, than by promoting Becker. What could be more irritating to Neaman than to have to accept directives signed by Izzy Becker? "It's like a mongoose taking orders from a snake," a financial reporter slyly observed.

But, then, of course, the speculation notwithstanding, the victory was psychological. Both men now had equally significant roles with immense plates to eat from. They would not bloody one another. The effect of the Riklis ploy, if its intent had been to boot Neaman, was to intensify the mutual awareness of all the principals and to sensitize their nerves.

The McCrory chairman remained silent during all the speculation, not reacting more than merely to send a curt congratulatory note to Becker. He kept his composure, stoically following his routine. It was as if he realized that he had gained his objective, to stay the ultimate merger, that of his own company into its parent. If an enemy at court had been jockeyed into a key offensive position, so be it. One made sure to win the war first.

But, unlike Neaman, Becker was quite willing shortly afterward to discuss the strategic change. He was so joyous over his promotion that he responded quickly to my request for an interview. He discussed the matter in terms so candid that it was obvious he felt a new flush of power and recognition.

Becker, it appears, prefers Italian restaurants. Since he agreed to an interview, he decided in the wave of good-will that he felt toward most of the world to invite the reporter to lunch and to grant the interview during it. As we entered the well-known, uptown restaurant, it was apparent that Becker was a well-respected, frequent customer. The cloakroom girl fussed over him, he pinched her cheek to her delight, and the maitre d' glided over to us. "I like this joint," Becker whispers. "It's no pasteria or pizzeria—they charge Four Seasons prices. But the food is *buono*."

As we ordered drinks, a cursory study showed that Becker had changed. He was more at ease than I had ever seen him. Somehow, away from the Riklis mystique of the triumphant, golden conglomerator, Becker seemed his own man. He spoke with authority to the wine waiter and with precise knowledge to the regular waiter. He greeted friends with dignity and a cautious warmth. After a while, asked what he particularly enjoyed about his new promotion, he hesitated, swallowed, and replied, "My mother's reaction. She's almost eighty, yet she's still got all her buttons. But she never thought that I was a big wheel until she saw my picture in the *Times* last week."

He spoke of his years with Riklis, his frustrations of learning first to adapt to the man's quixotic moods and then, after that level was reached, of keeping up with his restless ambition and drive.

"I think," Becker says, "that he's the greatest financier in the country today. He's done things that are creative in the extreme and yet he's the most honest man I know. The people who don't like him are jealous. They're jealous of what he's achieved, jealous of his style, and jealous of the way he likes to live. The trouble with a lot of you guys in the press, the reason that you give him the back of your hand is that you don't know. He's the nearest thing to a genius Wall Street has seen in a generation."

If every important figure must have an alter-ego, Becker assumes that he was Riklis's. As a C.P.A., he was put into a position of bringing some of his superior's concepts down to pragmatic terms. As a treasurer, it became his role to validate the balance sheet. As financial vice-president, he became the contact man with the banks, and it was here that he scored his greatest triumph. Solid and well-schooled, the type of former accountant who can explain a corporation's needs in banker's terms, Becker created his own acceptance with the lenders. The fact was that a financial entrepreneur like Riklis needed a strong back-up man with the banks. And no one knew it more than Riklis. And then, realizing that Becker's greatest fear was that he would always be considered only a financial man, Riklis had given him certain operating functions and then, in that move that was "just a great, sweet event in my life," made him corporate president.

"What can I say about a guy who does that for you?" asks Becker. "He's just a real *mensch*. There's nobody like him."

"What about Neaman?"

Becker stiffens perceptibly. The conversation then turns into a verbal form of a cat-and-mouse game. It consists of feints and withdrawals, of nasty thrusts, pained retorts followed by blazes of passion:

"How is Neaman taking your promotion?"

"What do you think? He's dying, that's how he's taking it."

"Why? He has his own empire, doesn't he? Why should he care?"

"Maybe I shouldn't get involved."

"Or is it that you two just never got along?"

"You can say that again."

"But didn't he once want you as his number two at McCrory?"

"Yeah, that's true. When Rik made him chairman of McCrory, Neaman told him he wanted me as his number two. But Rik told him, 'No, Izzy will be my own number two.' "

"Well, doesn't that show that Neaman respects you?"

"I don't care if he does."

"Well, what do you think of Neaman?"

"I think he's a very capable administrator. But he's very callous toward people."

"Would you explain?"

"He just has no feeling toward people. He's very cold-hearted and damned demanding. That's one reason he's made a lot of enemies."

"But you would have to admit that a lot of people swear by him."

"It's a question of whether they swear by him or at him, if you ask me."

Becker pauses, stares thoughtfully at his tall glass as if he is beginning to feel that he is getting in too deep. He drains his white wine, sighs pleasurably, and runs his stare around the restaurant.

"Well, all right, you've told me what you think of Neaman but how do you personally feel about him?"

He swallows as though it hurts, pauses, and then hoarsely it bursts forth: "I hate him; I hate him. I've always hated the sonofabitch!"

"Why?"

"He's untrustworthy and a liar," says Becker. "I think there's a good chance he feels he's gotta resign because of my promotion. He's not the kind of guy who can take a reversal."

So much seems to be implied rather than said that a lapse in the conversation follows and then the question: "I get the impression that you think he's not quite—is Neaman suffering from some sort of psychological problem?"

"No question about it. He's a paranoid and maybe worse. He's got no friends. He doesn't want to have any friends. He's just a person that is entirely alone—except maybe for his wife—and he suspects that the whole world is against him."

"Hasn't he accomplished a great deal in spite of all that?"

Becker responds with a vast shrug. "If he's so good," he asks "why isn't he proving out to be such a genius with the Klein's stores? The reason is that he can't solve their problems. Maybe no one can, but one thing we know is he can't. All he can do is solve the problems of the variety division. The others take care of themselves. You know what Old Man Lane said over at the Lerner shops, don't you? He said that if Sam ever came to his office to check on what was going on, he would personally take Neaman by the lapels and the coat collar and throw him out of the fifteenth floor window. Sam heard about it and he never came there again. That's the great Neaman."

"What's in store for McCrory?"

"I'm convinced that the future growth will come from the integration of the J.J. Newberry stores. This will bring the greatest profit growth for the company, combined with the continued profits from all the others except for Klein's. McCrory should have excellent potential. As far as the Klein's stores, they never made much money, and that's not going to mean one thing or another as long as everything else holds up. That's going to be the big challenge—to make sure that everything else holds up."

"With or without Neaman?"

"That's up to him."

16. "Wherever I Am . . . "

Neaman grinned. His jowls bulged. He laughed. If it was all, as Becker said, "up to him," then that was no real change, was it? He held himself upright at the head of the table, as if the ridiculousness of the situation would burst right out of him as I sat at the other end, ballpoint poised. There was, it seemed, nothing to write at the moment. His reaction to Becker's outburst was no different than it had ever been. When the head of the subsidiary company can hold at bay the heads of his parent company, then why worry about their rancor even "when it spits"?

In that spring of 1973, he was unquestionably riding high. He had produced eight consecutive years of profit advances for his company and was soon to report a ninth. He had taken the huge Newberry chain and swallowed it as a whale gulps a dolphin. He had just engineered a delegation of the management of the 1,100 store variety chain into a network of regional presidents, revamped the warehouse system, and regrouped the stores into their most effective combinations. Already, in a few short months, the Newberry stores were beginning to contribute their share of profits. The other divisions were purring along, with or without his intervention. The Klein's chain was also in the process of coming up for air once again under the prod of yet a newer effort to make its stores pay off.

But, perhaps the sweetest triumph of all was how he had handled Meshulam Riklis. He had taken everything that the golden, little conglomerator has thrown at him and done handsomely with them. Klein's? That, too, would come along. But, even more than all that, he had become the first one who could stand in Riklis's way and force it back into his teeth. Why? It was simple: a wall of success in achieving performance and in motivating people blocked any righteous anger and punitive action on Riklis's part, however fervently he desired revenge. Worry about the resentment and jealousy of one like Izzy Becker? It was to laugh. So Neaman laughed again before pitching in and demolishing his spartan lunch.

He wiped his lips carefully and said, "My friend, McCrory is Neaman. In fact, Rapid–American could even be considered Neaman. Wherever I am—that's the center of the world. That is the way things stand."

He studied me as if to ascertain whether I were repelled by such egotism. "It is not egotism," he explained, "but only a sense of the reality of the world I live in."

Neaman sat down and sipped from the large cup of tea that remained after Margit Bergklint had swept in and deftly removed the remains of the lunch. Now he became positively philosophical.

"May I explain my position? I think I can always talk to you," he said. "Riklis is a very intelligent man. People sometimes forget it. And they talk without thinking. All corporate chairmen are considered dictators, isn't it so? Rik's personality is volatile. He enjoys making constant little explosions in the press. Myself, I like to be inside. I can control things this way. It is my world. I don't like being the subject of juicy stories. He likes to make the headlines for Rapid, fine. But, even in spite of it, look what he has accomplished. Still, people don't give you credit after you have done something. You have done it, so what? That is the cynicism of the time. Analysts from Wall Street and everywhere tell Neaman, Riklis, Richard Nixon what they would do in their place—but we do what we have to do. The analysts' community should quit that. After all, you put the left foot forward, then the right foot, and then both feet—

"So we have our worlds that we rule. In my world, which sometimes becomes superimposed with Riklis's, it is very well-known that as long as I am around, there will be no merger. Why will there be no merger? Because he needs me more than I need him. Yet, we are really friends. I can work elsewhere, but where can he get another Neaman? So he needs me. Therefore, I am not about to leave and they are not about to merge."

But, couldn't the situation change so that he would lose the same strong position? He smiled. "Of course," he conceded. "It could be twenty years from now. Old Man Lane is now almost eighty-four, and he is still going strong. I, too, am going strong. If anything happens to me, if I should break my neck or die, they will rush into a merger. But not now. Not while this is my world. I have shut the door on them."

A few days later, in the basement auditorium of a major downtown bank, he worked his magic on stockholders at the annual meeting. As usual, his rhetoric produced initial tremors of resentment and uncertainty among some analysts and stockholders. But, as he proceeded, he began once again to hypnotize them with his logic, his facts, his assurance.

Staring out at his audience of about 200 persons, he told them of the improvement in profits for the first quarter, reflecting the integration of the Newberry chain. "We have," he said, "already started turning Newberry around, and now their profits are starting to reach the same plateau as our own variety division—almost seven percent before taxes. That's where we are going. We have acquired $300 million in business for only $53 million in paper. In a couple of years . . .

"All this, my friends, does not come by wishful thinking. We have developed management to help the Newberry store managers. There are no arguments, no debates, no fights. Everyone is showing excellent cooperation."

He paused, pouted a bit, removed his glasses, put them on again, and proceeded warmly. "All our divisions are doing well. We have exceptionally good results as usual from the Lerner shops. Our sporting goods and auto supply stores are doing better and better. But—as in every family—you have a black sheep. We have a problem with the Klein's group. Like all other promotional department stores, it is suffering from low markup. The day of just low prices is gone. The public is sophisticated now—what is the value? what does the dollar buy?—this is what it wants to know. We are moving Klein's out of the low markup and into the markups of the normal department store. This means new, better merchandising and new management responsibility, but we are doing it gradually. This is not to be a revolution, because revolutions spill blood and I don't believe in that."

Eyes in the audience brightened. There was a perceptible stir and a few backs of elderly stockholders straightened as Neaman said, his voice rising, "What I do believe in is our policy of staying with and improving the small store. We are the Toyota and the Volkswagen of the retail business—we believe in what I call the micro-efficiency store. What are we? We are 2,300 small stores all told—only 100 of them are above 25,000 square feet. The normal discount store, the normal department store is 100,000 square feet. But not us. We are taking exactly the same tack as the automobile business. Compact. Families may still own big cars, but they are mostly buying small cars."

Pausing again, he swallowed some water and said, "We are the only chain in America that is not trying to get out of the small store. And we are finding ways to identify our requirements without having to spend lots of money on computers and electronic equipment. Instead, we are relying on the human being and his capacity to merchandise. And, with this and a cautious but very aggressive program, we will be the best operators of small stores. Yes, my friends, small stores. Our 2,300 small stores have 2,300 young Americans managing and working in the private enterprise spirit—each one in effect owning his store. . . ."

Applause greeted him. Apparently surprised, he held up his hand and went on, ". . . And we will make sure that all these young men, each man, is a retailer by nature. Because you can't acquire it. You have to love people to be a retailer. You have to be outgoing. You have to love your store and you have to take it home with you. You have to want your wife to participate. You can't just have a store manager—you have to have a store manager, his wife, and his kids. And I want to tell you that they are all helping. And we have to make sure that they are well-paid—within three years, they will be making at least $15,-000 a year. Before I came to McCrory, the minimum wage for a manager was $4,000. Now, it is $8,000. That's why they are all happy. That's why they are all dedicated. . . ."

He invited questions, his eyes gleaming in anticipation. The first to rise was John Gilbert, one of the corporate gadflies. He was one of two brothers who represented others by proxy and were skilled at goading management.

Holding up the gaudy McCrory annual report, the questioner referred to page five and asked, "Who bought that Newberry subsidiary?"

"Who remembers their name?" asked Neaman with a grin. "The only thing is we sold it. That's the important thing to remember—to get the hell out of it. We sold everything we didn't want. The people who bought the subsidiary knew what they were doing. They're over twenty-one and good luck to them."

As the applause and laughter died down, the gadfly asked, "What about our bank loans? Are we paying the prime rate?"

"Yes. The banks consider us a prime customer and so they charge us the prime rate. They always did—from Chase Manhattan to everyone else."

"And as far as Stanley Kunsberg," pursued the questioner, "he's listed as president and treasurer. This is unusual—and I don't think that the president should also be the treasurer. . . ."

"Do you know," asked Neaman with an ever bigger grin, "what an unusual man he is? He can handle two jobs."

"Have we been buying our own stock?"

"No, we haven't. Rapid–American jumped the gun. They have been buying our stock because they recognize what a good company they have."

"I have a few more questions. But I will wait until later."

"Thank you," Neaman said. "John, you're great."

"What will you do if the economy turns down?" asked another stockholder.

"For eight months, I went from store to store and studied the situation in hundreds of communities and reached the conclusion that we must have the small store in the United States. That factor will help us greatly today. We're good in prosperity because the big store doesn't want to sell the fifty-cent item. We're good in depression because people don't have more than fifty cents to spend. We are the people's store. . . ."

"But, Mr. Neaman, don't you have to advertise a lot to tell the people where you are?" asked a stockholder.

"No, it makes no difference. We are next to—we sit next to the big store and live off their traffic. First, the shopper buys his big-ticket item in the big store, then he needs a pack of envelopes and there we are. Then he needs a can, a shovel, and there we are. No big lines; you don't have to walk a mile; everything is compact within 10,000 square feet. Don't forget, the working girl has only a half-hour to eat and shop. There we are, easy to shop, and she can walk through quickly. . . ."

The questions lapsed and Neaman said, "Any more questions? No? John? You want to wind up the meeting?"

John Gilbert arose, arranged the sheets he held, and asked, "What about the dividend? If you're doing so well, when will it go up? You know, a lot of these retired stockholders in Florida are worried about inflation. I think a little sweetening in the form of a higher dividend would be very welcome. Then they could come back into stores and buy more. Just a suggestion. You know, you're not allowed to raise it too much anyway."

"Yes, I accept the suggestion—and the members of the board will consider it."

A few minutes later, after tallies of votes were announced on routine matters, the meeting ended. Neaman consented, a public relations man told the members of the press, to a short press conference in a room nearby. It turned out to be a fencing session, primarily on the subject of the abortive merger of Mc-Crory into Rapid.

To questions from the reporters, Neaman said that there would never be a merger, not as long as he was there. He had a commitment, he said, an agreement with Meshulam Riklis that there would be no merger during his, that is, Neaman's tenure. He insisted that this was to be off-record. He didn't want to start any fights with anyone, he said. But he demonstrated some resentment at the press's insistence on the point. He did say, however, that Riklis had "prematurely and erroneously" stated that there would be such a merger. When he was told that the question would undoubtedly be raised at the Rapid–American annual meeting a week later, he shrugged and smiled. "All right," he said, "let's see what Mr. Riklis tells us about it at his meeting."

Several hundred stockholders of Rapid–American turned out at the parent company meeting. Some came prepared to do battle, others to defend or harass management. Lewis Gilbert, the second of the two gadfly brothers was also on hand. Riklis, dapper and relaxed, handled it all in his usual easy manner. But it had its difficult, even comic moments.

After introducing his directors and then the officers seated on the dais on his right and left, Riklis proceeded with routine matters. But a woman stockholder quickly arose to ask, "I would like to know how you decided what terms to give us on the merger of Glen Alden into Rapid? Just to steal the stock from us, in other words. I had 200 shares of Glen Alden and you gave me nothing in comparison. . . . I have here a copy of *New York Magazine* with salaries of leading men in the United States . . ."

"You don't need the magazine," said Riklis. "My salary is always in the proxy statement."

"Just to give you a comparison," she proceeded. "You are one of the six highest paid. What makes you better than anyone else?"

"I rise on a point of order," said Gilbert. "She's perfectly right to say anything she wants to. But this is not the time to do it. I suggest we proceed and she can . . ."

"All right, later—" she conceded and sat down.

Smiling at the gadfly, Riklis said, "You don't have to worry about my ability to . . ."

"I know we don't have to worry about you," the woman

said. "You know how to connive out of everything—" There was a scattering of applause and laughter.

The microphone suddenly hummed into everyone's ears. When it became normal, Riklis said with a sort of grim smile, "Young lady. I don't mind your saying anything you want. But you should say it nicely."

"I can say it," she pursued, "and it's much nicer than what you do!"

A stocky man got up in the center of the room. "Just a second," he said. "Can I have the floor microphone? I think I can satisfy her a little. I would ask the lady to be a little indulgent and wait until a little later in the meeting when we hear what will happen. If you look ahead and see earnings of $60 million this year and maybe $70 million next year, maybe you won't complain."

These words drew a brief silence. The stockholders knew this man, a schoolteacher who had invested his life savings in Riklis's companies and invariably defended him. A few moments later, Riklis said in a low, resigned voice, "I'm glad everyone is trying to protect my position over here. Let's proceed with the meeting. I will give the lady a chance to say what she wants to say. I will give the teacher a chance to answer her. We do it every year. Please be patient. The only thing is that the mike should cooperate."

After management named its slate of directors, Gilbert arose to question why the company's proxy statement failed to include a previous limitation of $500,000 on director's earnings. Riklis explained, patiently, "My salary is related to profits. When they go up, my salary goes up. When they go down, so does my salary."

"But, I don't think they should go through the roof!" said Gilbert.

The next questioner was a woman who suggested in vehement terms that a woman should be on the board. "Since many of your products are bought by women," she said, "don't you think a woman should advise you how to run your business?"

"Young lady," said Riklis, no doubt thinking of his recent separation from his wife, "I had a woman to tell me how to run my business all my life." The officers flanking him laughed loudly.

Another stockholder, a crisply speaking man, suggested that the backgrounds and other corporate directorships of all directorial candidates be included in proxy statements. "This will give us some kind of a warning in case there is a potential conflict-of-interest on the board," he said. Riklis readily agreed.

The woman who had complained at the outset about Riklis's salary got up to harangue him on the matter of directorial conflict-of-interest. The teacher interposed again, "Look, let's dispense with the trivia. Let's hear some important words on profits, sales, dividends." But Riklis told him, "Please, I ask you again not to defend me. I am fully capable of doing it by myself."

The female gadfly jumped up again, "So what are we gonna do about the directors? Especially when they are directors of other corporations and start washing each other's hands?"

"Miss," Riklis said, his face reddening, "let me ask you a question. Did you hear my answer to listing the full backgrounds of each director?"

"Yes. I believe that we should—"

"I believe what you believe," Riklis said, smiling painfully. "And I told him I believe in what you and he believe. And we will have it next time so that we can all believe." The audience enjoyed this, applauding again and laughing.

A vote was taken on the directorial nominees, and it was followed by a long discussion on the next order of business, an increased stock-option program. Riklis gave an eloquent defense of the plan as an incentive to middle-management employes. "Izzy Becker and I don't get any of this," he explained. Almost an hour of wrangling over the plan drew patience thin, and those close to the dais saw Riklis beginning to shift with growing fatigue and frustration.

Finally, the discussion and the stockholder fretting subsided, and the chairman presented his formal remarks. Rapid–American had completed its very best year on record, he told them. As he spoke, he seemed to loosen up. He used the adjective "very" six times in describing Rapid's fine performance during the recent fiscal year. "And I want to remind all of you," he said, "that this was in a year when the economy had lots of troubles and lots of companies had troubles."

He was questioned by the gadfly brother about a fee of almost $2 million to the company's outside auditors. "We are an active company," explained Riklis, "and we have been involved in a merger and several acquisitions over the last year. We have had a tender offer. So our auditor's fees are higher. Our legal fees are higher. We are a corporation in movement, aren't we? We are slowly but surely consolidating."

A stockholder in the rear asked, "What happened to the merger with McCrory?"

Riklis stared hard at the man, trying to make him out but apparently failing to do so. "A merger with McCrory," he replied slowly, "is not in the immediate future. It was easier to merge Glen Alden into Rapid. Mr. Neaman at McCrory, as chairman and chief executive officer there, wants his freedom to perform, and we are going to give it to him."

The same stockholder pursued him, "What about the Klein's chain? Why don't you get rid of them?"

"Mr. Neaman," said Riklis, "is grappling with that problem. Klein's is not doing well—it's like a retarded child, it needs lots of care—but Mr. Neaman has been very successful in solving other problems. We can only hope that he will be successful in solving this one, too."

No one really knew for certain why Neaman did what he did shortly after those two meetings in spring 1973. The McCrory chairman himself declined any rationale at the time. He didn't articulate any program to his staff. He merely issued instructions to various departments and specialists. He certainly didn't tell Meshulam Riklis, and he avoided the press. And later, when he explained why he had done those things, it was obvious that it was all veiled over by hindsight logic, the kind of narrative that is pinched here, expanded there, rounded or squared to support a convenient explanation. But it is not hard to reconstruct what he did and why against the framework of elements in flux.

Klein's, those twenty vast, awkwardly operating, and fumbling stores, had obviously become an urgent problem. There were several reasons for this. First, it was more and more obvious to Neaman that if he were to continue to exert his hold over Riklis, to maintain his ability to sway the little conglomerator from swallowing up his company, it was vital that he should continue to produce the degree of earnings that made him and his men indispensable.

Secondly, Klein's was sinking into even deeper problems because of the recession-inflation pressures. People just weren't buying household durables. They couldn't afford it. They couldn't even buy suits or coats, and they were buying even less at Klein's. Even Macy's was no exception, but the Herald Square store had fifteen profitable satellites. Klein's in Manhattan had eighteen branch stores scattered along the Atlantic seaboard, only a few of which made any money. So, in view of the business downturn, Neaman had to mount yet another attack on the chain's difficulties.

And thirdly, there is a very simple truth to a man's reputation. He cannot live on it indefinitely without reinforcing it. If he was still to be considered "the greatest nonmerchant in retailing," Neaman knew he could not long withstand a failure to make Klein's profitable. Already, he was well aware that there were a growing number of critics in both the parent company and his own firm who were scoffing at his real abilities in view of the recalcitrant Klein's. He hadn't wanted the damn outfit in the beginning. He had advised Riklis against buying it. But as always Riklis couldn't resist a bargain. That bargain, Neaman thought ruefully, could yet turn out to be the most expensive one Riklis had ever bought. And it could, Neaman became convinced, ruin a reputation that had already been earned many times over.

The situation called for some drastic actions, and he quickly set them in motion. Within a few weeks, working several days around the clock and fourteen hours on other days, he whipped together three basic courses of attack.

He greatly increased the use of the company's computer. The IBM 360 had been utilized by Lerner's and the variety division. Now, he issued a detailed blueprint for an automatic replenishment system of ordering and inventory-taking for Klein's. To his dazzled and dismayed staff at Klein's, he unfolded the glories and strategies of "MERZ," or a "Merchandise Early Replenishment System."

"Perhaps, you wonder," he said with a smile while eating his cottage cheese, "why I use a Z instead of an S for 'MERZ'?" No one knew the answer. "Sigmund," said Neaman, calling on a young German refugee who sat quietly nearby and who would program the new computer application, "please tell them why."

The intense, bespectacled young man arose. "Yez Zir," he said. "It iz becauze it iz a zyztem—a zyztem to remove the human errors."

Neaman grinned. "You see," he said, "Zyztem. Z, not S." He beamed at them all. They beamed back. Everyone understood his little ruse. The touch of humor, the injection of a light but barbed touch, would remove the rancor that any of them might feel that the boss had lost his faith in people and was placing it instead in a machine.

The fact was that MERZ had a difficult time until it became part of the Klein's pattern. Most of the old-time executives, merchandisers, and buyers had an innate conviction that the IBM 360 would do them out of a job. Then, in a test of four stores over a month, the results proved inconclusive. It was simple enough. If you told the computer that you had sold ten washcloths the week before and ten washcloths the week before that, it would then know how to order for the weeks ahead. The ideal, of course, was to have one washcloth on hand in every store, no more, with a truck already backed into the receiving bay with another washcloth in case it was needed. That, of course, was uneconomical and impractical. The singular had to be multiplied by thousands. But the buyers and store managers (who should have told the home office to tell the computer just how many washcloths they needed and when they were needed) never did quite trust the IBM 360 and failed to give it the kind of input it needed.

At the end of the month's test, Neaman was told that the results were inconclusive. He was stunned. "Inconclusive?" he burst out. "No test should ever be inconclusive. Either it is a success or it is a failure! It can be neither if you have done your job. Recheck your figures."

The figures were checked again and came back in a slightly different form. Neaman studied them carefully in his closed office. After an hour, he emerged with a radiant smile. "I am satisfied that they are conclusive," he declared. "The test is a success."

As the computer application under MERZ was quickly extended to the entire Klein's chain, several buyers complained. One said that it was "foolhardy" to involve his department in MERZ when it was still unproven. According to those who heard the ensuing explosion from Neaman, the buyer was "torn apart." Another whose responsibility was men's wear thought that he had some clout with Neaman and expressed some serious reservations about MERZ. He immediately found himself drawn into a serious debate with the chairman and stamped as "cowardly." A week or so later, the buyer was relieved of the major part of his duties and assigned only to buying lower-priced accessories—ties, belts, socks.

Within two months after MERZ was extended to all stores, the amount of inventory rose several million dollars at the chain. But sales did not rise commensurately. Suppliers, of course, were elated. Their orders were larger. They saw the latest Neaman move as a harbinger of new life at Klein's. The merchandisers and buyers were aghast. For many months, their orders had been held back and reorders pruned to keep expenses down and produce some profits. Now their functions had been replaced by an IBM machine and an EDP system nicknamed "MERZ" which had reversed the stock reduction. It was disillusioning, degrading, and confusing.

At a staff meeting, Neaman explained why he was not concerned by the abrupt rise in the amount of inventory. "The system—pardon me, zyztem—is obviously filling in the holes in our inventory which were created by people failure. So, naturally the inventory is up," he said. "And, further, how can you really expect a computer to correct the overstock in some departments committed by people? Give it time and it will do that, too. I am very pleased."

As he was transforming the merchandise array in Klein's from low margin to "department-store margin" by heavy reliance on the "zyztem," he also demonstrated dramatic acts of faith involving people and his reliance on them.

Isolating what he felt were Klein's most difficult problems, he in effect set up task forces to grapple with each. He didn't call them that, but he simply appointed more than the usual number of executives to solve such headaches as "merchandising mix," "store productivity," "waste space," "unproductive display," "advertising dispersion." In almost every case, people working on such problems found themselves falling over one another. Each offensive had about twice as many soldiers as it needed. "I am convinced," he told everyone, "that from the ranks we will find the answers." He was, in other words, still sold on the vitality, the dynamics of the average, although it was obvious that he wanted the computer backup, too.

But the men in each group did not seem as much gratified by the expression of confidence in them as they seemed irked by it. Perhaps it was because it is difficult to feel any surge of personal confidence when everyone else obtains the same expression of confidence. Given the same challenge, the same responsibility, the same corner of the same department, the situation naturally began to breed considerable in-fighting.

Neaman's second display of faith in people came when he commenced reassigning qualified executives from the variety-store division to the department stores. He was only "borrowing" them, he explained to the variety division. He needed the cream of the specialists at the attack point where he must solve his knottiest problem. These raids produced a complex set of effects. While they pleased some of those reassigned, because he raised their salaries and brought them in with some hoopla, those with whom they were joined resented their arrival. Soon, the reassignees found themselves uncomfortable. The glory of recognition lasted only a day or two. Almost immediately, they were under the gun. And, at the same time, certain key divisions and departments of the variety division found themselves almost denuded of their best executives.

Yet, controversial as all three of these moves were, it was generally conceded that the Klein's chain had never before been given such a direct and massive concentration of effort. It seemed possible as 1973 wore on that, for perhaps the first time, Klein's might not have a loss and might even earn more than a puny profit on its $230 million in sales.

But it did not. Why it didn't was suggested some time later by an executive who had worked for about two years at Neaman's elbow, one of the numerous "assistants" who were brought in to handle special assignments. These were tasks that the chairman felt could be better accomplished by alert, experienced men without any officer's or department-head's designation.

Mike Berdow was a thin, wispy executive of forty who had experience in both the retail and wholesale businesses, but he retained an objectivity about them. He also operated his own marketing company and had just sold it at a profit to a larger company when an executive recruiter contacted him. Offered a job so quickly after he had cut his own business ties, Berdow was pleased to accept a post as Neaman's assistant. He was hired, so he was told, to help the chairman solve the problems of the department-store division. He was hired on January 1, 1972, and resigned October 24, 1973. "It was almost two years," he said, "that I'm not very likely to forget."

In recalling those months when he worked closest with the chairman, Berdow said he found himself drawn into a deep study of the man. His methods were unusual enough. But the man was so much the father of his methods that knowing the man could help one almost to predict what he would do.

"A lot of Neaman's personality," he said, "is tied up with the scientific management that he espoused. But he was strange. Although he seemed to feel that people could do anything, he mistrusted them. And he allowed his mistrust to guide his decisions about people. Maybe it's true that you can trust people only so far. Neaman was the kind of guy who either trusted them too much—or not enough."

Such a case was when he used a lot of people to bear down on a problem. That made too many of them think of cheating, Berdow said. They would spend half their time politicking and the other half working. With so many given the responsibility of coming up with a solution, Neaman simply couldn't get the kind of efficiency out of them that he wanted. They would visibly put forth a lot of effort to assure him of their diligence and loyalty. And he would, despite his mistrust, fall for it, according to Berdow. He began to exhibit a methodology of advancing the business mainly by using people who were obviously loyal to him.

Neaman's next step, Berdow recalled, was to intensify his spy system. Here's how it worked: "If a buyer or merchandiser left the home office to visit a store," he related, "I or one of Neaman's other assistants would call the store manager to find what time the visitor got there, what he had said, and what time he left. The aim was to ferret out those disloyal types who would either bad mouth the home office, Neaman, or the guy's immediate bosses. But it was also intended to make sure that the man didn't waste time or go somewhere else to look for a job. And if the guy was even seen talking to someone else from another company, he immediately came under suspicion."

There was little doubt, Berdow said, that Neaman began to feel that he probably could depend more on the IBM 360 than on people. Perhaps it was because MERZ, limited as it was to what one put into it, had the reliability that Neaman found lacking in people. As far as the staff was concerned, at least then, no one seemed to understand that. The employes' attitude about MERZ was that it would somehow do them out of a job. Neaman's attitude about the computer was that the bugs in it would eventually come out in its usage, so there seemed to be no reason to delay an extended application.

"I've worked with computers before," said Berdow, "and they're an effective tool if used properly. Mostly, you get less out of it than you should because of the people's fear of it. But even then, even when it works right away, it takes two to three years to run it properly. And you should have a standby manual system in case the computer breaks down. Neaman didn't have the *sitzfleish* to test it out properly, and once he decided to go whole hog, the manual system was discarded.

"Faced with growing pressures in regard to the department-store chain, Neaman threw himself into its problems and he 'began giving the variety chain less and less attention.' That was a mistake. He had trained the staff in York, Pennsylvania, to take orders from him. When he no longer gave any orders, it became sort of like an army in disarray. But it was still going along on its momentum and not too much could go wrong with it. In the meantime, he was putting all that effort and attention into Klein's. But what he failed to recognize was that there were things that even he, with his great talents, couldn't do. No one I know ever grappled harder with a less viable property than Neaman with Klein's."

Why did he, Berdow, leave Neaman's employ so soon? "Well, I could have taken him longer but my wife couldn't," he replied.

Sarah Berdow was actually a very unassuming woman and a devoted wife. She rarely complained, except on those occasions when Neaman asked Mike to spend several weeks or months out-of-town on one of those special assignments. Sarah packed up and moved with her husband. The penultimate topper, however, came during the preparations for the annual staff luncheons when service awards were presented. This particular one was held in a country club not far from the York, Pennsylvania, home office. As with almost everything in which Neaman involved himself, detailed instructions were prepared for the event.

The plan called for Neaman to arrive in front of the country club via helicopter. He was to be greeted outside the plane by twin rows of executives, twelve in each platoon. It was somewhat on the level of a South American chief of state, perhaps, but as far as Mike Berdow knew, at no point did Neaman protest the ceremony. As far as the wives were concerned, they were to stand in a group several yards away from the parallel platoons. The program stated that wives were not to wear miniskirts or midiskirts but dresses just so long. Then, in the evening at the cocktail party, they were instructed to wear longer skirts but not cocktail gowns. That would be too ostentatious.

When Sarah Berdow heard the instructions on the lengths of the dresses she was to wear in the afternoon and evening, she did a very uncharacteristic thing. "She just about blew her top," Berdow recalled. "I remember her saying to me, yelling at me is more like it, 'I'll be damned if I will do that! What if I wear whatever I want to? You work for him, not me.'" But Sarah acceded to the plan, as Berdow knew she would.

But some months later, when Neaman asked him for the third or fourth time to spend several months out of town, Sarah would not move. "No more," she told Berdow. "This is it."

So he quit.

17.   The Plan Changes

Yet Neaman could hardly ignore the variety chain, despite the sense of urgency he felt in grappling with the department stores' problems. He had created a social concept in his working relationship with the thousands of variety-store employes, now augmented by the Newberry staff. It was a tremendous corporate family. There were approximately 1,700 executives in the variety stores and about 200 in the Klein stores. He was warmed by his closeness with them. After launching a new system of warehouses and warehouse relay points to service the 1,100 variety stores, he visited with managers from coast to coast, inviting them to dinner and eating in their homes. At times his worries seemed pleasantly remote.

As New Year's Day 1974 came and went, he worked his way through the upper Midwest, then across the Dakotas, Utah, and then to California. On a murky morning in mid-January, he took a call in a manager's office in a store in San Diego. He was surprised to hear that it was Harry Wachtel, one of the partners in Rapid's law firm.

"Sam," Harry said, "I just left Rik and he wanted me to call you."

"Yes?"

"Would you be interested in a merger with Interstate Department Stores?" Harry asked. "They would take over our variety stores and our department stores. They would close out most of their unprofitable discount stores and still have about 150 to 200 stores making money. You know, they're in specialty stores, junior department stores, toy stores. The total group with yours would be something like 1,400 units—"

"What's the big *kunst?*"

The line crackled a bit with silence and then the lawyer said quickly, "You would be the chief executive officer, the biggest stockholder—"

"I see. . . ."

"I thought you got that without my saying it, Sam. Forgive me. You see, the banks like the concept very much. Rik came up with it a few days ago and Becker checked the prime banks. They would be willing to give Interstate a full new line of financing if you ran the show. They would also work out a deal in which you would get 1 million of a new Interstate common so you could be the largest stockholder. Sam, you would finally have your own company, don't you see that?"

Neaman saw it, of course, and he found his heart pounding. "What," he asked, "would be with the rest of the McCrory operation—Lerner's, the sporting goods and auto supply stores, the Newberry department stores, the Canadian operations?"

"They'll be merged into Rapid–American."

So Riklis would still get his merger, Neaman thought. "Rik wins," he said softly.

He distinctly heard the lawyer draw in his breath, "No," Wachtel said firmly, "you win. You'll be on your own, Sam, completely. You'll be the operator and the owner. I say you win."

"Yes," Neaman admitted, "it has an attraction I admit it and yet—"

"Sam, can you meet with Rik and me in New York tomorrow morning?" the lawyer asked quickly.

During the six-hour trip back, Neaman sat through the night pondering the proposition. It was a stunning plan. The lawyer had given him additional details before they ended their conversation. From those and from what he knew of Riklis's match-making efforts and style, he could reasonably well chart its scope. He was forced to admit that it was one of the most creative financial deals, possibly the finest that Riklis had ever devised. It was built on several basic blocks, each of which supported the other to create an arch—the merger. One was the reluctance of banks to extend any more credit to Interstate, a troubled chain that had overexpanded and was close to insolvency. For months, its waning fight for survival had dominated talk in retail circles. Another block was the good profitability of at least half of the company's stores, which given an infusion of new capital might well allow the banks not only to recapture their previous loans but to successfully float new ones. A third was evidently Meshulam Riklis's great desire to merge McCrory into Rapid–American so that he could "simplify and capitalize on its corporate assets," that is, obtain full return on his subsidiaries. The final block was Neaman and his reluctance to allow himself to be submerged in a merger, a reaction that he and everyone else knew was basically a drive for independence. Like any well-built arch, Rik's Arch, as Neaman began mentally to refer to it, capitalized on the deadweight of each wedge building a lateral thrust to defy gravity in this case, things being as they were.

As he refused offers of food or liquor from the flight attendants, asking only once, "Perhaps a little tea or cottage cheese?" Neaman had little doubt that Rik's Arch had been stimulated by Riklis's rankling frustration over his inability to merge McCrory into Rapid. Given that frustration, Riklis could have been expected to emerge with some new scheme to end it. But what fascinated Neaman, as he stared out into an endless purple sky, was the cleverness with which Riklis had refined his scheme. Not only would he obtain his merger, but he would make Interstate pay for it. The tab for the buyer's right to purchase more than half of McCrory's business would be $150 million in a new preferred stock to be issued by Interstate. Thus, as a sixty-seven percent owner of McCrory, Riklis's company would itself cash in. Then, there was the matter of giving Neaman 1 million shares. Who would pay for it? Interstate, of course. It would mean a recapitalization, but the banks were willing to go for it. With an administrator like Sam Neaman running the show, the banks obviously hoped that they would once again be financing a very viable property. It was all, Neaman conceded, a marriage of the greatest convenience for everyone concerned.

He closed his eyes for a few moments, feeling an onrush of impatience and even ercitement. What Wachtel had not specified were the numbers of shares to be outstanding in either common or preferred stock under Interstate's recapitalized structure. Assuming that he would personally be the merged company's biggest shareholder, what portion of shares would be retained by Rapid–American? True, preferred stock such as Rapid's would receive no voting rights, but it could be converted—often on short notice—into common stock. Also, what percentage of ownership would the retiring management of Interstate retain?

As he pondered all this under heavy eyelids, faces darted across his mind. Frank Patchen, Harold Hughes, Ed Luedtke, Norman Mallor, Ben Litwak, Charley Gass, Charles Witz, the John Kings, Paul and Mildred McClellan, Marge Schiller, many others. He opened his eyes wide. Why shouldn't they and their 1,700 counterparts also share in the ownership of the new company? A tremor of excitement, of an overwhelming desire, whipped through him. Yes, why not? If they were willing to go that far, why shouldn't they go one step further? The rest of the way to Kennedy Airport, his mind was restlessly but happily occupied by the new thought. Once again, he thought with satisfaction, he would be able to counter Rik's offensive with an assault of his own.

The meeting the next morning, after Neaman had slept a full ninety minutes and opened his eyes, completely refreshed, was unlike any other that he and Riklis ever had. There was a palpable distance between them not, as was usual, because they were far apart, but because both realized that for the first time they were conversing as near-equals. But it was relaxed, too. Each had the other's measure, it seemed, and there was no point in any further delusions. Wachtel, the attorney, sat at Rik's right but remained silent. He had known both men for a long time.

"Why," asked Neaman, "should we invest our time and our guts in a dying company?"

"It won't be a dying company once we get into it," Riklis assured him. "What it needs is a new shot of confidence on the part of the banks. When you are head of it, they'll have their new confidence. They have a lot of respect for you—"

"And you can have your merger."

Riklis shrugged. "And you can have the variety-store division. You always had a paternal feeling for it and its managers. Once you're the head of Interstate, you can do what you want with the stores. Open, close, whatever you want."

Neaman lapsed into silence, Riklis stared out the window.

After some moments, Riklis observed, "Don't forget, Sam, you're getting Interstate without a dime on your part. You're getting the biggest block of shares on a silver platter. How many men ever get such a bonanza in their lives?"

Nodding, Neaman said, "Of course, I appreciate it. But, let's not fool each other, Rik. This is the price the banks and you are paying me to become part of this deal."

"Not to mention," said Riklis smiling, "that you will also get the same big salary you get now, plus deferred, plus retirement, plus survivor benefits, plus . . ."

Neaman lifted a pink hand. "Please," he said, his face pained. "There is nobody here but you and I and Harry." The implied reproof brought a widened smile to Riklis's tanned face. Neaman leaned forward. "I want something else, too," he said. "I want a generous stock participation for all my executives. I want them to own the company, too."

Riklis turned to stare briefly at Harry Wachtel. There was a grin on the face of the calm, stocky lawyer with the long hair down well below the middle of his neck. "Well, Rik, if you're agreeable," he said, "I don't see any legal reasons why something like that can't be worked in. But the banks have the final word, and they may balk at it."

"What is it that you are after, Sam?" asked Riklis. He laughed. "What do they call your operation lately? The Happy Centipede? You want so much to keep it happy?"

"It occurs to me," said Neaman, seriously, "that if you and Harry can convince the banks to go along with this idea, Interstate will be the one big corporation in the United States which is owned and run by its own executives."

Riklis and Neaman studied one another. It would have been difficult for Harry Wachtel in that moment to decide definitely that the entire proposal hung on that issue. But he couldn't say for sure that it didn't. Nonetheless, he was relieved when he heard Riklis say softly, "All right, Sam. I'm with you."

As the two men rose and shook hands, Wachtel said, "Sam, the banks and some of the insurance companies want to meet with you tomorrow morning. You better take an Interstate balance sheet with you and put in some hard brain-work tonight. They're planning to grill you on how you would keep the company alive."

Riklis accompanied Neaman to the door. "How's Klein's?" he asked, a small smile quivering on his lips, "Is there any progress?"

"We are trying to give it a real *shtip*," said Neaman, "but you should never have bought it. The one who sold it was smarter. But, we'll see."

"Don't bring it up at the meeting tomorrow," Riklis advised. "Talk only about future goals. Not current problems. Bankers get ulcers just like human beings."

The next morning, Neaman faced about forty stiff faces, but on some he saw the hovering warmth of pre-acceptance. That would mean more than the stiffness. Introduced around the long, oval table in the board room of a Wall Street branch of one of New York's largest banks, he sat easily amid the discussion of plans to finance a merger between a near-insolvent company and one with nine years of consistent growth. He did not involve his mind more than superficially in the discussion. He felt a looseness and a coolness in him that he had long ago come to equate with discipline. Neaman knew that by not unharnessing his consciousness to take sides in the debate he would be reserving his emotional and intellectual strengths for the time, soon enough, when they would be needed. But his sensitive antennae, geared to twitch rather than jangle at the tremors of opposing attitudes, responded to what he could best consider as sonic precursors arising from the discussion. There were about four of them: a basso-profundo rumble (direly negative); a fruity baritone, well-fed, well-drunk (hesitantly positive); an earnest tenor (definitely positive); and a shrill tenor, almost counter-tenor (negative, negative). As he pondered these with an intense awareness that there isn't really a hell of a lot of difference among people but among the times, the place, the pressures, he heard his name called: "Mr. Neaman, would you care to make some small observations about the company's situation?" He would, of course; his abrupt rise from his chair indicated that. But he realized that his voice *cared*, convincing them all immediately that he considered it all so *vital*. He spoke in very definite terms about the company's balance sheet, its debts, its assets, its losses, and its hidden reserves. It was not necessarily all financial. Although he had had less than a day to pour over the papers, he had asked Marvin Shenfeld, his main computer expert and programmer, to stay through the evening. Marvin and an assistant had remained at the end of a telephone and conveniently near the IBM 360 as he, Neaman, phoned in a barrage of questions and calculations to be recalculated. So, to an audience that was the most likely to appreciate it, he was equipped to deliver his conclusions data-substantiated. Moreover, as he posed probable results to hypothetical actions, he was able to honestly report, "This checks out on the computer, gentlemen. I have already taken that precaution." And, as he went on for some thirty minutes, he spied that the stiffness on a few faces eased and that the very air over the darkly red tabletop had changed. And when he closed his eyes for a few moments and became silent to induce the pregnant pause, the hiatus after the electric storm, his ears detected a shift in the chorus undertone. It consisted entirely of earnest tenors now. He decided to conclude with the pause, nodded curtly, and summarily sat down. A moment after he did, the entire assemblage rose to its feet and applauded.

Ten days later, on a late January afternoon, an hour after the New York and American Stock Exchanges had closed their trading for the day, the following announcement appeared on the financial ticker:

RAPID–AMERICAN, MC CRORY, AND
INTERSTATE ANNOUNCE JOINT TRANSACTION.
    N.Y.—RAPID–AMERICAN CORPORATION,
MC CRORY CORPORATION, AND INTERSTATE DEPARTMENT STORES
INC. JOINTLY ANNOUNCED AGREEMENTS IN PRINCIPLE
HAVE BEEN REACHED FOR THE TRANSFER BY MC CRORY
OF A PORTION OF ITS OPERATIONS TO INTER-
STATE AND THEREAFTER FOR THE MERGER OF RAPID–
AMERICAN AND MC CRORY ITS 62 PC OWNED
SUBSIDIARY.
    MESHULAM RIKLIS, RAPID–AMERICAN CHAIR-
MAN, SAID "UPON COMPLETION OF THESE TRANSAC-

TIONS RAPID—AMERICAN WILL HAVE FURTHER
SIMPLIFIED ITS CORPORATE STRUCTURE. THIS
LONG-TERM GOAL ANNOUNCED SEVERAL YEARS AGO
IS NOW WELL ALONG THE ROAD TO COMPLETION."

DIRECTORS OF MC CRORY AND INTERSTATE
HAVE AGREED IN PRINCIPLE THAT MC CRORY WILL
TRANSFER TO A NEW SUBSIDIARY OF INTERSTATE
ALL OF MC CRORY'S VARIETY STORE AND DEPART-
MENT STORE OPERATIONS EXCEPT FOR CERTAIN CAN-
ADIAN OPERATIONS FOR SECURITIES OF SUCH SUB-
SIDIARY.

IT IS EXPECTED THAT INTERSTATE'S SUB-
SIDIARY WILL ISSUE TO MC CRORY A $4\frac{1}{2}$ PC
PREFERRED STOCK. THE PREFERRED STOCK WILL
HAVE A LIQUIDATION VALUE EQUIVALENT TO THE
NET BOOK VALUE AT JAN 31, 1974, OF THE MC CRORY
NET ASSETS ACQUIRED, WHICH IS EXPECTED TO
BE APPROXIMATELY $150 MILLION.

SAMUEL NEAMAN, CHAIRMAN OF MC CRORY, IS
EXPECTED TO BE ELECTED PRESIDENT AND CHIEF
EXECUTIVE OFFICER OF INTERSTATE FOLLOWING
THE TRANSFER THE ANNOUNCEMENT SAID.

IT IS ALSO CONTEMPLATED THAT NEAMAN WILL
ACQUIRE A MILLION SHARES OF INTERSTATE
COMMON STOCK FROM INTERSTATE UPON OBTAINING
REQUIRED APPROVAL OF CERTAIN ASPECTS OF THE
TRANSACTION BY INTERSTATE STOCKHOLDERS.
IF SUCH APPROVAL IS NOT OBTAINED MC CRORY WILL
HAVE AN OPTION TO REACQUIRE THE TRANSFERRED
OPERATIONS THE COMPANIES SAID. . . .

Savoring halcyon days, Neaman felt himself at the height of
his powers. Some men function at their best under adverse pressures. Others find hidden wellsprings of accomplishment when
their fortunes are brightest. Neaman felt he was always at top
form. But there was little doubt among his closest associates that
he was at his peak in those first months of 1974, when he was
the object of considerable admiration even among those who
disliked him. The superficial reason was obvious. Few men are

powerful or fortunate enough to create convulsive changes in three major companies. Mergers usually regurgitate people. Here was a case in which one man was regurgitating mergers. Neaman was evidently so proficient and important that several corporations and forty of the country's largest banks and insurance companies had arranged to erect a corporate vehicle for him.

But there was another reason, not as superficial, which lifted a halo over his round, bald head. It was understood best by many executives of McCrory, as well as by other competitive concerns. Having created a company in his image while shaping it to a social concept that had worked so well, he was now in the process of extending it to another company and carrying the process yet one step further. Not only could average people combining their average talents achieve above-average performance, but now, it seemed likely, that they would also be able to own their own company.

Naturally, the admiration for him in York, Pennsylvania, was boundless. A delegation of merchandise men and buyers called on Frank Patchen to ask how they could demonstrate their support. He telephoned Neaman, who told Patchen that it was not necessary to do anything at this juncture. "Just tell them to pray," he said, "in whatever church they like. Who can know for sure? American business may never have been so close to God before." Mildred McClellan sent another of her odes, this one more effusive than the others. The press waited uncertainly. The principle seemed too idealistic to come true. But the Neaman critics, not unjustifiably perhaps, suggested that it was all another of his grandstand plays, like his annual gifts of bouquets and $50 bills to employes on their birthdays or wedding anniversaries.

He was extremely busy in the meantime. Besides the new network of warehouses and relay points, he had worked out a new system of reallocating home-office costs, making a separate profit center of them and thus removing their burden from the divisions. He spent much time with the management of Interstate Stores, the chairman and the financial vice-president in particular, advising them and preparing the groundwork for the anticipated merger. He also renewed his intermittent attempts to find a president for the Klein's chain, some skilled executive who could come in and with a few adroit moves put the ungainly stores on the right track.

Some months earlier, on an impulse, he had called one of New York's most respected retailing consultants, Milton Goldberg, and asked him, "Why are you wasting your time being a consultant when you can come in here and be my president of Klein's?"

As Goldberg later recalled the incident to me, "I told him that I appreciated the offer, but I had made up my mind after leaving Altman's that I would never work full-time again for any company. Neaman said he would still like to talk to me. I visited with him and Kunsberg, and they both worked on me. But he let Kunsberg do most of the talking. Neaman said, 'You talk to Kunsberg and I'll listen. If you talk direct to me, I'll talk too much and I won't find out much from you.'"

As he spoke, the consultant found Neaman at ease, aglow with his recent triumphs and full of hope that it also meant he could solve the stubborn problems of the department stores. Kunsberg, on the other hand, was testy. "He showed a temper, especially when Sam needled him about this or that," said Goldberg. "They asked me, after they saw I would not be enticed into coming full-time, if I would be a consultant for them. I agreed, of course, and I saw them often."

Goldberg continued to see them as things progressed, even during the period when the proposed merger with Interstate was being negotiated. "Neaman was in a wonderful mood," Goldberg said. "He acted as though he had the world under control. I used to leave hilarious after my sessions with him. He used down-to-earth similies along with flat, dogmatic statements that made you double up. Typically, he would say, 'What does a store manager do? If you don't watch him, he'll go out to a motel with his secretary and screw her. But if he knows you're watching him, he'll leave his secretary alone and go home to his wife.'"

They would frequently disagree on things, especially on Klein's and its executives. "He regarded the chain as his cross to bear," the consultant recalled, "and he didn't have as much patience with people there as he did at the variety division. But he felt under pressure at Klein's, and if a man didn't perform within a few months he was gone. 'How can you expect a man to give you any real results in less than a year?' I used to ask him. 'A year is much too long,' he would answer. 'The situation here can change in a week or a month. We got a merger to make, and we need the results to show everybody.' "

Many times Goldberg would find Neaman difficult to sell his ideas to, and he wondered why the chairman retained him. But, every so often, Neaman would suddenly implement one of Goldberg's suggestions and then behave as though it were his own original idea.

"Candidly, I don't think that Neaman will live too long," Goldberg said in concluding his talk with me. "He's too intent, he spends all his time and energy on his job and he's really not his own boss. He's got all his eggs in one basket and that can be a mortal mistake if you're as involved as Neaman is. Riklis calls the shots, and no matter how much Neaman fights him off, I can't see the situation changing. Riklis and Henry Kissinger are the world's best two salesmen."

But Goldberg was wrong about Neaman's survival ability. The consultant, who had had several mild heart attacks, had a severe one very early in 1974 and didn't survive his long night. Neaman attended his funeral.

Less than a month after the announcement of the proposed merger with Interstate, Riklis phoned Neaman to tell him that the deal was foundering. "The insurance company bastards are trying to bow out," Riklis said. "They're not so much in hock with Interstate's $70 million financing as the banks, so they want the banks to buy them out and the banks say no. We gotta find some way of convincing those insurance guys that this is a hot deal for them."

Neaman mulled it over and decided that he was in a strategic position to help. He spoke to Harry Wachtel, Riklis's lawyer, and to his own lawyer. He contacted top executives of the two insurance companies and had long talks with them. He gave them both the same message: "I have never been so sure of the rightness of anything I have ever come in contact with as I am about this."

But they were still noncommittal. He brooded on it for several nights, hardly sleeping. He spoke once more to the lawyers and told them of his decision. What he decided was simple enough. In order to convince everyone, not just the insurance companies, how deeply committed he was, and to be free to negotiate the deal without arousing any suspicion that he was abrogating his responsibilities at McCrory, Neaman proposed that he resign from the company. He would then devote himself entirely to making the marriage between the two companies as its president-to-be. The lawyers were first puzzled, then intrigued, and then they concurred in the plan. Riklis agreed and said he thought it could be "a very strategic gesture."

So in mid-February, Neaman resigned. For the first time in thirteen years, he was out of a job.

18. Conceptualizing: A Company with a Conscience

Riklis moved quickly to fill the void. He assumed the added posts of chairman and chief executive of McCrory. Stanley Kunsberg remained president, but he was instructed to operate as though he were the chief executive. Izzy Becker promptly declared a detente with Kunsberg, with whom he had always had a tacit rapport. Otherwise, there were no personnel or philosophical changes. Everything seemed to be waiting for the two simultaneous mergers, one of which would permit the other. All eyes were on two focal areas: the banks, the insurance companies, and their discussions; and Neaman and his movements.

Neaman kept his office at McCrory. But, in personal instructions and memos, he made it clear that he was only a tenant now and would only have an advisory capacity at McCrory, a capacity he hoped would not take up much of his time. Neaman had already put most of McCrory's 1974 annual report to bed. The only thing left was the auditing process, which would continue until April when the final quarter's net income could be computed from the spot-check audit of physical inventories. He was to all intents and purposes no longer connected with Mc-

Crory. He was a free agent whose entire function was to bring about the merger with Interstate Stores.

He restricted his communications with the outside world, his colleagues, his competitors, and the media. All his contacts were with the lenders, those forty stiff faces. They had warmed to him but managed to retain a wariness that convinced him he would have to continue to sell them hard. But as determined as he was to avoid his executives at the variety division and Klein's, they couldn't leave him alone. Amid their euphoria over the prospect of "owning" their own company, many of them felt reservations and fear over their future. Neaman, after all, no longer had any official supervisory role over them. In reality, he could no longer protect them, although nothing had developed to threaten them since he had resigned. But it was well-known that he held only a tenuous relationship with Interstate's top brass. After they had made repeated efforts to contact him, Neaman passed the word along to Frank Patchen, Harold Hughes, Ben Litwak, Charley Gass and Steve Jackel: "Stop being nervous. You should think like Columbus—round not flat. Here we sit to await a historic achievement. We will be the first to own a big company, a company that will be the first to have a conscience. And you are biting your fingernails. Consider what we have already accomplished."

In those weeks when others felt uncertain, Neaman himself was full of hope. Yet he lived in a two-tier world. On one level, he was isolated. On the other, he was impatient for what he sensed would be the ultimate act of his life. He was fifty-nine years old but he felt much older. It seemed to him that he had carried a momentous weight on his back for many years—people, their problems, their failings, their gropings, their sweaty inadequacies, and their occasional triumphs. It had been hardest at McCrory, and yet it had been productive. The principle had been proven. Now, he was poised for that final step from productivity to proprietorship. The employe would be the owner. The owner would be the employe. At times, he was stirred by a vague sense of alarm that it must all be an exercise in futility. But he knew that as long as he remained in the strategic role augured for him he would not permit the situation to decline into futility. That went against his grain. He would just not allow it.

As he came and went from meetings with the lenders—walking down the halls of his own building with a detached expression or riding in his Cadillac through the streets of Manhattan and eyeing the pedestrians and wondering how many of them could look forward to as profound a change in their lives as his colleagues—he quivered under an occasional flicker of fear. Had Riklis and Becker outflanked him, outmaneuvered him? The double merger—a merger within a merger—was too pat. One door opened, edging open a second, closing a third, prying apart a fourth, slamming shut a fifth. The neatness and the meshing of parts within parts had all the earmarks of a Riklis strategy engineered by Becker. And, if so, who would it benefit but them? But invariably, as those cold flashes went through him, his lip stopped pouting, his rapid heartbeat slowed and he couldn't help smiling. What difference did it make who had engineered what? The irrevocable fact was that he had forced them into their move. Unable to exert their power through the usual pressures of parent company structures on the subsidiary, he had compelled them to go into contortions to accommodate him in order to accommodate themselves. Staring with satisfaction at the back of his chauffeur's head, Neaman could only imagine what fear and self-doubt also must be going through Riklis's and Becker's heads during this period of negotiations. He was happy, too, that he had insisted on the protective clause of a cancellation of the deal if the Interstate stockholders disapproved the granting of shares to him. It was a final card he held, a bit of whipped cream happily cast on top of the sundae.

Many watched the proceedings. The world didn't exactly stand still as the players circled. Overshadowing it all was the energy crisis, Vietnam, oil-rich countries buying everything they could, a rapidly developing Watergate scandal, and Secretary Kissinger winging back and forth across the world. But in the small worlds which it touched and among the thousands involved and among just plain observers of corporate behavior and human strivings, the ongoing merger negotiations in New York held a fascination. Businessmen, sociologists, academicians, minority group advocates, financial men, personnel recruiters, journalists, and others were drawn to the developments with mingled feelings of hope, doubt, cynicism, and idealism.

In the past, of course, there had been some pockets of communal ownership of an American business, created for religious, ethnic, or political reasons. But here was a possible formation of a $1 billion plus enterprise strictly for the purpose of economic and social objectives. A principle in the act of becoming a reality. For the first time in years, the likelihood of a new, large-scale, employe-owned business enterprise raised the possibility that American business wasn't just a cannibalistic, profit-hungry exercise. But most of those interested doubted that it would ever materialize, mainly because the matter of whether American business has a conscience had never been fully resolved.

Neaman was so excited by the promise and the closeness of the formation of the new company that there were nights when he could hardly sleep. As Cecelia placidly slept on, emitting gentle but deep snores, he would get up and pace the apartment. He would sit in his study in front of the elaborate communications system that he no longer used and wonder whether such an ideal could come to pass in the self-hate syndrome that gripped Americans in that year of inflation and recession. The only thing he really had going for him was performance. Controversial as his methods were, they had produced results while helping society. Would banks and insurance companies that had been under so much attack lately for their so-called lack of social conscience participate in the formation of a company with a conscience? He would sit at his penthouse window, chest and teeth bared, and ask himself how they could do otherwise?

But the nagging thought kept intruding; would the problem with S. Klein be held against him? Would that one black mark make them do otherwise? All he needed was more time, although eight years had gone by as he had grappled vainly with the big, ungainly stores that Riklis had wished on him only to see their losses grow. No, Neaman reassured himself, that would not, could not be held against him in the light of his otherwise great performance.

And, as he sat by his penthouse window and wondered, he was warmed by his recent experience with Herbert Siegel, the financial vice president of Interstate Stores, who had come to him in a deliberate and odd confrontation. The brash, chunky

44-year old Siegel had simply taken it on his own initiative to see if he could live with Neaman if the merger were to take place and evidently to try to prod the Neaman "edifice" to see if it could squirm, just like any other human.

Intrigued, irked and yet curious about Siegel's unusual behavior, Neaman had invited him to dinner. Strangely, that dinner had reaffirmed everything Neaman believed in, perhaps because at that time he had needed it.

The dinner had been a strange affair after a surprising first meeting. A day after the merger news had crossed the ticker, Herb had sought out Neaman, who had readily agreed to meet him. Sitting across from one another in Neaman's office, they had taken each other's measure. "I'm glad you called me," Neaman said. "It will save time. You impress me. Most of the time, a man like you, the financial vice-president who would work under a new chief executive, waits until he is summoned. But you came to me. You have initiative, my friend."

Herb smiled. "Sam—I hope I can call you that now?—initiative is my middle name," he said. "Tell you the truth, I've heard so much about you that I could hardly wait to meet you. I wanted to see the man behind the legend."

Neaman smiled. "You are worried if you will have a job with me?"

"No," Herb said. "I don't give a damn. I've already spent two years keeping this business alive—and I could work in a half-dozen other places that are also trying to stay alive for more money. No, Sam. Mainly I'm here because I'm curious as hell about what makes you tick. You got a reputation that's ten feet tall. Personally, I don't believe it, but I figure let me see the man for myself."

Neaman straightened in his chair. The man was youthfully brash. Did he think that this would impress his new boss? If so— But then Neaman remembered how Siegel had propped up the fading founder of Interstate Stores whose dynamism and entrepreneurial virility had been tragically sapped under the onslaught of financial reverses and possible insolvency. Siegel (a C.P.A., a former NYU athlete, and a man still muscular, clear-eyed, and strong) had proven to be more than just a sturdy crutch to the crumbling entrepreneur. Perhaps the financial man's independence and self-respect were well-founded.

"All right," Neaman said. "I accept what you say even though it is disturbing to hear that you are not anxious to stay in your job. I myself prefer people who are motivated."

"Motivated—or scared?"

Neaman glared. Siegel really was unusually candid or just plain foolish. Neaman smiled and relaxed. "I see through this that you are testing me," he said. "Good. I think maybe we will get along, after all."

"I hope so," Herb said. "You see, Sam, I knew I wasn't taking much of a chance. I know that the one thing that a tough man respects is another tough man. . . . So tell me, I know what I want out of life, but what the hell do you want?"

As Neaman's steadfast gaze took him in, Herb could not help but admire the man. He knew something about how the descent from success (as in the case of his own chairman, Sol Cantor) or how the hazards of fostering a principle (as in Neaman's case) could affect a man. He knew enough about the situation in which the ex-McCrory chairman found himself to sense that Neaman stood in shifting sand. But the man's manner exuded confidence, resolve, inevitability. "Could I also tell you," Herb said softly, "how much I admire what you're trying to do?"

Neaman invited him to dinner a week later. When Siegel arrived, he was not surprised at the sumptuousness of the penthouse. Neaman, resplendent in a gold leisure jacket, a velvet-like turtleneck, and sleek brown slacks explained, "Cecelia, my pigeon, is ailing and stays in her nest. I will cook dinner. But, first a drink." He made what seemed to Herb a gigantic scotch-and-soda for him, eschewing anything for himself, and then invited Siegel into the kitchen as he prepared dinner. Incongruously wearing an apron over his striking clothes, he deftly prepared a large tossed salad, inserted generous portions of veal scallopine into the microwave oven, and let a variety of what seemed interesting Mideastern vegetables simmer on the regular gas range. As he hovered over his cooking, Neaman invited Siegel to "satisfy your curiosity about the creature, Neaman."

"Okay," Herb said, "so let's begin where we left off. What do you want out of life?"

"Good. After almost sixty years that I have lived, I have come to some conclusions. People need a goal. If they wander through their lives without one they drift. All I have tried to do at McCrory is to give everybody a direction—to point out an objective to them. If God gave you only a certain amount of ability, of skill, you don't have to fall back on self-pity. If you can work with others toward a common objective, you can exceed even yourself. And this is as true about me as it is about anybody. I give everything to what I do because I know that if I work with my people toward a mutual goal, my effort will reward me and it will reward them."

"Fine. That I already knew. But, I have to insist, what do you want out of life, Sam?"

As he gestured at Herb to help him carry the food into the big dining room, Neaman replied, "Work. That's all, work." They ate and the food was delicious. "You're a hell of a chef," Herb said, his mouth full. "Where did you learn how?"

Neaman shrugged. "I am not even a good amateur, Herb. But, over the years, in Israel, Europe, Mexico, South America, one learns a few things. Cecelia, she is a cook. Usually, she is healthy as a horse. Today," he said with a shrug, "maybe she indulges herself. But I allow her after so many years of marriage."

Herb ate silently for a while. Then he said, "You mean work is everything for you? Isn't there anything else?"

"Work for me is everything, and there is nothing else," Neaman said. "I am at work usually at 7:30 in the morning and I leave at seven at night. After dinner with Cecelia, I am back at my work at home at eight until ten. Then I sleep."

"That's almost fourteen hours. Why do you need fourteen hours to get a job done that you should do in only eight hours? I get fourteen hours work accomplished in eight hours. What is it, Sam, are you just plain inefficient?"

His host's head snapped back. The sudden glare turned to a warm smile. "Herb, Herb, you are trying to provoke me," Neaman said. "Aren't you afraid I'll fire you even before I hire you? No, you are not. You are a hard-skinned young man. But I'll try to explain. Cecelia and I have no children. There is nothing to divert me from my work. It is my work and my hobby and my social life and my great diversion. If I didn't have to sleep, I would spend even more hours at it. Do you understand?"

As Neaman abruptly gathered up the dishes and darted into the kitchen, Herb pondered the words. Maybe Neaman sensed it or maybe he didn't. Actually, Herb wasn't much keen on working with him in the new setup, if it should ever materialize. He felt that he was ready for a new challenge. He had gone through two grueling years with a failing, desperately unhappy Sol Cantor, and he would just as soon move into a new environment. As a result, he didn't care a hell of a lot whether or not Neaman decided to chop him. But he had been fascinated with the man's style and philosophy, and he had wanted to ascertain himself how much substance there was to it. At this point, however, he had to confess to himself that he was vaguely disappointed.

Neaman returned with—wouldn't Herb have predicted it?—two dishes of baked alaska. "For you, for this occasion," Neaman admitted, dipping happily into the melange, "I am temporarily giving up my rigid diet. You have intrigued me, my friend. Either I will hire you or fire you, I don't know which yet or in what order."

Herb asked him to explain his management philosophy. It was as though he had opened the floodgates of an overloaded dam. For almost the next two hours, Neaman spoke, propounded, clarified, posed, and expostulated. The tide was so overwhelming that even a few days later Herb recalled only some of it, globs of things Neaman said, but they pasted themselves to his mind and almost gave him a sort of mental indigestion.

". . . There is no theory of retailing, no school for retailing because they teach generalities. They do not produce a buyer of brassieres, a merchandise manager of toys. They teach generalities which don't help when you are sitting there and making decisions on how you are going to commit money and units for hundreds of different stores, each having its own personality. Each one reflects the environment, the neighborhood. Some stores will never sell an item that comes in green. How do you know that and when it will change? In the past, it was a matter of experience, of memory, of communications between the man on the floor and the man who did the buying. But now with chain operations, it's impossible. Nobody came up with that knowledge. But we in McCrory did. We wrote the book. . . .

"Now, let's talk about McCrory and Interstate, the soon-to-be-married lovers. Like McCrory was, the new company will be a smorgasbord of retail outlets. But it's not cafeteria smorgasbord where you put out the things that you wanted to put out. It's accidental dishes. That was what was on the market at that time at a price the purchaser could afford. Now, beside this problem there is another mixture—the mixture of noncohesive units of people who don't know each other, who don't know how to work with each other. And then there are also accidents of location. All the theories of the world fall by the wayside if you have the right location. And when do you know it is the right location? When you make money at it. And that is what we are faced with—the management of accidents. . . .

"We know how to handle such problems because we had many, so many in McCrory, yet we achieved the highest profit margin on sales in the variety-store business. That's proof, right. So you want to know my management philosophy? What will I do with your company? All right, here it is. No one can sit in a central place and tell people how to make a profit. No one can control the minds of hundreds and thousands of people. But if you make it simple enough, just the way the army teaches you how to strip and clean a rifle, even if you are a civilian you will learn soon enough how to do it by the numbers. And it remains with you forever maybe. I broke the big problem of loss stores into small problems, and then the store manager could tell the home office not only where he was losing money but also detect what areas had a chance for profit. It was beyond experience. But it was knowledge, rough knowledge, crude knowledge, but knowledge just the same. . . .

"So what do the managers have and what will yours have? They will have the tools to operate. Each one has got his own tools or will have them. Some will use those tools to help themselves and their employer. Their employer will have to help himself and them, and sometimes people will raise their eyebrows at those tools. Others will be too damned lazy or too afraid to use them. Some will get a kick out of using their tools; others have the talent but don't enjoy the music. And these people blessed with the talent are less than those who don't have any but are willing to work, because the ones with the talent and without the will have the capability but they are not interested. They don't get a kick out of it, and they are less than useless. . . ."

Having neither slept nor remembered what he wanted to, Herb Siegel kept his appointment with Norman Mallor. The chunky, reserved McCrory financial man greeted him with a smile and a certain amount of warmth. They were, after all, identical in function. The likelihood that one might replace the other, since there would be no need in the combined company for two financial vice-presidents, did not appear to exert any sort of constraint. Norman ordered coffee for Herb as they sat at a sofa across the room from his desk.

19. The Interlock Snaps

As the banker came to the end of his long, nasal monologue, not even pausing for that parenthetical bit of sympathy to soften the blow, Meshulam Riklis held on to the telephone moments after he had heard the click at the other end. Over the years, he had learned to roll with the punches, it had become vital to do so, but a few still managed to come right through to the temples. This, he told himself as he released the phone, was one.

The banks, it appeared, did not want the McCrory–Interstate deal. Not in the form that it had been presented and maybe not in any form. They were, it seemed, horrified over the Klein's losses —$3.4 million, then $9.6 million, and then . . . who knew except that it would certainly be more. And wouldn't any merger, they asked, which included a bottomless pit like Klein's be symptomatic of a lack of synergy and wouldn't a chief executive who had failed to turn Klein's around also be unable to turn Interstate around? So they didn't want Klein's or any deal that had Klein's in it. And they didn't want Neaman.

And that, of course, Riklis knew, would spell the end of Klein's—and the end of Neaman. All nineteen Klein's stores were finished, *kaput*, and so was Neaman.

Alone, Riklis leaned back in his chair, his head whirling. He closed his eyes and Neaman's smooth, round face immediately came into view. It startled him to realize how much Sam had changed, how far he had come. In ten years, Neaman had undergone a complete metamorphosis in personality and behavior. The diffident but eager, indifferently dressed European-Mideast businessman with one foot in the kibbutz and the other in the French garment industry was now the impeccably dressed, smooth but hard American business tycoon who proudly offered as his calling card his own idiosyncratic *chutzpah*. In that decade, Sam had progressed all the way from pleading for a part-time assignment so that he could prove himself to threatening to resign and taking fifty of his top executives with him if Riklis insisted on a merger. "You have to hand it to Sammy," Riklis told himself. "He came all the way from an ass kisser to a ball breaker."

He thought about the self-effacing things that Neaman had done. Back in 1967, for example, Riklis had phoned to congratulate him on the year's profit gain and told him, "I love you, Sammy. You were the best idea I ever had in my whole life. What can I do to show you how I feel?" And Neaman's reply, with the matter-of-factness of humility, "Nothing, believe me. Just give me the opportunity to do all the things I need to do." And, almost four years before that, spending eight months on the road for the company, living out of his suitcase in Pascagoula or Muncie or Colorado Springs, so he could find out just where the dry rot was coming from in the variety division. He thought about all the endless hours Sam had given his job, the concentration and heat of his thinking process, and the guts he had shown from the beginning all the way through. And the many people who looked to Neaman as though he was God Almighty, whose lives he had touched and enriched. To know him was not exactly to love him, perhaps, but few whom he came into contact with remained unchanged. "Even hating Sammy is some kind of education," Riklis said aloud.

He thought, too, about the other things Neaman had done. How he had created his own empire-within-an-empire. How he had pushed Riklis into giving him one job after another, always manipulating that edge of his performance and his indispensability to gain himself another notch of power. How he had often said derogatory things about Riklis to his own staff, even in the later years threatening to throw Rik out should he have the crust to appear in McCrory's home office. And along with the grandiosity, the penchant for silly and vainglorious extravagances: the Man-of-the-Year dinner with guess-who as the first man of the year; the Samuel Neaman Tulip; the immense map of all the McCrory units, blinking and flashing so as to blind you; the Manager-of-the-Year dinner where Sam sat in state as the chief-of-chiefs, pontificating to platoons of sycophants; and, not the least, his resistance to the merger, his pleasure in sticking it to Riklis.

Eyes closed, mind open, his body perspiring, Rik thought about all these things. Why is it, he wondered, that a man becomes his own worst enemy, his bitterest self-saboteur? It would be easy to abide by the power corruption principle—it evaded no man—but that was much too simple. Maybe it was a matter of when you change the rules, you soon also begin to make them, warping them to your biases. Neaman had had the whole world and it wasn't enough. Whose fault was that?

Riklis opened his eyes. Half turning, his gaze came upon the large portrait on his right wall in which he and Neaman were shaking hands. It had been taken right after the board meeting when Neaman had been elected McCrory's corporate president. Staring at the portrait, at the glazed good-will permanently captured in it, Riklis felt heat churning up in him, anger rising in his chest cavity. "We were locked together, Sammy, you and I," he muttered out loud, "for better or worse, only I kept hoping it would always be better and better. . . ." He broke off, swallowing painfully and thinking, what the hell was wrong with people?

Rik phoned Neaman.

"The bankers are all upset, Sam."

"Upset? How much?"

"They're climbing the walls."

"So?"

"So."

"They don't want to discuss the problem?"

"No, they discussed it."

"What does this mean—that I am out?"

"That's it, Sam."

Neaman hung up. So quickly that Riklis did not hear the huge sigh.

Five THE AFTERMATH

20. The Void Is Filled

The news had a stunning impact. Among McCrory's thousands, it was as if the head-of-state had suddenly been deposed without even the slightest warning or an explanation. There was a terse announcement from the parent company that afternoon, hours after Neaman had physically departed. His top executives who tried to reach him could not, while phone calls from York, Pennsylvania, and the trade were unavailing. It emerged later that he had packed his papers and left within fifteen minutes after his phone conversation with Riklis. He had not said a word to anyone.

In the home office, the paralysis among the executives produced a plastic appearance and behavior. For days afterward, everyone went through the motions of normal activity, but it was entirely synthetic. Kunsberg, who waited impatiently for some word from Riklis, was caught between happiness at Neaman's departure and frustration at not being able to tell the others that he had heard from the parent company. Steve Jackel, Ben Litwak, Norman Mallor, Charles Witz, Charley Gass in

New York and Frank Patchen, Harold Hughes, John King and Ed Luedtke in York, Pennsylvania, could scarcely do their work because the decision-making process, committee-style, could not function without its chairman, even though it was supposed to. It was all like a bottle uncorked, but nothing was coming out.

Many managers in the field phoned to seek instruction and information. All they were told was to carry on until the situation clarified.

The impact on those closest to Neaman lingered because it had no way of dissipating itself except through the passage of time. Neaman could not be reached. Riklis wasn't talking. The trade scuttlebutt was unreliable. The market talk ranged to extremes, stating that Neaman would be back in a few days, ending what was only another play for position, and that he had absconded with a sizeable amount of company funds and was no longer in the country.

At Rapid–American, everyone seemed to be walking around with tight lips and a far-off expression. Riklis, the word came, was bemused and busy in meetings. Izzy Becker appeared alternately delighted and grim. Among the faces of the rest of them there was a stillness and yet a disquiet. An awesome figure at court had been decapitated. It would all come out later, perhaps, but in the meantime no one quite knew why it had happened and what would come after.

After a few days, several events filled the vacuum. They put things into focus, but they failed to answer the basic questions.

McCrory and Interstate announced that their merger plans would resume but with a somewhat different rate of exchange. However, the Klein's chain would no longer be involved. That company would undergo a comprehensive management study to determine whether some or most of its stores should be closed.

The merger of McCrory's into Rapid–American would continue under negotiations, despite the changes in the other merger.

Stanley Kunsberg, McCrory's president, would continue as the operating chief of that company. Lorence Silverberg, a senior vice-president of Rapid–American, would be the new president of McCrory's variety-store division.

That was that on that spring day of 1974. Doors had been closed and then shut. Outwardly, everything seemed to have fallen into place. The only major difference was that Neaman, who had occupied a tremendous role in that world, was gone in actuality and in essence, apparently having vanished off the face of the earth. The listed telephone at the upper East Side apartment had been disconnected. Even the private line did not respond. Security guards at the desk of the lush highrise condominium referred questioners to the office where the reply was, "Sorry, we have no information."

Within weeks, however, there was word of Neaman. He had been seen in Mexico City, Tel Aviv, and Paris. Had it really been he? No one was certain.

In the meantime, attempts were made to repair the broken lines of normality and confidence. Riklis, accompanied by his choice to run the variety division (the fifty-five-year-old Lorence Silverberg), visited the York, Pennsylvania, center, met with the executives, and assured them of his confidence. "You know Lorence," he said, putting his arm around the thin shoulder of the scholarly looking retailer, "he's one of you—a merchant. You'll get alone fine with him, just fine."

Silverberg, who had been around the Rapid and McCrory retail circuit for thirty years, was almost the Neaman antithesis —calm, undemonstrative, almost bloodless. Riklis trusted him, having given him responsibility for some of the former Glen Alden subsidiaries, and even allowed him to supervise some of the companies in which he, Riklis, had personally invested. The bland Silverberg was more like Frank Patchen than Neaman. But Frank Patchen felt both an irreconcilable loss over Neaman's departure and a sense of being unwanted. He could only regard Silverberg as a pale replacement. Harold Hughes, John King, Ed Luedtke, and almost all the others had difficulty in the beginning relating to Silverberg.

Tall, courtly, soft-spoken but troubled with a light lisp, Silverberg took over in York, Pennsylvania, and declared the new direction as "a return to basic retailing," adding, "We'll go by the book. And, please—do not think I am not implying any criticism of the previous management."

Frank Patchen decided to end his thirty-three year career with

McCrory. He bought a major interest in a small New England department store and was soon gone. To close friends he confided, "I knew they didn't want me after Neaman left. I can't blame them too much. I was his emissary to the troops. When the general leaves, who needs his aide-de-camp?"

Executive posts in York, Pennsylvania, were shifted. Ed Luedtke, who should not have needed Neaman, missed him greatly and showed it. He was soon given a field assignment but without change in rank. He remained, querulous but full of pride. Harold Hughes, who missed Neaman perhaps more than anyone else, continued as administrative vice-president, but he found that Silverberg preferred following through on many details himself. His own role thus circumscribed. Hughes returned to a certain extent to his old habit of introversion. But he tried to respond with interest to Silverberg's requests. He spoke less and less and frequently kept his office door closed. He would sit at his desk, staring out at the heavy traffic on Market Street, and dream with open eyes about his approaching retirement. His life post-Neaman was over.

In McCrory's New York office, the effect of Neaman's departure produced many actions and developments. Norman Mallor, the financial vice-president who had gotten his second chance under Neaman, was promptly fired. Marvin Shenfeld, vice-president for systems and methods, resigned after being given some clear indications that his work was now unnecessary. Two executives borrowed from the McCrory variety division to prop up Klein's were returned to their former posts. In the process, they experienced a serious dislocation in their plans and aims. One of them, Ben Litwak, forlornly regarded it as a confirmation of his "ordinariness." If he had had more to offer, he told himself, he would not be going back to York, Pennsylvania, when the job was still undone in New York. Yet, as the professional optimist which every merchant must be, he realized that he was still valuable to the company and that was gratifying. "I've done pretty damn well—considering," he confided to friends. And the other, Charley Gass, whose Silver Star still hung proudly in his den, unhappily faced up to the fact that life seemed to be a never-ending gallery of challenges for the display of courage, physical or moral. But he longed for Neaman, having established an almost filial relationship with him that had become deep, warm and secure.

Charles Witz, the department-stores' controller, remained for a while but like the others so close to Neaman he had come under a cloud. He contributed to his severance by withdrawing into himself, exhibiting a depression over what had happened to his sponsor and thus presenting a personnel problem to Kunsberg. Six months after Neaman left, Witz was working for another retail chain and appeared happier.

The biggest change in New York involved Klein's, a chain which since Neaman's forced resignation from the pending merger had come under its most serious cloud. Steve Jackel, the peppery vice-president for stores, was convinced that his chances to become Klein's president had boomed with Neaman's leaving and Litwak's transfer. With all of the Klein's problems, it was clear to everyone that Jackel could not be faulted for his efforts or his initiative. But, as it turned out, his association with Neaman (reluctant, sour-sweet, and almost consuming for the young executive) hurt him. A new man was appointed president of the department-store chain.

His name was Kenneth Grey, and he was a burly, matter-of-fact discount-store career executive who had been quietly working for Meshulam Riklis for almost a year. He, too, took over his new post with a pronouncement, "We'll go back to basics—the things that once made Klein's world-famous." Everyone, even the resentful Steve Jackel, immediately liked Kenneth Grey. How can you dislike a man who immediately calls attention to the warts on his face and hands, admits that his career has been dogged by financial reverses and grunts, moans and shuffles like the old pals you remember from the days in the schoolyard? But, it seemed that while Riklis had him stashed away in some tiny office at Rapid's headquarters he had been understudying Klein's for months and had correctly called some of that company's problems before they had surfaced. Riklis, it became clear, often hired aspiring executives on a contingency basis, posted them away in tiny cubicles, and kept them in a type of farm system in case they were ever needed. If a reasonable time elapsed and their services weren't required, they were let go.

As things fell into place, Stanley Kunsberg made it clear where he stood. One of Neaman's problems, he said, was that he had constantly fought with the parent company management, and this had proved "counterproductive." "Now," he stated, "the climate between Rapid and McCrory has improved considerably and this has helped morale. There are no longer any internal wars. We have a new team spirit in New York and in York, Pennsylvania."

There were other changes of different types.

Margit Bergklint, Neaman's lithe secretary who had intrigued many of the executives in New York, abruptly got married and left.

Within days after Neaman's removal, every office in the organization that had prominently featured large-framed reproductions of Neaman's photo and his credo no longer had them. Also discarded were the thousands of cards containing the four keys to successful management, as well as the cards listing directives to supervisors.

MERZ, the merchandise early replenishment "zyztem," was changed in nature and in name. The young man who had suggested "zyztem" as a way of rendering the inventory-control system more memorable quaked for months in fear of his job. But nothing happened to him, and he was vaguely disappointed. He left, too, for a more promising career elsewhere.

Staff cutbacks were substantial. In New York, at least one-third of all the executives and office workers were let go. In York, Pennsylvania, the overhead was substantially cut, mainly by reducing the 3,000 workers to about 2,000. Warehouses and relay points were closed and sublet to other companies.

For months, no reporters were invited to Rapid–American's or McCrory's offices. But visitors to the latter spoke of it as a ghost town, almost a "cemetery." Phone calls from the press were denied. Once, a McCrory executive agreed to have lunch with this reporter and then changed his mind, admitting, "It could be my job to meet with you."

The reluctance to make any more disclosures was understandable. Worse bad news was indicated. McCrory's profit decline for the fiscal year 1973–1974, already indicated in the much-disputed advanced financials, was almost ninety percent compared to the year before. This produced a disastrous effect on Rapid–American's results for the same year. Riklis and Becker, their concern over the highly erratic stock market already great, watched in dismay as the stocks of both companies plumeted in response to the huge profit declines.

Months later, it was possible to meet with some of the executives and discuss Neaman. The heat was off, so to speak, and a few, such as Stanley Kunsberg and Steve Jackel, didn't mind discussing the circumstances involving Neaman's ouster.

"Starting about two years ago," said Kunsberg, "Neaman seemed to change. He became power-hungry. He wanted to have his own company. He fought with Riklis, wouldn't even talk to him unless he had to. Sam had no use for anyone. He didn't trust people. Eventually, that's why he relied so much on computers. He mechanized everything so that he could count on them instead of on people. . . . He created a buffer between the people and the variety-division president. He moved people from one division to another, putting lots of them in positions in which they weren't happy. A good man from one division was transferred to another so the original division lost out.

"I don't believe in normal people with normal talents as a guiding rule. I believe in normal people with above-normal talents—people like me who started as a stockboy and became president or chairman of the board. People with drive, dedication, and imagination."

Kunsberg's dislike for Neaman was, of course, well-known. Yet, he admitted that in his view his former superior had "great qualities as well as great faults." Kunsberg said, "Sam had a capacity to motivate people, and he has an unbelievable mind. He is, I have to admit, a brilliant man. But there's the other side of him. He thought that only he was right about everything. The result turned out that the computer created overbuying and excessive inventories. Sure, he had his downfall over Klein's, but he let the variety division get out of hand on inventories and expenses with too many people, too many marginal stores, and too many warehouses. He was building an empire. Rik wanted to talk, to communicate, but Sam wouldn't have it. Now, Rik has exactly what he wants."

Several months after Neaman had gone, Steve Jackel still had deeply mixed feelings about him. No one had received more brusque treatment at Neaman's hands than Steve. But he had often asked for it by being brash and offensive toward Neaman. Yet, some people who had watched them both for years suspected that the older man had a paternal feeling toward Steve, secretly had great affection for him, and would have protected him down to the last impossible moment. Steve had reacted to Neaman's demands by working harder and longer than anyone else around him. But, after Neaman, things were different.

Jackel himself appeared much changed, chastened, matured. He had that strained look of a man who had gone virtually to his outer-limits and then come back, an improved retread. He still had some of the mid-thirties jauntiness, some of the baby-fat around his cheeks, and the jutting chin that made him seem always ready to break out with a string of moderately obscene jokes. But one trait seemed to be gone, his penchant for being the resident loyal opponent.

"What happened with Neaman?" he repeated the question. "I worked with him all those years, and yet I still find it hard to come up with a simple answer.

"Sam failed because he was so rigid. He thought that inventory replenishment could be accomplished by computers, and he relied on them even though all they could do was to be programmed based on already indicated trends. In other words, if you planned to go for an increase in sales, it was damned near impossible to get the computer to program more inventory. And under Neaman's rigid inventory system every purchase order around here had to be okayed by a committee.

"Maybe Sam was right," Steve said. "Maybe it's true that by the year 2000 retailing will be entirely conducted by machines. But he didn't take into account the interim steps—the experience and the know-how of all the people who made the company tick. How could he ignore that in preparing for the future takeover by the machines? But he did. I guess he just lost patience."

In retrospect, Steve said, Neaman lived on "a kind of mountain top." He was so demanding and his criteria were so high that losing his patience with people was almost preordained. "He went, what I mean is, from never wanting any one person to have much responsibility so that if they quit he wouldn't lose too much—he went from that to wanting everyone to have an understudy so that there would be plenty of backup depth in case anyone defaulted. And then he began to entrust more functions to the machines and the systems. If he had only stuck with his principles of giving every man a chance to show what he could do— But maybe there just wasn't enough time. Time can be a helluva luxury."

And with it all, Neaman remained on that mountain top, a man cold and remote. "He made no friends so that when the axe fell," Steve said, "it was left to every man to react in direct proportion to how highly he regarded Neaman and how important Sam was to his life. . . . When I learned that he had been kicked out of the Interstate deal, I tried to get through to him. I guess I was just about the only one who succeeded. He happened to pick up the phone when I called. I said, 'Sam, probably everybody is calling you to ask what will happen to them now. But I'm not worried about myself. What I want to know is, what can I do for you?' I guess maybe I was pulling a Kennedy, but I was sincere. Do you know what he answered? Like a recording: 'There's nothing, but thank you for the thought.' "

But when the end came, Steve Jackel said, "he didn't treat us right, those of us who knocked ourselves out for him. He more or less walked out, leaving all the rest of us to sit and sweat. What could he have done? He never gave any of us a contract, never assured us in any tangible way that our efforts would be rewarded. Only that we would better ourselves by working together and pooling our talents. Worst of all, he made a lot of promises of things we would get, rewards, this, that, and few of them ever came about.

"I myself put in a seven-day week with him for years. I would spend all day Saturdays with him, hitting the stores, checking things, and then he would call me at 11 A.M. on Sundays, and keep me on the phone until seven at night. When I would kid him or complain about it, he would say, 'So don't answer the phone when I call you.' But can you imagine how he would have reacted to that? I still think he was one of the most brilliant and unusual men I ever met, but I guess when you are as rigid, as demanding, and as cold as he is, you don't leave any way out for yourself. Personally, I think the crowd at Rapid was always angry with him because they basically don't often have real faith and trust in anyone as they did in him, but they feel he let them down.

"As for me," he continued with a grin, "I don't put in a seven-day week anymore. I spend a lot more time with my family. My wife is very happy and so are my kids."

In mid-May of 1974, it was announced that the merger talks between McCrory and Interstate Stores were being dropped because the lenders could not agree on the terms of the re-financing of the latter's debt.

A week later, Interstate filed a petition for court protection under the bankruptcy laws.

One month after, Rapid–American and McCrory suspended their merger talks because of the high cost of money and the very uncertain stock market. But the merger, both companies announced, would eventually take place.

21. "Good-Bye, Sam"

Three months later, after a number of unsuccessful attempts, Neaman consented to see me. I would interview him once again, probably for the last time.

After he disappeared from view, I called every few weeks, trying his private line. Mostly, no one answered. Once, I left a message with a woman who had a foreign accent. Once, his wife, Cecelia, answered. When I said, "Is Sam around?" she replied, "Yes, he's getting very round." Neaman came on and explained that Cecelia had let him off his diet as a therapy for his psychic wounds so that he had just put on weight. Would he allow me to come and see him? No, he replied. He was going away again. I might try to call him in a month.

When I called again, he invited me to lunch at his home. It was apparent that he had decided that he had something more to say or, perhaps, that there were a few more things left that might be said.

The luncheon was lavish, consisting of an avocado and to-
mato salad, a thick steak covered with mushrooms, Pilsen beer,
and a rich ice-cream sundae accompanied by a sugar cookie.
Cecelia served with a smile. She was at ease and seemed pleased.
In the kitchen an elderly woman, who occasionally peeked out
at us, prepared the meal.

Neaman had obviously put on weight. His middle had thick-
ened and his jowls were softer. I searched for signs of bitterness, resentment, trauma, and found none. He appeared
complete, that is, more fulfilled than I recalled him last. With
Cecelia, a plump, smiling package of good-will, he gave the
impression that he was happy and that they were more together
than they had ever been.

Asked about his activities since that fateful April, Neaman
began to speak, and soon the words poured out:

"I'm a private citizen now. After I left New York, I went
back to Israel and spent a week on the Dead Sea. I recommend
it highly to anyone who wants to reflect. The Pan American
Hotel is quiet and the sea—there's no life, there's nothing,
there's silence. We ate. We walked. I got peace-of-mind.

"I'm sixty-one years old. I'm fine. I had an experience for ten
years. The day after that relationship ended, I took my suit-
cases and went away. I spoke to no one. I saw my brother in
London, and then I spent four weeks in Israel. It was a wonderful experience. Perhaps it was because I locked the door on
all that happened. It's like my mother—she's dead—I can't talk
to her anymore."

The now-ended merger with Interstate Stores was almost
all an accommodation, he said, rather than a synergistic action.
The resulting company would have consisted of a reshaping
of McCrory to allow Riklis to carry out the merger that
he really wanted. "I'm not a fool," he said, "nor am I the
most intelligent man in the world. But there is a big difference
between strategy and tactics. The tactics was the merger with
Interstate, but the strategy was the merger of the rest of
McCrory into Rapid–American. I didn't like the association to start with, yet I had to make the gamble so that we
could have our own company, my colleagues and I. It was an
eye-for-an-eye. But it was always like that between Riklis

and me. I contributed more than $200 million in cash toward his company. And for that he agreed to let me alone to do my work. I said to him, 'Call me whatever you want, but don't ever sit in judgment on me. You were down and out and I took over, and after that you didn't have a sleepless night.' That was good for ten years. The only trouble was when Riklis got greedy and bought Klein's for a bargain price. I told him, 'I don't want that fucking business. It's a pit without a bottom.' When I saw what I had, I tried like hell to get rid of it. I told Riklis, 'Get rid of it for book value or for any price.' He said, 'You can handle it.' Why not? I had the headache and he lived the good life."

Accidentally, purely accidentally, said Neaman, he "stumbled on a bunch of nice people in the variety-store division." They responded to his management, his credo, his manner of doing business and the initial bigotry changed. "Some of them used to say, 'The bastard Jew is on the way,' when I would visit them. After I showed them how to improve themselves, it became, 'Jesus Christ is on his way.' I had a beautiful thing going with them—I wasn't too near to them but near enough to enjoy it.

"I came to understand that my success was that I turned the pages back a few decades to create a patriarchal society," he observed. "The psychologist who tested all the McCrory people before promotion said that I had convinced them that I knew all their names, their birthdays, the names and birthdays of their families, their anniversaries. I hit a chord in personal relationships, and the people reacted by doing their best in the worst time the country had in years."

As he spoke, I couldn't help wondering if some of his critics weren't right about the fallacy they perceived in his great social experiment. The fallacy in having average people performing their average talents in the hope that the sum will be greater than the parts may be that all will go well as long as the leader remains steadfast in his beliefs and actions, or as long as he is around. Once the leader falters or leaves, the direction is gone. Then it is time for the talented, the above-average to surface. But if there has been no environment for them to develop, where will they have come from? The increased reliance on computers and electronic systems was patently an indication that Neaman lost confidence in the conviction that averageness could make all the difference. And in a field like retailing, where you have to sense what people want and crave, when they mostly do not know it themselves, reliance on computers could be fatal.

When I mentioned all this to Neaman, he did not respond directly. But there was a subtle shift in his tone, almost to a minor key as he said, "My teaching won't survive. That's what is so sad. I created a different structure. It has to be the thing of tomorrow. The young generation has rejected automation and computers. They don't believe in them. But for ten years I showed how it could be done. I gave an opportunity to the good and the mediocre. Don't forget, I turned the variety division around in one year and Newberry in even less. . . ."

Did he think there will always be a little corner of Neaman left in them? I asked with a smile. He shrugged and frowned over the obviously sentimental question. "I hope so," he replies, his dourness easing, "but I don't think I will ever know it."

"Why were you pushed, kicked, and shoved out of the Interstate deal?" he was asked.

He shakes his head at the typical newspaperman's nasty phrasing. "After eighty to eighty-five percent of all the problems were solved, I was suddenly out of the deal," he said. "I made the mistake of falling in love with my job. What do I now care about the deal? I fell in love with the people. Now there is a death in the family. I am gone. But as long as I was the chief executive, I had to worry about them twenty-four hours a day. So now I am out. I am totally committed as an executive but when I'm out, I'm out. . . . I'm not an elephant who goes into the jungle when he is hurt and lies down to die. I want to put a barrier between what has happened and what I am now. I must make the break—period, paragraph, chapter. And I'm not writing my next chapter now. I am merely waiting."

So *why* was he chopped? I insisted. His round face darkened again and he scowled. "I don't know," he replied. "One week the banks want me and the next week they don't want me."

"Of course," I insisted again, "of course you know, Sam. Couldn't Riklis and Becker have saved you? Did they finally decide to stick it to you?" He was angry with me now. He got up from the sofa where we were sitting after the meal, and he paced around. "You know already," he said, his voice harsh, "and you keep asking me what it is? I don't want to get involved with personalities at this late stage. What do I care what it is? I told you, it's a closed chapter—it is like death!"

When I asked why he was angry with me, he relaxed a bit and sat down again. "I'm not angry," he said, "just excited. It's my high blood pressure. I have to watch it. A little excitement and it jumps up in a minute. I don't want to have a stroke, so please, do not excite me."

I apologized, then asked him what he was doing currently. "Not much," he said, "I'm a consultant for a little company, but I don't get a nickel for it. I'm just there a few days a week. But already people are coming to me and telling me that I am making them see things a new way. And already they are working late, weekends, for the first time."

Had he had any offers to become chief executive of any companies since he left McCrory? He smiled as though the question were too simple. "I have had twenty offers," he reported. "All sorts of offers—solar energy equipment, mortgage banking, a large retailer. But I have accepted nothing."

"Why?"

"The jobs don't have the scope I want," he said, "but I am not actively seeking anything at this point."

He got up again and went to a wall cabinet where there was a long row of bound volumes. "These contain everything ever printed about me," he said. "Now here is a brand new volume. It contains hundreds of letters, telegrams, cards, and other things from people who wrote to me when I left. Look, here is a typical one, regretting that I am no longer at McCrory. Here is another that says he will never forget my teachings. Here is another that says I changed his life. You see that large, crystal vase over there? That's from a group of McCrory wives. . . ."

"Would you go back to McCrory if they wanted you?"

He shrugged. "If they would, maybe I would. The only thing that I miss is the people, my 'family' in the variety division. But it will never be. I volunteered to serve as a consultant to them in York, Pennsylvania. But Riklis refused me. He said that if anybody there wants to see me, he will not stop it. But I cannot interfere with the new management."

The conversation lapsed. He picked it up. "Financially, I am secure," he said. "I can sit on my backside the rest of my life. I will not have to work for money. Cecelia will always be taken care of. I am not mad at Riklis. I don't even hate Izzy Becker. I don't understand him. But I don't hate him."

As I got up to go, Neaman came over and shook hands. Cecelia gave me a friendly good-bye. He accompanied me to the elevator.

"Good-bye, Sam," I said.

"Good-bye," he said warmly. "Good-bye."

As the months passed, I phoned him occasionally. Once when I reached him to ask what he was doing, he said, "What does a has-been do? Nothing." He answered two more calls of mine, each time replying more cryptically. Finally, I stopped calling. In my mind's eye, I can still picture him. He sits in his big, expensive penthouse apartment, eating more than he should, smiling or frowning over his letters and mementos, and perhaps above all, waiting for the telephone to ring. For the call that will return him to glory. Only when it rings it is usually for Cecelia. Sometimes it is a wrong number. Sometimes it is for him from someone who still wants something. And mostly, it does not ring at all.

On March 12, 1976, or slightly less than two years after Sam Neaman was ousted, the merger between Rapid–American Corporation and the McCrory Corporation was voted on by stockholders of both companies. Separate meetings were held in the Hotel DuPont in Wilmington, Delaware. The vote in favor of the merger was overwhelming. There was little discussion.

APPENDIX

The People

Rapid-American Corporation

Meshulam Riklis, Chairman of the Board
Isidore Becker, Vice Chairman of the Board
Leonard Lane, Vice Chairman of the Board
Harry Wachtel, Legal Counsel

McCrory Corporation

Samuel Neaman, Chairman of the Board
Stanley H. Kunsberg, President
Norman Mallor, Financial Vice President
Charley Gass, Vice President, Internal Audit
Marvin Shenfeld, Vice President, Electronic Data Processing
Cecelia Neaman, wife of the Chairman
Margit Bergklint, secretary to the Chairman
Mike Berdow, assistant to the Chairman
Sarah Berdow, his wife
Milton Goldberg, consultant

S. Klein Department Stores

Samuel Neaman, Chairman of the Board
Duffy Lewis, President
Ben Litwak, Senior Vice President
Steve Jackel, Vice President
Charles Witz, Controller
Hi Leder, Vice President, Advertising

McCrory-McLellan-Green Variety Stores

Samuel Neaman, Chairman of the Board
Frank Patchen, President
John King, Executive Vice President
Mary King, his wife
Harold Hughes, Administrative Vice President
Ed Luedtke, Vice President, General Store Manager
Paul McClellan, Vice President, National Merchandise Director
Mildred McClellan, his wife
Earl Powers, Buyer Supervisor
Sheila Powers, his wife
Marge Schiller, Buyer
Robert Schiller, her husband and division Purchasing Agent
William Wasserman, a Store Manager
Johnny, the company driver

Lerner Stores

Harold Lane, Sr., Chairman of the Board
Harold Lane, Jr., President

J.J. Newberry

Walter Straus, Chairman of the Board

Interstate Department Stores

Sol Cantor, Chairman of the Board
Herbert Siegel, Financial Vice President